The Vampire Hunter's Field Manual

A Survivors guide to Narcissistic abuse

Matt Davis

Cover design by Oliver Brooks

Dedication

This Field Manual is dedicated to all
the Survivors of Narcissistic abuse out there,
and the Targets who still suffer in it.

There is always hope.

By understanding the nature of
Narcissistic abuse and abusers,
we can help each other to heal,
and to take back our freedom.

Special mentions to some wonderful people
without whom this book would not have happened.
My Therapist, Deborah Bennett: Thank-you.
Justin Wynne, Ross McIntosh, Jo Hadley-King:
for your kindness, love and support.
Erol Kentli & Ceejay Sargent:
for all that, and a home.

Angela Newman:
Teamwork, innit?

Contents

Foreword	4
Introduction	6
The Basics	11
The Mind of the Vampire	49
The Vampire's Attack Cycle	83
The Weapons of the Vampire	117
The Tactics of the Vampire	157
Drama and the "Drama Triangle"	209
How the Vampire Trains their Target	237
The Biological effects of the Attack Cycle on the Survivor	260
The Psychological effects of the Attack Cycle on the Survivor	286
The Emotional effects of the Attack Cycle on the Survivor	304
How Targets are made, and how they can become Survivors	329
The Key Skills of the Survivor	349

Foreword
by Gemma Oaten

I first made contact with Matt when a dear friend advised he would be able to help me...help me rebuild my life in the aftermath of a relationship with a Narcissistic abuser. Well, if 'relationship' is ever the right word to use when you are in the grips of what feels like hell from Narcissistic abuse. Sadly, like so many in these relationships, you don't realise you are in it until it's too late.

I felt like I'd been in a hit and run; totally broken at the hands of a man who one minute swept me off my feet, telling me I was the love of his life and amazing, to telling me I was worthless, a victim, pathetic and more. A man who would make me believe I was going crazy and I was in the wrong constantly.

Matt, hand on heart, picked me up and helped put me back together. He helped me understand, he helped me remember who I was and that this wasn't my fault: it was abuse.

There is so much terminology when it comes to a Narcissistic abusers' behaviour and sometimes it's overwhelming. 'Love bombing', 'Gaslighting', 'Cluster B personality type'; the list goes on. What Matt does in this book, and what he did for me, is explain it all in its simplest form, whilst helping the Target of such behaviour learn and restore themselves.

Knowledge is power and Matt gave me that and does so here. I can't recommend this read enough to anyone recovering from abuse. Indeed, I'd advise anyone to read it, not just in the aftermath, but if they have any shadow of doubt that they themselves are in a Narcissistic relationship.

What I also love is how he ends each chapter on a high, makes the reader laugh, it's so important. A Narcissistic abuser wants to darken the soul... Matt ensures that although the subject matter is serious, we still find the laughter and the heart we once had and do still have.

Matt reminded me that I am a warrior. Thank you.

Introduction

There will be any number of reasons why you're reading this. Hopefully, it's because you've bought the book. Whatever the reason is, I'd like to take a moment of your time to explain a couple of things about this book and why it is different from other self-help books out there.

1) It is called "The Vampire Hunter's Field Manual" because it is a practical guide to help Survivors and Targets of abuse make sense of what they have been through, and how they can avoid going through it again. It is designed to be a plain English explanation of all the jargon and psychobabble surrounding a subject that often confuses people.

2) I use the term "Vampire" to refer to those individuals who abuse their romantic partners, family and friends. The reason I do that is because abusers behave in a very similar way to the old-fashioned Vampire. They "suck" the life-force from their Targets, care only about themselves, never about their Targets, and will go from Target to Target without a second thought, just like a Vampire.

The Vampire is a personality disordered individual. Specifically, they qualify for a diagnosis on the "Cluster B" spectrum of personality disorders in the Diagnostic and Statistical Manual of Mental Disorders (DSM). They are pathological, and they are dangerous. I don't use terms like "Narcissist" or "Borderline" for several reasons but the main one is that I don't think it helps. Survivors often obsess about whether their abuser would qualify as this-or-that type of "Narc" in order to try to understand them and their behaviour.

In all the important ways, all abusers behave the same way and I believe it is enough to know that the individual in question is an abuser. The best and only advice in dealing with such individuals is always to get the hell away and stay the hell away from them anyway, so what matters now is not the label they are given. What matters is that we deal with the abuse.

The second reason is that I am absolutely not supporting the notion that terms like "Narcissist" or "Borderline" should be bandied about at will. In my view, there are currently dangerous levels of this kind of practice going on in popular culture. To qualify for the diagnosis of a Personality Disorder, individuals must be found by a qualified clinician to meet sufficient of the criteria laid out in the Diagnostic and Statistical Manual of Mental Disorders. The diagnosis for these disorders is based on behavioural traits, and if an individual has enough of them, they may qualify for a diagnosis but I am not in a position to provide such a diagnosis, and neither are most of the population.

The final reason is related to the second. Since it is possible to display all the traits of a disorder without having been diagnosed with that disorder, the term "Vampire" can be usefully applied to individuals who behave in ways that simply add up to abuse, regardless of whether they have a diagnosis or not. Most Narcissistic abusers are never seen by clinicians anyway because, for reasons that will become clear, they don't think there's anything wrong with them. What does apply, however, is that the individual in question refuses to change their abusive behaviour. Therefore, when I say "Vampire", I am talking about severely personality disordered abusers. I neither know nor care what their specific disorder is.

If they're abusive, and they refuse to change: They're a Vampire.

3) I use the term "Target" to refer to anyone who has been the subject of abuse in a relationship. I don't accept the term "Victim" for a number of reasons:

a) Victims are helpless; Targets are not.

b) Victims stay victims; Targets can become Survivors.

c) The "Victim" position in relationships is often adopted by the Vampire, so if they want it, they can have it.

4) I use the term "Survivor" to refer to anyone who finds themselves at the end of an abusive relationship. I base this on the dictionary definition that a survivor is "a person who survives, especially a person remaining alive after an event in which others have died." Some people think that's over-dramatic. I don't. As a conservative estimate, 23% of Survivors of domestic abuse attempt suicide (compared with only 3% of the rest of the population) and many succeed. People develop life-threatening illnesses as a result of being in abusive relationships.

What happens to Survivors is so egregious and so devastating that people can die as a result. That's not hyperbole. That's a fact. Survivors reading this book have clearly remained alive after an event in which others have died. Some have lost their lives to the Vampire; the Survivor has not.

This Field Manual is written in Chapters and Interludes. For every Chapter, there is an Interlude, and there's a good reason for that. The Chapters contain information to help Survivors understand the Vampire, and themselves. They can get a bit heavy at times, though, because of the serious nature of the subject, so the Interludes are designed to give a bit of "light relief". With a bit of luck, you should be able to finish a Chapter with a laugh or two because let's face it, if you're a Target or a Survivor, you'll need it.

I should warn you, however, that I can be a bit "sweary". I won't be pulling any punches because I'm not a fan of the Vampires behaviours to say the least, and I am a firm believer that maintaining a positive outlook and seeing the humour in things is fundamental to recovery from abuse. I make no apology for my use of swearing and cussing. I don't use it to shock, I use it as punctuation and in all honesty, if my language is what offends you about the subject matter, I think you urgently need some perspective. People die at the hands of Vampires, so let's not fret about the odd F-Bomb, OK?

Chapters 1 to 6 are about the Vampire and provide information that Survivors and Targets need to make sense of what they have been through, or are going through. A lot of it may be difficult to take in, and much of it may be unfamiliar.

You may find that it goes against everything you thought you knew about people, but all of it is true and all of it matters. When dealing with a Vampire, nothing makes sense and this book is designed to help you make sense of it. People who become involved with a Vampire have their sense of self destroyed, their sanity eroded, their resources exhausted and their entire world turned upside down.

Part of recovering from abuse at the hands of a Vampire is to understand what they are, how they behave and why they do what they do. By the time you get to the end of those Chapters, you should have a better understanding of what you're up against, and be in a position to start taking action to protect yourself.

Chapters 7 to 12 look at the experience from the point of view of the Target and Survivor, and are designed to give a better understanding of what you've been through and why you feel the way you do. There's also great news: Chapters 11 and 12 address what you can do about it. By the time you finish the Field Manual, you will not only understand the Vampire better; you will also understand yourself better. When you're finished reading, you will know what you need to do to start your recovery and make sure that what you have experienced never, ever happens again.

Given that lot, what you're got here is a book for Targets and Survivors that is designed to help them understand what they've been through and what to do about it. It's factual, it's funny, and it's sweary. If you fancy some of that, let's get started. I'll see you on the other side of Chapter 1.

Chapter 1

The Basics

Understanding the Vampire is a process of getting your head round some basic, but surprising facts. I say surprising because most people are unaware that Vampires even exist and those who are attacked by one often attempt to figure out what happened to them using traditional "normal" standards for understanding people. That simply won't work. The Vampire is nowhere near "normal" and they require a whole new language and new ways of understanding people if we're to try to explain who and what they are. What follows is what I call "the basics". It is designed to give an overview of the most significant aspects that need to be taken on board in order to begin to understand the Vampire and why they behave the way they do. These aspects fall into what I call the 3 Factors and the 10 Truths.

The 3 Factors are:

1) Toxic Shame (or just Shame)
2) Self Respect
3) Narcissistic Supply

Toxic Shame

Toxic Shame arises from experiences of abuse, trauma and neglect in which the individual comes to believe that they are unworthy and lesser to those around them.

Those who experience abuse, trauma and neglect (especially in childhood) come to believe that they somehow deserve it in order to explain why it occurred. A child that is constantly criticised or invalidated will come to believe that what they are being told or shown is true because how could it be otherwise? Children learn what adults tell and show them. If they are shown abuse, trauma and neglect, they will come to believe that they are only worthy of these things. Individuals who carry high amounts of Toxic Shame feel at their core that they are worthless and they loathe themselves.

The Vampire has enormous amounts of Toxic Shame, so much so that to experience it all consciously would overwhelm them and lead to a total inability to function in the world. Most people experience Shame to some degree, but the Vampires levels of shame are off the chart. Probably as the result of childhood abuse, trauma and/or neglect, the Vampire has come to believe that they are unworthy, unlovable, inferior to those around them and shameful.

However, in order to deal with those feelings and beliefs, the Vampire has buried them deep in their unconscious mind. Effectively, they have cut off from those feelings and spend their entire lives actively denying that they exist at all.

Self Respect

I use the term Self Respect to also refer to Self Esteem and Self Love. I do that because people who love and hold themselves in high esteem treat themselves with respect. So, when I talk about Self Respect, I am effectively talking about all three.

Self Respect is the antidote to Toxic Shame. It is simply not possible to have high levels of both because it operates as a set of scales; the higher the level of Self Respect, the lower the levels of Toxic Shame and vice versa. People with high levels of Toxic Shame have low levels of Self Respect, and therefore behave in ways that are harmful to themselves and others. People with low levels of Toxic Shame have high levels of Self Respect, and therefore behave in ways that are beneficial to themselves and others.

The Vampire has chronically low levels of Self Respect. Their core feeling about themselves is that of Shame and, just like their Shame is off the chart, so is their Self Respect but in the opposite direction. Despite the fact that they have buried those feelings of Shame arising from their history of abuse, trauma and/or neglect, they still experience them, but cannot explain why they experience them because they have disconnected from them, and buried them in their

unconscious minds. They are unable to generate Self Respect, and instead rely on others to provide that for them.
People with high levels of Self Respect like themselves. They behave in ways that are in line with their values, they take responsibility for their actions, they do not seek to hurt others and their feelings of Self Respect is not contingent on what others do or say, or how the world responds to them.

What is crucial to understand is that Self Respect is just that: it comes from the Self. People with high levels of Self Respect do not rely on outside sources for their sense of who they are, or their value to others. Instead, they know that they have value for exactly who they are, and this knowledge comes from within them, not from people around them.

The Vampire is self-loathing. What is occurring is that their levels of Toxic Shame, and their levels of Self Respect are in direct opposition. The first is extremely high, and the second is extremely low. Completely unlike people who can generate Self Respect, and therefore reduce their own Toxic Shame, the Vampire is entirely dependent on others for their sources of Self Respect in order to hold their Toxic Shame at bay.

Narcissistic Supply

The term "Narcissistic Supply" occurs frequently in the literature on Narcissism and personality disorders in general. It has even managed to make its way into popular culture and is often understood to mean "Attention from others".
In fact, it is far more than that. Narcissistic Supply actually refers to the meeting of emotional needs. It is what gives

people a sense that they matter, are cared for, are worthy and lovable and helps them avoid feelings of Shame.

Narcissistic Supply provides attention, admiration, approval, affection, validation and gives us a sense that we are special. All people have emotional needs, and we'll be looking at those later on. For now, it is fair to say that if we cannot meet our own emotional needs, we are more likely to need Narcissistic Supply from others in order to validate and feel good about ourselves.

People with high levels of Self Respect can provide well for their emotional needs. When life throws them curveballs, they have the ability to self-soothe (to calm themselves at times of emotional difficulty). They are not "phased" by criticism, insults or failure because their ability to generate their positive feelings about themselves counteracts any negative emotional experience they may be having.

People with high levels of Self Respect have little need for Narcissistic Supply from others. People with low Self Respect struggle to meet their own emotional needs. If life throws criticism, insults or failure at them, they have a hard time counteracting that with positive feelings about themselves. Their ability to self-soothe is limited, and they experience feelings of Shame in response to negative feedback about themselves far more readily. People with low Self Respect have high levels of need for Narcissistic Supply from others. Narcissistic Supply is therefore necessary to fill the void of unmet emotional needs. Individuals with high Self Respect need little. Individuals with low Self Respect need a lot.

Because of their extremely low Self Respect, and extremely high Toxic Shame, the Vampires need for external sources of Narcissistic Supply is also extreme. In the same way as their Self Respect and Toxic Shame are off the chart, so is their need for external sources of Narcissistic Supply. In fact, as we'll see later, they are so dependent on external sources of Narcissistic Supply that they are permanently and irredeemably addicted to it.

For the Vampire, Narcissistic Supply is the only way by which they can stave off their feelings of Shame. Without it, they feel inferior, unworthy and unlovable. But the Vampire doesn't simply need Narcissistic Supply to feel validated, they need it to feel superior. Their disorder compels them to constantly seek to place themselves in the "one-up" position in their relationships in order to avoid feelings of Shame. If they can feel superior, they feel safe. This is clearly pathological, but that is the nature of the Vampire. They are disordered individuals and so behave in disordered ways.

The 10 Truths

Vampires are developmentally arrested. They do not think or feel like "normal" people.

The Vampire is emotionally arrested; the full range of adult emotion is not present in them and they are driven by the more primal emotions of Shame, Rage, Envy and Fear. This state of affairs usually comes about as the result of abuse, trauma and/or neglect in childhood and the result is an individual who does not feel or behave the way that "normal" people do.

Because of their early experiences the Vampire never reached, and never will reach, emotional maturity. As I said before, abuse, trauma and/or neglect in childhood shows and tells children their value in the world. The Vampire has been treated in ways that have taught them that they do not deserve Self Respect. What has taken its place is Toxic Shame. Healthy emotional development requires the development of Self Respect, but this has been denied to the Vampire. Therefore, during a crucial period in their development, they did not develop Self Respect and that "window of opportunity" is now closed.

From an early age, Vampires know that they are different in some way. As they grow up, they become aware that they think and feel differently to others and have to find a way to cope. At the heart of every Vampire is an overwhelming sense of Shame. The abuse, trauma and/or neglect they experienced led them to internalise it and feel eternally unworthy. They have suffered psychological damage so profound that it has destroyed any sense of Self Respect they may once have had.

Their sense of Shame is so profound that even the slightest imperfection, criticism or failure wounds them to their very core and is a feeling so overwhelming that it threatens to destroy their entire sense of who they are. The Vampire uses Narcissistic Supply not only to stave off feelings of Shame, but to allow them to feel superior to others. In the Vampires mind, if they feel superior they are not Shameful. It serves to validate them that they can make themselves feel better than others because if they are the superior person, the other person must be inferior and in that way they avoid feeling shameful by comparison.

What exists in the Vampire on an emotional level is a child in an adult's body that requires constant attention in the form of Narcissistic Supply in order to relate to others. While they exhibit all the intellectual traits of an adult, their emotional capacity is that of a child. This is often what is so confusing to the Target or Survivor because the Vampire appears to be "normal" in many respects. However, the first Truth is that the Vampire is emotionally arrested and they are not capable of the full range of human emotion.

Vampires are incapable of Love, Empathy, Compassion and Reciprocity because they see other people as objects.

The capacity for Love, Empathy, Compassion and Reciprocity develop during childhood. Since the Vampire is developmentally arrested, they never developed the capacity for these things. The abuse, trauma and/or neglect they experienced resulted in a developmental arrest during a critical phase in their emotional development. In the normal development of a child, the idea that other people exist in their own right is something that is learned through experience.

Young children start out by seeing people as objects, no different from their toys. It's why you don't leave toddlers and dogs together unattended. As they develop, children gradually come to recognise that people and objects are different, which can take many years to learn fully. People have feelings, just as they do. Objects don't. The gradual understanding that people and objects are different is part of normal development but the development of the Vampire is massively hindered by abuse, trauma and/or neglect, potentially on an on-going basis. This prevents the development of the understanding that people and objects are different in any meaningful way.

For Love, Empathy, Compassion and Reciprocity to develop, children must come to understand fully that other people have the same emotional experiences that they do, and therefore the same value in the world that they have. The Vampire never comes to understand this because they are too busy dealing with the abuse, trauma and/or neglect they are experiencing. If they do develop an understanding of others at all, it is through the lens of their own emotional experience and that is how they come to understand the emotional experience of others.

In other words, since their own emotional experience has led to the destruction of their Self Respect, they cannot respect others. Since they view themselves as worthless, unlovable and shameful, they cannot conceive of others not feeling these things. They do not understand that others can have healthy Self Respect and, in fact, fear those that do.

They actively seek out others that lack Self Respect because those individuals can be dominated, controlled and manipulated easily, which is the ultimate goal of the Vampire in any relationship. They seek to do these things in order to feel superior and thus avoid their feelings of Shame. For the

Vampire, people are objects to be controlled and manipulated in order to meet their own emotional needs. Healthy people with Self Respect can engage in Love, Empathy, Compassion and Reciprocity. They understand that people exist as separate individuals with their own emotional lives and are not simply there to meet their needs. The Vampire simply does not understand this, which is why this is the second Truth: Vampires are incapable of Love, Empathy, Compassion and Reciprocity.

Vampires are incapable of having relationships but they keep trying (and failing).

The next few chapters will discuss this in more detail, but for now, all we need to do is examine why the Vampire is incapable of having relationships. Given that the Vampire is developmentally arrested and has never developed the capacity for Love, Empathy, Compassion and Reciprocity, they lack the fundamental emotional skills to engage in adult relationships.

Healthy relationships involve two individuals that are emotionally developed to the level of an adult. If one or both lack this emotional development, the relationship will fail because it will be torn apart by constant emotional instability.

No healthy relationship can last when one or both partners are emotionally inconsistent because neither partner can ever be assured that their emotional needs will be met. Such relationships are characterised by chaos, drama, unmet emotional needs, emotional pain and betrayal. They lack the fundamental emotional skills of Love, Empathy, Compassion and Reciprocity. Relationships that feature an emotional child require an emotional adult in order to manage the emotions of that child because they cannot manage their own. Clearly, the Vampire is incapable of being the emotional adult and so the burden of the emotional management in the relationship will always fall on the other partner.

The Vampire approaches relationships in the only way they know how: as a child. They bring absolutely no capacity to relate as an adult to the relationship at all. Since that is the case, what the Vampire looks for in a relationship is not an adult; it is one of two things. Either they are looking for another child, or they are looking for a parent. The extent to which their partner functions in either of these roles will determine the "success" of the relationship. I know.
That sounds weird, right? That's because it is weird. Vampires don't have "normal" relationships; they have weird relationships.

Whenever the Vampire encounters another individual, they will consider them to be either another child or a parent figure. Therefore, anyone involved with a Vampire will be cast in one of these two roles because of the Vampires inability to do anything else. In intimate relationships, the Vampires Target will be cast in the role of parent. Others may be cast as children. What's more, the Vampire only sees others as a means of providing Narcissistic Supply.

Therefore, the Target will be cast in the role of a parent whose sole responsibility is to provide for the Vampires emotional needs through the constant provision of Narcissistic Supply. It's a full-time job, completely unsustainable, utterly exhausting and will always lead to the destruction of the relationship.

This is why I use the term Vampire to refer to these individuals. Their disorder renders them completely incapable of engaging in relationships in any meaningful way other than to drain their Target of all their emotions. In addition, they also drain all other resources. Whether that is money, property, friendships, businesses, interests or whatever doesn't matter. Any and all resources the Target has will be drained by the Vampire in their endless and unquenchable thirst for Narcissistic Supply. The parents of small children pour all their resources into raising their children and helping them grow. The Vampire is that child, but they never grow. They remain an emotional child with all the demands of a child but those demands never end.

For as long as the Target remains in the relationship, the needs of the Vampire will be centre-stage in the relationship. The needs of the Target are irrelevant to the Vampire, and will also become irrelevant to the Target. This is a pattern that will never change. The Vampire repeats this way of relating in all their relationships because it is the only way they know how, which accounts for the Third Truth: Vampires are incapable of having relationships but they keep trying (and failing).

Vampires live in a False Reality and have created a False Self. Their very survival depends on forcing others to believe that these False things are True.

The Vampire is in complete denial of what they are. In order to deal with all that Shame, the Vampire creates a False Self that they present to the world to justify their existence. This False Self is what they want the world to believe about them, and it serves to protect their enormously fragile True Selves. The False Self is what they believe about themselves, and they will never accept any other version of who they are. To do so would be to accept their True Selves, and they have disowned that version to spare themselves all those feelings of Shame.

The False Self is an identity, a disguise, a mask. Many commentators talk about the "Mask" of the disordered individual, and that's what I'm talking about here. Because the Vampire has no means of meeting their own emotional needs, they are compelled by their disorder to secure others in relationships to meet their needs for them. They use the False Self to do this.

What the Vampire projects into the world is an illusion, a carefully crafted facade of a "normal" person that they use to trap others into relationships with the express intention of dominating, controlling and manipulating them into becoming a constant source of Narcissistic Supply. This False Self is often very attractive, interesting, charming, seductive and so on because if you're going to use bait, why not use the best, right? A False Self that is not attractive isn't going to be effective in luring the Target into the relationship is it?

This is why Survivors are so shocked by the whole experience of having a relationship with a Vampire, because the disparity between the False and True Selves is so vast.

What the Survivor saw in the beginning was the False Self, the bait. What they increasingly saw during the relationship, and certainly saw at the end of it is the True Self. If the Target saw the True Self at the start, they would never have got into the relationship in the first place and the Vampire knows this full well. In other words, they know they're doing it. The Vampire knows that the False Self is false but they cannot admit to that because doing so would be to accept the True Self. That would require the Vampire to face all their feelings of inadequacy and Shame, which would be psychologically devastating and is never, ever going to happen.

What the Vampire lives in, therefore, is a False Reality in which the False Self is real, and the True Self is hidden from the world. If it ever came to light that the True Self is in fact true, the Vampire would have to admit all their feelings of inadequacy and Shame, which would lead to psychological self-destruction. The Vampire cannot afford to have the world know about the True Self, so they force their version of reality on those around them. For many people who do not know the Vampire well, this is easy. It's simply a case of image management. The Vampire keeps up the act of the False Self around others that don't get too close, and the vast majority of them buy it. In fact, the Vampire needs such others because the more those people believe the False Self, the more the Vampire can convince themselves that it is true. Those who buy the act are kept around by the Vampire for this purpose. Those who do not are systematically discredited and removed from the Vampires life.

It's why the Vampire engages in Smear Campaigns (more on those later). By undermining the credibility of people who do not support the False Self, the Vampire retains a coterie of people who do, and this allows them to constantly prop up the False Self. By doing this, the Vampires version of reality becomes a feedback loop in which they find support for the False Self, eliminate those that contradict it, attract and retain those that support it and continue to live in a False Reality that they can convince themselves is true.

The problem arises when the Vampire enters an intimate relationship. Who is most likely to notice that the False Self is false? The Target. It is crucial for the existence of the Vampire that they convince the Target that the False Self is real, despite any and all evidence to the contrary.

It's why relationships with Vampires are so crazy-making, and why they go from being wonderful at the beginning to being a total nightmare by the end. They don't just expect that the Target buys the act, they force them to. The full range of the Vampires weapons and tactics are brought to bear on the Target to make sure they never get the chance to point out the True Self. Any and all actions on the part of the Target that indicate that they are going to do that are met with a very nasty array of behaviours on the part of the Vampire to bully the Target into buying into their False Reality. If the Target submits, the Vampire will keep them around for the purpose of providing Narcissistic Supply. If the Target resists, they will be Smeared and brutally Discarded. The Vampire will attempt to destroy the Target's credibility because they pose a threat to their False Reality.

For the Vampire, it's not a case of "my version against yours", it is a case of "my version or nothing". Any version of reality in which the True Self is true represents the psychological annihilation of the Vampire and this accounts for the fourth Truth: Vampires live in a False Reality and have created a False Self. Their very survival depends on forcing others to believe that these False things are True.

Vampires are predators. Never assume that they are anything else.

Vampires prey on their Targets. They need the Narcissistic Supply the Target provides to validate the False Self and assure themselves that they are superior and they know they need the Target more than the Target needs them. They know that if the Target ever caught on to what was really going on, they would leave the relationship and the Vampire would be left without a source of Narcissistic Supply. They will not allow that to happen.

What ensues is a sustained campaign of domination, control and manipulation to make sure that the Target does not leave until a new Target can be acquired. I call it the "Attack Cycle" and I'll be going into more detail on it later. For now, I'll stick to explaining why the Vampire is a predator.

From the very beginning of the relationship, the Vampire attacks the Target. At first, the attack takes the form of Idealisation, in which the Target is shown the False Self but, crucially, they are shown themselves. The Vampire uses a tactic known as "Mirroring" to reflect back to the Target all the best qualities they possess.

The Vampire knows that they can attract the Target into a relationship if they share similar qualities, but they also know that they don't possess those things, so they fake them; whatever qualities the Target possesses that the Vampire finds attractive are mimicked. In other words, the Vampire becomes the mirror-image of the Target. Whatever the Target likes, they like. Whatever the Target values, they value. Whatever is important to the Target is important to them. That's why it's called Mirroring, because the Vampire is simply holding up a mirror to the Target and allowing them to see what they want to see.

While this is going on, the Vampire will be "Love Bombing" the Target, a process of showering them with attention to make them feel special. In effect, the Vampire is smothering the Target with Narcissistic Supply. That's why people with high Self Respect don't fall for it, because it feels weird, excessive, desperate and creepy.

Once the Target has been lured into the relationship, the Vampire continues to attack but the tactics change. From here on, it's about making sure that the Target serves as a source of Narcissistic Supply, never catches on to the truth of what is going on and never leaves. That requires the Vampire to systematically grind down the Targets ability to trust their own judgement and to destroy their Self Respect.
People with low Self Respect are easy to control and manipulate, and that is what the Vampire will try to turn the Target into. What the Vampire wants is not a healthy relationship because they can't have healthy relationships. What they want is a dysfunctional relationship that they can control. They are not interested in the Target as a person

because they don't see them as a person; they see them as an object that exists to serve their emotional needs.

The inevitable outcome of a relationship with a Vampire is that the Target will suffer. They will be drained of their resources and have their emotional and psychological world destroyed. That is why the Vampire is a predator. Predators destroy others to fulfill their own needs, and so does the Vampire. For now, that's enough to explain the fifth Truth: Vampires are predators. Never assume that they are anything else.

Vampires cannot be reasoned with. They do not think rationally and consider rational thinking from others about their behaviour as abusive (no, really).

The Vampire lives in a False Reality and has created a False Self to protect themselves from feelings of inadequacy and Shame. They simply cannot tolerate any version of reality that contradicts their False version. Since their False Reality and False Self are such, they simply don't stand up to objectivity and reason. Any attempt to subject them to reason will result in the Vampire engaging in a vast array of emotional tactics to defend them. The Vampire lives in fear of 5 things:

Abandonment
Feeling or appearing Inferior or Inadequate
Loss of Control
Loss of Resources
Public Exposure

If the Vampires behaviours, beliefs and thinking are exposed to objective analysis and reason, one or more of these fears will be triggered and they will defend themselves with every fibre of their being. A Vampire defending themselves against their fears is a very dangerous thing indeed because it's not simply a case of discussing their behaviours, beliefs and thinking. For them, it is a choice between either the False Self being true or psychological annihilation.

For the Vampire, if the True Self is true, then they are inadequate and Shameful, something that they will never accept for all the reasons already outlined and therefore, they will do everything in their power to enforce their version of reality regardless of how crazy that process is.

Where "normal" people are critical reasoners, the Vampire is an emotional reasoner. Their version of themselves and reality are both false, so they cannot reason critically about those things because this would inevitably lead to their exposure. Instead, they reason emotionally. That means that, to them, what they feel are facts.

To the rest of the population facts and feelings are different things, but to the Vampire feelings are facts and they will twist the facts to fit their feelings. If the Vampire feels a certain way, they will find a reason outside of themselves for feeling that way and in most cases, they will find that reason in the behaviour of others, most notably their Target.

This makes it impossible to have any meaningful discussion about their behaviour and any attempt to do so will result in a bizarre array of emotional tactics being employed against the person attempting to do so. The Vampire will respond to critical thinking about their behaviour with emotional reasoning aimed at the other person. When the Vampire feels attacked in this way, they really do believe that they are being abused, and will have absolutely no qualms about saying so.

What you end up with is a situation in which any attempt to discuss the behaviours of the Vampire (which are usually abusive) will result in the other party being accused of being abusive. The Vampire really does believe what they are saying at this point because they have to. Anything else would lead to a state of affairs in which the True Self is true, and that's psychological annihilation to them, which explains the sixth Truth: Vampires cannot be reasoned with. They do not think rationally and consider rational thinking from others about their behaviour as abusive (no, really).

Vampires don't change. Assuming that they will miraculously change their behaviour and thinking is naïve at best and hugely dangerous at worst.

In order to effect change, people have to be able to reflect on themselves. They need insight into their behaviours, thinking and beliefs because thinking and behaviours are based on beliefs. If an individual believes that they are worthy of love and respect, they will not tolerate abuse. If an individual believes that they are not worthy of love and respect, they will. Changing the way we think and behave therefore requires the ability to reflect on what we believe about ourselves, and without that change is just not possible.

"Normal" people are capable of that insight. It might be difficult, even painful, but it is possible. The offices of therapeutic professionals the world over are rammed with people who are actively engaged in examining their core beliefs about themselves, changing them and going on to lead happier, healthier lives. What you won't find in those offices are Vampires. The Vampire is not capable of the insight required for change. For them, the False Self and the False Reality are everything and anything that contradicts those things is rejected out of hand.

The Vampires core sense of inadequacy and Shame lead them to blame anyone and everyone around them for their problems, never themselves, and they are extraordinarily adept at surrounding themselves with manipulatable others who support their False Self and False Reality. Such individuals are referred to as "Flying Monkeys" and it is a universal fact that wherever you find a Vampire, Flying Monkeys are never far away. I'll be examining them later on, but for now it is enough to understand that their purpose is to support the Vampire in maintaining their False Self and False Reality.

With sufficient Flying Monkeys in place, and sufficient discrediting and removal of others that contradict the Vampires reality, they create for themselves a version of reality in which they are never the one at fault as far as their behaviours are concerned. Through doing this, the Vampire sets themselves up in such a way that they never have to examine themselves, something they avoid at all costs because, as has been pointed out already, it would lead to questioning the False Self and entertaining the possibility that the True Self is actually who they are. The core sense of the Vampire is inadequacy and Shame. The very first thing they will do if anyone attempts to point out that the False Self is false is to engage in an attack on that individual that will involve as many Flying Monkeys as possible and as many abusive tactics as are necessary to make that individual stop or go away.

The only way the Vampire might eventually be forced to look at themselves is if they have lost all access to Flying Monkeys and have no-one else to blame for their behaviours. If that is going to happen at all, it will be when the Vampire has driven all others away from them by their abusive behaviours and there is no-one left to blame.

Since this pattern of behaviour is a constant in the life of the Vampire, it accounts for the seventh truth: Vampires don't change. Assuming that they will miraculously change their behaviour and thinking is naïve at best and hugely dangerous at worst.

Vampires are addicts. Anyone in a relationship with one will also become an addict.

In order to maintain the False Self and False Reality, the Vampire needs a constant source of Narcissistic Supply. They are unable to provide for their own emotional needs and must engage others to provide for them. According to Psychology Today, "addiction is a condition in which a person engages in use of a substance or in a behaviour for which the rewarding effects provide a compelling incentive to repeatedly pursue the behaviour despite detrimental consequences".

The behaviours of the Vampire in pursuing Narcissistic Supply fit this definition perfectly. They repeatedly pursue behaviours that will yield Narcissistic Supply because their disorder compels them to. The detrimental consequences of their behaviour are mostly felt by their Targets, but ultimately are felt by the Vampire as well through the destructive effect their behaviours have on their relationships.

But sadly, that's not all. Because of the nature of their disorder, Vampires engage in what Dr. Tara Palmatier calls "The Fearsome Foursome". These are:

Victim Identity
Entitlement
Control Freakery
Emotional reasoning

In the Vampires False Reality, they are the Victim. I'll talk about this in more detail later on, but for now it's enough to understand that they really do believe that they are victims in their own lives. They refuse to accept responsibility for their actions because responsibility means potential failure, and that could mean that they are inferior to others. If that were the case, it would be dangerously close to the True Self being true, which they completely reject. Therefore, as I pointed out earlier, anything that indicates that their actions are negative or hurtful is interpreted as abuse and they maintain the status of being the victim. It's crazy-making to be around and makes it impossible to engage with them in any meaningful way.

They also feel entitled. Because they reason at the emotional level of a child and see others as objects to provide them with Narcissistic Supply, they feel that they have the right to extract that supply by any and all means necessary. In exactly the same way that small children do not understand why they can't have what they want when they want it, the Vampire does not understand why they can't have Narcissistic Supply when they want it. This sense of entitlement leads them to abuse those around them, notably their Target in order to have their emotional needs met and they feel under no obligation whatsoever to engage in reciprocity. Children don't, and therefore neither do Vampires.

Control Freakery is related to the Five Fears mentioned earlier. In order to feel superior and avoid the things they fear most, the Vampire engages in behaviours that are specifically designed to control those around them. Again, these behaviours are primarily aimed at their Target. Any time the Vampire fears any of the Five, or they feel inferior, they exert control over the Target in order to re-establish their sense of safety and/or superiority. Their disorder compels them to do this and, as I pointed out earlier, that's not going to change.

Emotional reasoning has been touched on already, so I won't dwell on it. It's enough to remind ourselves that Vampires do not engage in critical reasoning about their behaviour, only emotional reasoning.

What that all adds up to is an individual that behaves in ways that are bizarre, counterintuitive, unpredictable and abusive. Anyone who attempts to have a relationship with a Vampire will find themselves living in an environment of constant drama and chaos in which the Vampires behaviours and needs are centre-stage at all times.

I'll be describing the way that leads to addiction in more detail later on, but for now I'll go back to that definition from earlier. "Addiction is a condition in which a person engages in use of a substance or in a behaviour for which the rewarding effects provide a compelling incentive to repeatedly pursue the behaviour despite detrimental consequences".

Whenever the Vampire requires Narcissistic Supply, they engage in whatever behaviours they have learned are effective in securing it. Usually, this involves creating drama and chaos. But this is not what creates the addiction in the Target; what creates it are the times in the relationship when the Vampire is behaving positively towards them. In an environment of chaos, drama and abuse, the Target lives for those moments when the Vampire returns to the behaviours they first exhibited at the start of the relationship, which only occur when the Vampire feels superior and/or safe and over time become less and less frequent. In simple terms, the Target ends up chasing the "high" of being treated well by providing whatever Narcissistic Supply the Vampire demands.

The detrimental consequence for the Target is that in order to get that "high" they must endure more and more abuse, and that only gets worse over time. This accounts for the eighth Truth: Vampires are addicts. Anyone in a relationship with one will also become an addict.

Vampires lie. All the time.

Vampires are pathological liars. When you consider that the entire self they are trying to convince you is who they are is False and therefore their identity is built on a lie, it's not a huge leap to accept that pretty much everything they do and say is also a lie. The Vampire is a lie. A walking, talking lie.

Ask any professional who has to detect lies and they will tell you that the best liars believe their own lies, which is why some of them can fool lie detector tests. The bottom line with lying is that the first person we have to lie to is ourselves. If we can do that and believe what we're telling ourselves, we can lie to others with ease. Vampires do exactly that. They live in a world where they tell themselves lies about themselves and others, about their behaviour and that of others, about their intentions and those of others, about their beliefs and those of others and they believe it. All of it.

Therefore, to the Vampire, what they're doing isn't really lying. It's simply a reflection of a reality they have created for their own purposes. That it doesn't match your reality is your problem, not theirs, according to them. Remember that the False Self must be preserved at all costs, and that includes all the lies that are required to achieve that.

Vampires lie to gain Narcissistic supply, to make themselves look good, to avoid being blamed for their bad behaviours, to protect the False Self, to gain sympathy, to gain control over others and they will even lie just for fun. There is a concept called "duping delight" that refers to the thrill that Vampires experience when they get away with lying to their Target and being believed. It is often accompanied by what I call "the smirk", that look of smug delight that crosses their face when they think they've got away with something.

Many people have asked why the Vampire lies and the fact is that there are many reasons, as many reasons as there are benefits of lying in any particular instance. If it would serve the Vampire better to lie than to tell the truth, they will lie without a second thought. Sometimes they will lie even when telling the truth would serve them better because they like lying and it has become second nature to them.

The bottom line with Vampires is that they almost never tell the truth. Because they lack Empathy and see people as objects, they have no remorse when they lie and they feel entitled to lie whenever they want to. Their twisted thinking about others tells them that if they are lying to you, it's because you don't deserve the truth. In other words, they justify their lies to themselves by believing that you are the reason they are lying to you.

I think the simplest way of explaining why the Vampire lies is to consider why other people don't. Normal, healthy people tell each other the truth most of the time. We may tell the odd "white lie" to save another's feelings, but overall we are truthful. Why do we tell the truth? Because we know that lying is wrong. We have a moral compass. We have Empathy and we can understand what it would be like to be lied to, so we don't do it. Vampires don't have a moral compass and they don't have Empathy.

Oh, they know right from wrong. It's not like they don't understand the concept of morality and that lying and cheating to get what you want is considered to be "bad". They know that, they just don't care. Where normal, healthy people would feel remorse if they lie, Vampires don't. It's absolutely vital to get your head around this one. It is an alien concept but it is a fact, and the ninth Truth: Vampires lie. All the time.

The words and actions of a Vampire don't match. Watch them very carefully and you'll see it.

This one follows from the last. Because Vampires are essentially two selves: the True Self and the False Self, what they say and what they do are often two very different things. Considering that pretty much everything the Vampire says is a lie, it's really no surprise that their behaviour doesn't match. That we often don't notice just reflects the normal human tendency to not think that everything we hear is a lie. Sometimes the gap between the Vampires words and behaviours is subtle and easy to ignore such as when they say that they don't like a particular person and then are lovely to them to their face.

That kind of hypocrisy is fairly common and easily dismissed. Other times the gap is definitely not subtle and our jaws hit the floor when we see what the Vampire is doing or has done. Many Vampires claim to be highly moral, for example, and then conduct affairs. Or they may declare their love and commitment to their Target days or even hours before a brutal discard.

The reason for all that is really straightforward. The Vampire talks from the position of the False self and behaves from the position of either the True Self, or the False Self with a different motive at that point in time. They can't help it and don't care anyway.

What they say reflects what the False Self requires, and the False Self is the definition of an opportunist. Whenever the Vampire sees an opportunity to gain Narcissistic supply or resources from others, they will change their behaviour in order to obtain it. Whether the behaviour required at that point in time is in line with what the Vampire has said about themselves previously is irrelevant. All that matters is the Narcissistic supply they are chasing at that point.

The Vampire will also manipulate the Target according to the needs of the False Self. If the False Self wants you to be deeply in love, they will spout declarations of love. If the False Self wants you to be admiring, they will say things to gain that admiration. And let's not forget that the Vampire is just a pathological liar anyway, which all adds up to a really toxic soup of words that have no basis in reality and are almost always lies. Therefore, the Vampires behaviours cannot possibly agree with their words because their words are all toxic lies soup.

The bottom line with the words and actions of the Vampire is that they do not match because they cannot match. The Vampire will do and say whatever is needed to secure sources of Narcissistic supply and if those words and actions don't match, they simply don't care. If they are challenged on that, they will lash out with Rage. That's why it's usually a smarter move not to challenge them, but to watch them instead. Inevitably, when you watch a Vampire for any extended period of time, their hypocrisy will surface. The gulf between their words and actions will become apparent, which is why this is the tenth and final truth: The words and actions of a Vampire don't match. Watch them very carefully and you'll see it.

So there we have it: The basics of the Modern Vampire. It's a lot to take in, so I think we'll pause for a moment for the first Interlude.

Interlude 1

"A laugh can be a very powerful thing. Why, sometimes in life, it's the only weapon we have." - Roger Rabbit, "Who Framed Roger Rabbit?"

Hello, dear Survivor!

Well, here we are at the end of Chapter 1. I've read it all back and, quite frankly, if I hadn't been there myself, I would think the whole thing was Batshit Crazy. I really don't care whether people who've never been there believe me. I've had my time trying to explain the Vampire to people who've never been attacked by one and I just don't bother any more. Too many "WTF?" faces.

If you're still reading, there's every chance that you get it because you've been there. Good to have you here, fellow Survivor. Since you've made it through Chapter 1, I think you deserve to have some positivity. So here we go...

I believe that laughter and humour really are the antidote to the misery and negativity that Vampires spread in the world. I get them, I really do. I get why they do the things they do. I get that they had bad childhoods. I get that their existence is really unpleasant and they can't possibly hope to have decent relationships ever. And it's not that I don't care, because actually I do care. The last thing I want to see in the world is suffering. But does the Vampire care about their Target? No, they don't, and that's where they and I part company as far as my sympathy goes.

Now, while we can't do anything about them, what we can do is look after each other, spread the word about who and what the Vampire is and do our level best to take good care of ourselves and each other and stay positive. Why? Because that's exactly what they don't want us to do and if we allow them to make us miserable, they win. I'm not having that, folks.

These Interludes exist to help fight the darkness and despair that the Vampire spreads around by offering an alternative, and occasionally funny commentary on what could otherwise be quite grim reading material, so with that in mind, a word about how I think we might have a rethink about how to deal with the Vampire.

For my money, one of the first things we can do is to recognise that having relationships is not a right, it is a privilege. We don't let people drive cars until they've learned how, do we? And we happily disqualify people from driving if they behave dangerously or hurt other people. How is that different? No-one says "Oh poor you, you lost your licence for hospitalising someone with your car" do they?

Once we get our heads around the notion that being in a relationship is not something everyone is entitled to, maybe more people would feel better about speaking out when they've been abused in one. We wouldn't think twice about telling people we got run over, right? I want to see a world where people feel the same way about speaking out about Vampires.

The analogy I like to use is that of the leper. Did lepers ask to have leprosy? No. Is it the lepers fault they have leprosy? No. But do they expect for other people to treat them like they don't have leprosy and get all intimate with them? Hell No! The Vampire is the relationship equivalent of a leper. Does it suck to be them? Yes, it does.

But do the rest of us have to lay down our right to have a happy, healthy life because of it? No, it absolutely does not. And does it mean we shouldn't point out the lepers in our society? No, I don't believe it does. Vampires won't ever change anyway, so it's not like we're doing them a disservice by pointing out what they are.

What we're doing is helping those people who understand that relationships are a privilege to have them with other people who feel the same way. Should we have Vampire colonies where we could contain them? Maybe on an island surrounded by Great White sharks and populated by Velociraptors? I'll leave that for you to decide, but I for one am not going to stand by and let those who seek to hurt others to serve their own sick agenda get away with it any more. If it takes for me to write daft interludes with a bit of comedy in them to achieve that, bring it on.

And that's enough about the Vampire for now. They get more than enough airplay anyway. This next bit is about YOU, dear Survivor. I reckon you deserve to have the spotlight on you for a change. In my experience there are a number of "burning questions" that Survivors struggle to answer once they have escaped their abuser. They ask them because they feel guilty and not good enough because their Self Respect has been shredded by the Vampire. These questions kinda haunt them and they ruminate endlessly about them, which sucks. I am going to answer these questions in first 6 Interludes and I think you'll like the answers. With any luck, it'll cheer you right up.

The questions are:

1) Did the Vampire really love me?
2) Will the Vampire be happy in their new relationship?
3) Even if that new relationship fails, is there someone out there with whom the Vampire can be happy?
4) How can the Vampire move on so quickly as if I never mattered?
5) Does the Vampire miss me?

6) How much of this is my fault, and what could I have done differently?

Sound about right? Thought so. OK, here goes with answering the first one:

Did the Vampire really love me?

No. I'm really sorry to have to tell you this, but the Vampire never loved you. The Vampire cannot feel love as normal people do. The Vampire is incapable of sustaining the healthy sense of real, honest-to-goodness love for another that you yourself felt. I know that sucks, but there comes a time when all Survivors have to face the truth. Having said that, there is HUGE optimism to be had from that, so please read on....

Bear in mind that the Vampire is insane and therefore sees you very differently to how normal people see you but they are not stupid, and they can and do appreciate the qualities that make you attractive to normal people and Vampires alike.

In the Idealisation Stage (see Chapter 3) the Vampire saw something in you that they did not and never will possess. They thought you were enormously attractive, both physically and emotionally and they wanted each and every inch of you all the time. All day, every day. I shit you not. That is God's honest truth.

Think about it for a minute. Why would an individual that cares only about how others perceive them choose anything other than a partner that makes them look amazing? Why would an individual that cares only about how their Targets make them feel about themselves choose anything other than the very best possible source of positive emotions? Why would an individual that cares only about securing the best possible source of Narcissistic supply bother with anything other than the best possible source of Narcissistic supply? If you are not appreciated by others as their partner, if they can't show you off, if you embarrass them or make them look bad, that's criticism to the Vampire and they are not going to do that to themselves.

The Vampire did not take some random, scattergun approach when they chose you. These individuals are not stupid, and they are not interested in anything other than the best. They chose you because you are physically and emotionally attractive. Gorgeous in fact, and don't you dare ever doubt it. I'm not kidding.

Just follow my logic for a moment while I do something I hate doing: Seeing things from the Vampire's perspective. I hate doing it because I feel, in the words of Jack Sparrow "sullied and unusual" afterwards but here goes: "I am a Vampire. I go for the most beautiful, most intelligent, most caring, most compassionate, most sexy, most funny, most kind, most witty, most charming and most amazing individual I can get my hands on. Why? Because I'm a fucking Vampire! If I can possess those things in the form of another person, it means I AM those things, and if I can dominate and control that person, I can feel like that whenever I want"

Bleuch! I hate doing that. Time for a shower to wash all the Vampire off. Here's the thing, though: The Vampire Mirrored your qualities and prayed to God that you wouldn't notice what a pile of shit they are when they had you in the Idealisation Stage. Because they used Mirroring, which I'll talk about later in the book, the Vampire reflected back to you what you are. By carefully watching you and adopting your mannerisms and preferences, they became you. What that means is that the person you fell in love with was YOU. Did you think your Vampire was pretty or handsome? That's YOU. Did you think they were smart? That's YOU. Did you think they were funny, sexy, charming and so on? ALL OF IT IS YOU. That may take a while to sink in, but I promise you it is true.

And once the Vampire secured you, a switch flipped in their fucked up little head. They found themselves in a position where they had sourced this amazing person and now had to figure out how not to lose them. From that point on, it's all about Domination and Control. In the Devaluation Stage, the Vampire did everything in their power to enslave and control the staggeringly beautiful person they had secured so that they could have you all to themselves. In a weird way, that's actually a compliment. The Vampire was paranoid about having you stolen away from them and they were terrified that you would abandon them because you are fucking gorgeous!

The Vampire knows this. The rest of the population knows this. The only person who doesn't know this yet is you and that's because the Vampire has fucked up your Self Respect in an effort to keep you from abandoning them.

Trust me on this one please. Vampires ONLY choose the best, and that's what you are. The Vampire tried to control you by fucking with your Self Respect, which is why you can't feel it yet, but you will. If you don't believe me in all this yet, dear Survivor, then do yourself a favour and just take it on trust please. I am not making this up and I have nothing whatsoever to gain from lying to you.

Also, please, please, please do NOT allow this knowledge to inspire a belief that any future engagement with the Vampire would in any way be different to the way it was before. The Vampire will NEVER change and will only inflict more harm if you engage with them. Once the relationship with a Vampire has ended, NEVER, under any circumstances, go back.

And that's it from the first Interlude. Here's hoping you've cheered up some and are ready to dive into the next chapter. See you on the other side!

Chapter 2

The Mind of the Vampire

Now that we've had a look at the basics, I'd like to take some time examining the real reason why having any kind of relationship with a Vampire is an impossibility. The underlying reason for why Vampires destroy all their close interpersonal relationships (and I mean all of them) is because they have a personality disorder.

Now, to reiterate a point I made at the beginning of the book, I am not referring to all individuals with personality disorders when I use the term Vampire. Personality disorders are on a spectrum from mild to malignant. Many people suffer with personality disorders, know they have one and do their level best every day to deal with it. These people are possibly best described as having "traits of" the disorder. In other words, they display some disordered thinking, feeling and behaviour but have sufficient self-awareness to be able to handle themselves and seek treatment where appropriate. I have enormous compassion and admiration for these people because theirs is an on-going struggle. What's more, I don't have a problem with such individuals because they don't abuse their nearest and dearest and, if they do and it is pointed out to them, they seek to make amends.

This chapter, and in fact the entire Field Manual does not refer to such people. It does refer to Vampires - those individuals whose personality disorder is so severe that they have no insight into their own mind, do not believe there is anything wrong with them, have no empathy, no remorse, no compassion and in most cases are sadistic - they abuse and destroy others and they actually enjoy it. As the brilliant Kris Godinez puts it, in such individuals "there is no there there". What she's referring to is that the mind of a Vampire does not contain a significant part of what we would consider a "normal" operating system; the empathy part.

So, as I go through this chapter and refer to the mind of the Vampire I will be referring to the malignant ones. The ones with no hope of change. The ones that are only capable of destruction.

In order to understand what's going on in the mind of a Vampire, we need to look at what a personality disorder is, and in order to do that, we need to understand what personality is, so here goes.

The American Psychological Association (APA) defines personality as "individual differences in characteristic patterns of thinking, feeling and behaving." In other words, an individual's personality is composed of how they think and feel and therefore what they do. According to the APA again, a personality disorder is "a way of thinking, feeling and behaving that deviates from the expectations of the culture, causes distress or problems functioning, and lasts over time."

In other words, the personalities of such individuals are maladaptive. While that may sound simple (and possibly obvious), it is the single most important piece of information any Target or Survivor can possibly get their hands on. Why? Because it provides the cornerstone of understanding the Vampire: Their personality disorder is so severe that it is no longer a case of having a personality disorder. It is a case of being a disordered personality. In other words, while the Vampire does have a personality disorder, it's more a case that they are their disordered personality. I'll say that again... While technically the Vampire has a personality disorder, their disordered personality is actually who they are. Without getting your head around that, you can't go anywhere with understanding the mind of the Vampire, so if you struggle with the contents of this chapter, please come back here and remind yourself of that one basic fact. It's so important.

OK, so once we've got a handle on that lot, we can go forward and examine what's actually going on inside the mind of the Vampire. I'll warn you now, some of this won't make sense simply because they are disordered and you're not. Or possibly because you have empathy and they don't. Or possibly because they are crazed sadists and you're not. Whatever the reason is, if you find yourself pulling a "WTF?" face, don't fret. Let the information settle and have another go. I'm going to break the mind of the Vampire down into the 4 primary emotions and the all-important lack of Empathy.

The 4 Primary Emotions

While the Vampire can feel some emotions outside of the Primary 4, they tend to be fleeting and they can't generate them for themselves. What they feel ALL THE TIME are Fear, Shame, Rage and Envy.

Fear

The Vampire is fearful. Because they are emotionally developmentally arrested, they are unable to provide themselves with the necessary reassurance that they are safe in the world. Any mask of confidence and grandiosity they wear is hiding a small child that is terrified of a number of things.

First, they are afraid of Abandonment. They don't show it of course, that would require them to be vulnerable, which would threaten their sense of superiority but they are deathly afraid of being left without someone to take care of their emotional needs because they simply cannot do that for themselves. The fear of abandonment goes all the way back to early childhood where, for whatever reason, they never learned to "self-soothe", to be able to regulate their own emotions. In other words, they know full well that they will go into total meltdown if they don't have external sources of Narcissistic supply and it scares the living crap out of them. It's why they need their Target to be terrified of abandonment.

Their twisted logic dictates that if they can make the Target dependent on them and more scared of abandonment than they are themselves, the Target won't abandon them. The

Vampires fear of abandonment inevitably makes the Target afraid of abandonment, often where none existed before and always more than that of the Vampire.

Second, they are afraid of feeling or appearing inferior or inadequate. The Vampire's True Self feels inferior and inadequate all the time. Therefore the Vampire does everything in their power to avoid those feelings and that's what the False Self is for.

One of the greatest fears of the Vampire is that people will see behind the mask of the False Self, see the truth of who they really are, find them to be inferior or inadequate and thereby confirm that the True Self is, in fact, true. This is why they engage in smear campaigns to discredit anyone who may be able to see the truth, why they cannot take criticism of any kind, why they keep harems of Flying Monkeys, why they systematically destroy their Targets Self Respect so that they appear superior to them, why they won't associate with anyone they deem "less than", why they seek to associate with people of high status, why they seek power, money, resources and status at every turn and why they always wear the mask of the false self in public, if not constantly. The Vampire is a slave to their fear of appearing inferior or inadequate and anyone in a relationship with one will become a slave to it too. Third, they are afraid of loss of control.

The Vampire has little to no control over their internal emotional state at any given time. They are consumed by fear, envy, shame and rage and that means that they are basically an emotional mess all the time. Since they can't control their emotions, they turn all that outward and try to control the emotions of others. They reason that if they can do that, the other person (usually the Target) will serve to provide them with the self-soothing they cannot provide for themselves. In other words, by controlling the emotions of others, they make their world "safer" and thereby can control their own emotions.

The problem with that is obvious: There's another person involved, and controlling the emotions of other people is emotional abuse. And the more emotionally deregulated the Vampire becomes, the more they try to control their Target. It's like a cat with a mouse - when the mouse tries to move, the cat pounces or drops the paw. If the mouse stays still, the cat keeps it there. The cat retains control and the mouse loses every which way. To the Vampire, loss of control over the Target represents a threat of existential proportions.

Without a Target, they are unable to regulate their emotions or self-soothe and they use the Narcissistic supply they gain from the Target to stave off the truth of the True Self. As with the other fears, the Vampire is a slave to the fear of loss of control and therefore so will the Target be.

Fourth, they are afraid of the loss of resources. To the Vampire, resources of any kind be they financial, emotional, physical or whatever are a shield against the harsh reality of the world: that their False Self is indeed false. Resources help the Vampire prop up the False Self and a lack of resources represents a threat to that. It really is as simple as that.
Any and all resources the Vampire can lay their hands on will be used to prop up the False Self and they will consume those resources remorselessly to do so. Sadly, people are on that list

too, in particular the Target. Whenever the Vampire feels a threat to the False Self, they draw more and more resources to prop it up again. That could mean money being spent on gifts, dinners, holidays, new possessions etc. It could mean emotional attention from the Target (good or bad). It could mean emotional attention from others outside the relationship.

Basically, anyone and anything the Vampire can draw on as a resource to prop up the False Self, they will and they will have absolutely no problem with continuing to do so until there is nothing of that resource left. Where to normal, healthy people resources are just that: resources, to the Vampire they are necessary on an existential level. Where normal, healthy people can lose resources and know they will be OK, the Vampire believes that loss of resources is literally a loss of identity and in their case, that identity is the False Self. Again, the Vampire is a slave to this and they will make their Target a slave to it too.

Finally, they are afraid of public exposure. This one chills them to their very core. The idea that other people might catch on to the fact that the True Self is who they really are is the equivalent of psychological annihilation. The Vampire hates their True Self and believes that everyone else hates it too. They hate all that they hate in themselves in others after all, so they expect that in return. The Vampire spends all day every day creating, reinforcing and propping up the False Self in order to avoid even the remotest possibility of public exposure.

They also expend enormous amounts of resources (usually not theirs) doing the same thing. Imagine being presented with all the things you've ever done that you're ashamed of all at one point in time by someone who hates you. Now imagine that happening in front of people who hate you. Basically, the experience would be akin to an emotional sandblasting in front of a hostile crowd. Don't fancy that? Neither does the Vampire. The fact is that for normal, healthy people that's just not going to happen and they know that.

The Vampire doesn't know that. In fact, they believe that public exposure for what they truly are would mean that all their Shame is laid bare for the world to see. That's what the False Self is protecting them from. Even as I write this, I feel empathy and compassion for that individual but I've just had to remind myself and I'll remind you too - the Vampire isn't with us on this one. You try offering empathy and compassion to a Vampire and they'll take you for everything you've got. Harsh, but true. As with the other fears, this one will suck in the Target. The Vampire's fear of exposure is so all-consuming that they will drag in the Target as an accomplice in their public deception and endless promotion of the truth of the False Self.

So much for Fear. It is a massive motivator for the behaviours of the Vampire, but it is not the only one. Neither is it the worst. I know. I thought the fears were bad enough too, but it's more complicated than that. To get a better handle on the mind of the Vampire, we're going to have a look at Shame.

Shame

The message that has been delivered to the Vampire (probably in early childhood) is that they are not good enough as a person. This is where we need to take a brief moment to draw the distinction between guilt and shame. Guilt is feeling bad about something you've <u>done</u>. Shame is feeling bad about something you <u>are</u>. Families that include Shame are toxic. Deeply, deeply toxic. They don't know the difference between Guilt and Shame.

I'm not kidding. Adults in toxic families talk to their children in terms of the child being bad, instead of <u>being</u> good and having <u>done</u> something bad. It's a simple distinction, it's massively important, most families get it right and it's the defining feature of a Vampire breeding ground that they get it wrong all the time. Not only that, they usually get it wrong on purpose. They send the message to the children in the family that they are not good enough, that they don't deserve unconditional love and in extreme cases that they don't deserve to exist at all.

Shame based families create Shame based individuals and it's as simple as that. If children grow up around adults who operate from a position of Shame, they send the message day in, day out either overtly or implicitly that the child isn't worthy of love, must earn approval, can do nothing right, is inherently wrong and defective and must put their emotional needs second to those of the toxic adults in the family.

Now, I think that's a tragedy of Shakespearean proportions. I'm not religious at all, but I'd like to believe that there's a special Hell for adults who engage in Shaming their children because it doesn't just make the child feel bad for a bit, it permanently destroys them on a fundamental level. It takes an innocent human deserving of unconditional love and affection, a child of the universe with the inalienable right to live a life free to experience all the wonders the world has to offer and trashes them.

Shaming children is unforgivable and you know who does it best? That's right - the Vampire. Shame is what Psychologists would call "generationally transmitted". In other words, it's passed down in families. Vampires are Shame based, they Shame their children, who become Shame based and on and on it goes. Just as an aside, if you're ever unsure about whether a romantic prospect might be a Vampire, watch their parents. If there's Shame there, that's a Red Flag.

But it goes deeper than this. Toxic Shame is so insidious, so pervasive and so malignant that in the case of the Vampire it cannot be cured. Apart from anything else, the Vampire doesn't believe there's anything wrong with them and that their relationship with Shame is just "normal" because they've never experienced anything else. In fact, the average Vampire simply doesn't get families or individuals that are not Shame based. They just don't make sense to them.

You'd think that might be a good thing, right? That maybe showing the Vampire that Shame doesn't have to be the only way to relate to others might help in some way? Yeah? No. That's not how that works because of one of the other basic emotions coming up shortly: Envy. The Vampire envies anything they can't have or be and that includes non-Shame based individuals. More on that later.

The emotional reality of the Vampire is that of the Shamed child who grew up never feeling good enough, only receiving love under certain conditions if at all, feeling undeserving of attention and affection and hating themselves simply for being who they are. They live in that reality all day every day and that is what composes the True Self.
It is tragic, yes. But it is also extraordinarily dangerous. All that Shame must be contained. It can't possibly be the everyday reality.

Think about it - would YOU like to live like that? If you went through every moment of every day thinking and feeling utterly worthless, hating yourself and everything you are and do could you even get out of bed? That's why the False Self was created. It's a matter of basic survival. The True Self of the Vampire as a child was assaulted constantly by Vampire parents or "caregivers" and reduced to a being composed of Shame that has no way of providing for their own emotional needs. Imagine that child going out into the world and trying to have others meet their emotional needs. That is one helpless, needy, clingy child right? That's a Vampire, that is.

The Vampire is completely incapable of meeting their own emotional needs and once we understand the nature of Shame it becomes obvious why that is the case. Children are not capable of looking after their emotional needs. Why? Because they're children! It takes nurturing and teaching and good parenting to show them how to manage their emotional needs.

Children who receive all that learn that they are good people who sometimes mess up, are worthy of love and don't accept abuse. When healthy people feel bad, they figure out why and deal with it. Whenever the Vampire feels bad about anything, they experience Shame. The message is so deeply ingrained in them that the only thing they experience when they feel bad is Shame. It doesn't matter where the bad feeling is coming from, they feel Shame.

It doesn't matter who did what or why, if they feel bad, they feel Shame. And that's not gonna fly, now is it? Essentially, you're taking an adult Vampire all the way back to their Shame filled childhood every time they feel bad about anything.

The way the Vampire deals with all that is to lock up the True Self and hide it away from the world. That way, all that Shame is contained and they can go about some semblance of a normal existence. In its place, they develop the False Self and craft that as a means of surviving in the world. It also serves to lure Targets in to be trapped in a one-way relationship where they will be used with the express purpose of supporting the False Self regardless of the consequences to them of doing so. The True Self is denied completely. The Vampire does not want to recognise it, has banished it into their unconscious and they certainly don't want anyone else to notice it, however briefly.

They never deal with their Shame, they simply turn their back on it and the True Self and deny that it exists at all. This is what Psychologists would call "splitting". It's the process of seeing an individual (including one's self) as either all-good or all-bad, Black or White, and it relates to another piece of psychological terminology: "Whole object relations". This refers to the ability of a person to understand that another person can be good and bad at the same time, a good person who made a mistake for instance, or a bad person doing good things in an attempt to change.

In normal, healthy development children start out using Splitting a lot. Look at their early friendships, or family interactions. Gradually, as they learn "Whole Object Relations" they start to be able to understand that people are not Black or White but shades of Grey. They can keep the thought of loving someone in their mind even though they may be hurt by them or angry with them, so they stop Splitting and don't do it as adults. Healthy adults demonstrate that they have "Whole Object Relations" all the time. It's the idea of "I love you, but you've hurt me and I'm unhappy with you right now". If you hear that from an adult, they're probably not a Vampire, because Vampires can't do that at all. They simply never made it through that part of their development and so didn't learn "Whole Object Relations". As a consequence, they use Splitting all the time. Basically, if you're supporting the False Self, they Split you White. You are reflecting back what they want to see about themselves and they like you.

However, if you stop doing that, or God forbid point out the True Self or cast doubt on the False Self, they Split you Black and they hate you. You're not reflecting back what they want to see, you're reflecting back the truth and they simply will not deal with that. Any deviation from the "reality" of the False Self can only lead to one place: all that Shame.

That's why there's a Jekyll and Hyde personality at play in the Vampire. That's why they can't stand criticism. That's why they appear to hate you and then love you. That's why their abuse goes in cycles of idealisation and devaluation. That's why Targets always feel the push-and-pull in these relationships.

That's why Targets never feel safe and "walks on eggshells". It all comes down to the Splitting reflex of the Vampire because they lack "Whole Object Relations". They deal with their Shame by Splitting, creating a False Self and then relating to the world through the "White" False Self. If other people reflect back the False Self, if they buy the act and behave accordingly, the Vampire Splits them White and all is well. If they fail to do that, the Vampire Splits them Black and treats them appallingly.

It's a point worth repeating that this is never, ever going to change in the Vampire. It's who they are. The way they deal with their Shame dictates how they relate to others and always will. They simply cannot and never will be able to hold two versions of any individual in their minds at one time. I have seen this happen first hand. I witnessed a Vampire standing right in front of me actually telling me what was going on in their head as far as their understanding of me went. They did exactly what I've described here - they explained that they had two versions of me in their mind and could not reconcile the two. It was one of the weirdest experiences of my life because I was witnessing someone having a psychotic meltdown right in front of me, I was within arms-reach, and according to the Vampire it was all my fault (of course). The Vampire cannot accept that there is anything wrong with them, so what caused the two versions of me in their head? That would be me. Weird.

So much for Shame. Once you get a handle on that, the picture starts to become a little clearer. However, we still need to examine Rage and Envy in order to get the whole picture.

Rage

Earlier, I drew the distinction between guilt and Shame. Here, we need to look at the distinction between Anger and Rage. Anger and Rage are both forms of defense from attack. If we are hurt, we get angry and that's completely normal. If we didn't get angry when we're hurt, mankind's life expectancy would have been close to zero. It also stands true of guilt because guilt is also a form of hurt. It's a hurt to our sense of self, if you like. If someone were to draw our attention to something we've done wrong, it would be quite normal for us to be angry with ourselves for having made a mistake, right? We might even be angry at them. The anger is the response to the hurt of guilt.

It's not unusual for normal people to feel angry at someone else who has made them feel bad either. If your boss points out a mistake you made in front of others, for example, you may be angry at them, but it's in response to the guilt you feel, not their behaviour. If you didn't care about the mistake, there would be nothing to get angry about, right? So anger is a normal response to feeling the hurt of guilt.

Rage, on the other hand, is the response to Shame. The purpose of Rage is to remove whatever or whoever is causing feelings of Shame because that's not about what we've done, it's about who we are. Someone causing us feelings of Shame is a threat to our identity and psychological safety and so Rage comes into play to defend us from that.

Rage is basically Anger on steroids, and it's operating within the mind of the Vampire pretty much 24/7. The reason is simple: Anything that triggers the Shame felt by the True Self results in a release of Rage. It doesn't matter where that trigger came from, who did it (or didn't) or how little sense it makes, as soon as the Vampire feels Shame, Rage ensues. It's a primitive defense and it's incredibly dangerous. It really doesn't take much to cause an injury to the Shame of the Vampire that will result in Rage.

Here's a very short list of some of the things that might do it:

The Vampire doesn't get their way

The Vampire is criticised, or thinks they have been

The Vampire is asked to be accountable for their actions

The Vampire's sense of entitlement isn't supported because they are not being treated as "special"

The Vampire is caught breaking the rules

The Vampire feels that they are losing control of a person or situation

That's just a few. There are loads more. Basically, anything that does not support the False Self can only do one other thing, right? It goes straight to all the Shame we talked about earlier. And that means that the world is throwing that stuff at the Vampire 24/7 because that's the nature of actual, objective reality. The one who doesn't live in reality is the Vampire themselves, so they are at odds with the world all day every day and are surrounded by potential attacks on their False Self 24 hours a day, 7 days a week, 365 days a year.

Any and all of them will result in Rage. It might not be "smashing the place up, homicidal Rage", in fact it's almost certainly not going to be that because Vampires are really good at knowing the rules of behaviour. What's more likely is passive-aggression, resulting in silent treatments, seething sulks, plotting to hurt others and extended campaigns of manipulation, hurt and stealth attacks designed to allow the Vampire to express their Rage in ways that won't be noticed by the general public. That doesn't mean that they won't express their Rage directly of course. Many do, but they usually do it behind closed doors and they always try to make sure that they come off as the Victim.

What you end up with is an individual that is full of Rage pretty much all day every day. They are never happy and nothing is ever good enough. Why? Rage. Sound familiar? Thought so. The world and everyone in it are at odds with the Vampire's False Self because the False Self is made up! It's a fabrication in the mind of the Vampire and only in the mind of the Vampire.

The only alternative to the False Self is, of course, Shame. And the response to Shame is Rage. That's the equation, ladies and gentlemen and yes, it really is that simple. Oh, I know there will be subtle variations between individual Vampires but the basic formula remains the same.

Once you get your head around the fact that the average Vampire is feeling Rage pretty much all the time, a lot of their behaviour starts to make sense. Why the sudden Silent Treatment? Why the cold shoulder? Why the argument from nowhere? Why the withdrawing of affection? Why the bad moods? Why the criticism? Why the constant feeling of not being good enough? Why the temper tantrums and explosions? Why the gossiping about others? Why the constant nagging feeling of "something wrong"? Why the feeling of walking on eggshells? That's all based on the Vampires Rage in response to their feelings of Shame.
So there's Rage. For the final piece of the puzzle, we need to take a look at Envy. I'll warn you now, this one's weird...

Envy

The reason I say that this is weird is because for most normal people, Envy is an alien concept. Oh, we get it on an intellectual level but because we don't feel it every day the way a Vampire does, it can be hard to get your head around, especially as it relates to a way of life. Mostly when we think about Envy, we think about jealousy instead because we don't really have a handle on what Envy really is, and we don't live it. However, just like with guilt and Shame and anger and Rage, we need to have a look at the difference between jealousy and Envy. Here goes...

Jealousy is about what other people have. We might look at someone else's lifestyle, job, partner or whatever and think "I want that, or something like it". Most normal, healthy people will then set a plan in motion to achieve that. Envy is different. Envy is not about what other people have, it's about who other people are. Where a healthy person will look at someone and say "I want to be like you", the Vampire will say "I want to be you". It's a very different and very dangerous proposition. What's more, Vampires believe that other people feel that way about them. I'm not kidding. They look at other people and want to be them and they believe that other people want to be them. How messed up is that?

And as if that wasn't weird enough, once the Vampire figures out that they can't be you, they will do everything in their power to discredit you and destroy you. Basically, they reason that if they can't be you, then neither can you. If they can't have what you have because you're you, then neither can you. Now that's the really messed up bit.

I saw this one first hand too. I've witnessed a Vampire looking straight at me and the progress I was making in therapy (for the issues they had induced, by the way) and they ended our relationship because I was getting healthy. The Vampire couldn't be me in the relationship, so there was no relationship. That's what Envy gets you.

At its heart, Envy is the earliest form of hate. Think of it like this: a small child, say 2 or 3 years old and the first in the family gets introduced to the new baby. Normal reaction? Envy. Little kids will often regress at that stage, maybe bedwetting, maybe becoming clingy, basically doing whatever they can to reclaim their parents attention that is now divided between them and their new sibling. Do they love their new sibling? In all shocking honesty? No, not really. They hate them because they are stealing the attention they've come to feel entitled to.

Do they get over it eventually? Healthy kids in healthy families do, yes. Vampires don't. Vampires in Vampire families never get over that Envy because the drama that leads to makes the Vampire parent(s) happy. As we all know, Vampires love drama, and what better drama is there than to pit two siblings against each other? Normal, healthy families encourage peace and the resolution of the Envy that exists, which is why healthy siblings don't grow up to be envious. Vampire families foster Envy. They encourage it and let it grow like a tumour, which is why Vampires never, ever get past the experience of Envy and live with it every single day. What's more, they actually think that's normal.

I'm not kidding. In exactly the same way they think their relationship with Shame is normal, Vampires think that their relationship with Envy is completely normal and that it is the rest of the population that is wrong. That's why they honest-to-goodness believe that other people are envious of them. They simply cannot conceive of a world without Envy. Think about it for a moment. Remember that moment when you realised that you'd spent the whole relationship with a

Vampire because you didn't know they existed? It's like that. For the Vampire to come to terms with the fact that Envy isn't normal would be the same bottom-falling-out-of-your-world experience that you had and that's just not going to happen because the only thing more resistant to change than the Vampire is the law of gravity.

In a relationship with a Vampire, Envy plays out in all sorts of cruel and sadistic ways. From the very start of the relationship the Vampire envies their Target. The Target always has something the Vampire wants. That could be money, resources, status, empathy, kindness, whatever. It doesn't matter what it is, the Vampire wants it. But they're not jealous of it, they're envious of it. They go through the whole relationship trying to be the thing they Envy, in other words, the Target. They are trying to be the Target. Sound weird? Sure, but is it true? Yes, it is. I told you this would be weird.

But what does the Vampire do when they figure out they can't have what the Target has because they're not the Target? They seek to destroy them. They reason that if they can't have that thing, no-one can. If they can't be that thing, no-one can. It's the original cutting off your nose to spite your face. Vampires excel at that. That's where the real damage gets done, and it's why the best advice I ever heard about identifying Vampires is "pay attention to what they do, not what they say".

The Vampire will lie about their feelings and intentions but their behaviour will betray their Envy every time. Why does the Vampire not support anything you do to better yourself? Why does the Vampire sabotage all your attempts to improve? Why does the Vampire isolate you from friends and family? Why does the Vampire undermine you at every turn? Why does the Vampire smear you to their Flying Monkeys? Why does the Vampire treat you with disdain so that you turn against yourself? That's all based on Envy. They Envy you and seek to destroy you just for being you. It's vile, despicable and inhuman, but then so are Vampires.

So, after all that lot, what have we got? Individually, it's all pretty bad but put all that lot together and you end up with an individual so pathologically disordered as to be almost unrecognisable as a human being. I know. I've been in relationships with two of them. I was raised by one. The mind of the Vampire is a very, very dark place. It's driven (and I do mean driven) by Fear, which makes them seek to control others, Shame, which drives them to create a False self that they insist is true against all evidence from the outside world, Rage at anything and anyone that contradicts that False self and Envy of all that is good and healthy in the world because that is exactly what they are not.

I firmly believe that Vampires know that they are different. They don't know they are Vampires but they know they are not normal. They just choose to believe that makes them "special" and better than others. Nothing could be further from the truth but let me ask you this: If you knew that you were different from everyone else would you choose to believe that makes you better than them, or worse than them? That might be hard to answer because you're not a Vampire but I've been inside their head and I know exactly which answer they chose...

Just before we leave this area of the 4 emotions, I'd like to clear something up. Targets and Survivors often ask "Do they know what they're doing?" Given everything I've laid out here, one could be forgiven for saying "No" in answer to that because how could anyone so pathological possibly carry out their awful, abusive, sadistic behaviours in the knowledge of what they're doing? Surely their pathology blinds them to what they're doing? Surely they are too wrapped up in their own emotional turmoil to pay attention to the impact their behaviours have on others? Here's the fact: They know exactly what they're doing.

Are they wrapped up in their own emotional turmoil? Sure. Are they blind to what their behaviours do to others? No. No they are not. The Vampire is far from stupid, which is often what makes them so dangerous. But what makes them so utterly chilling is that they know exactly what they're doing. They just don't care. What's more, in many cases, they enjoy doing it. They have no capacity to care even if they wanted to because they lack the very thing that makes humans human: Empathy.

In order to fully understand the mind of the Vampire, we're going to have to examine what it means to have Empathy and, more importantly, what it means not to have it.

Empathy

There are loads of definitions of Empathy out there, and they pretty much all say the same thing. This one comes from Psychology Today: "Empathy is the experience of understanding another person's thoughts, feelings, and condition from their point of view, rather than from your own. You try to imagine yourself in their place in order to understand what they are feeling or experiencing."

Read that back once or twice. Sounds obvious, right? The ability to see the facial expression of another person and feel what they are feeling. The ability to look at the situation of another person and infer what they must be feeling. The ability to hear another person speak and hear the emotion in their voice that moves us. The ability to simply look at a child learning about the world and feel their confusion. It's all so basic as to not be worth mentioning. It would be like pointing out that the sky is still there.

We've all been there, right? We've all seen people stub their toes and winced because we know how that feels, right? We've all watched a movie and cried because we can feel a characters pain when they lose the one they love, right? Everyone does that without thinking, right? Wrong.
It is absolutely vital to understanding the mind of the Vampire that you abandon all belief that they have any scrap of Empathy whatsoever. They don't. Not one bit. They know that they have emotional experiences; they know that they have feelings. They know that they feel Fear, Rage, Shame and Envy. Oh dear me, yes. They know that alright. They also know that on an intellectual level, so do you. They just don't care. That bit is so important that I'm going to say it again:

The Vampire knows that you have an emotional life and that you experience the same emotions they do. They just don't care.

There is a misconception about Empathy that goes like this: If people understand that others feel emotions the same way they do, they will understand what the other person is going through. On an intellectual level, I see why that works. On an emotional level it just doesn't, and it's the emotional level that really counts. Just because one person can understand the emotional state of another does not mean that they care necessarily, and that's what Empathy is really about. Knowing and caring are completely different things.

This one goes back to early childhood. Small kids are what psychologists would call "Egocentric". What that means is that they only care about their own experience. Ask any parent who's tried to break up a fight between two toddlers about egocentrism and they will tell you it's like dealing with feral children. Each child simply doesn't care about the other child.

Thankfully (for parents) that state of affairs changes as the child matures. Gradually, they come to realise that others exist in their own right and, with good parenting, they come to appreciate that others have the same emotions they do and that events in the world affect others the same way they affect them.

Often, parents (and other caregivers) will ask the question "How would you feel if that had happened to you?" when challenging what one child may have done to hurt another. It works because it challenges the child to actively question their egocentrism and develop Empathy in its place. Sometimes, they don't have to. I have watched that moment happen and it was a thing of beauty. A small child of my acquaintance looked at another child who had fallen over and they themselves cried. When I asked why they were crying, they replied "That little girl hurts". That's Empathy. Not just knowing; feeling.

As children mature, Empathy continues to develop and they gain the ability to relate to others through shared emotional experience and mutual understanding. Those children develop into healthy adults who are capable of true Empathy. They can feel the emotions of others and respond accordingly. They can appreciate the impact of their actions on others in terms of how it makes the other feel. They know when another person is in pain, or is happy, or is doubtful or whatever and respond accordingly. In other words, they are human.

The Vampire cannot do any of this.

Through Vampire parenting / caregiving, trauma, neglect or whatever the Vampire simply never moved on from egocentrism. They are the Empathic equivalent of a toddler. Now, that doesn't mean they don't understand emotions; they do. They also understand that other people have them. They simply never learned how to put themselves in the other person's position and feel what they feel, and they never will.

Imagine asking a toddler to appreciate why you are crying. Imagine asking a toddler to feel the pain of your loss. Not going to happen, is it? And it's not going to happen with a Vampire either. And because it's developmental, even if they really, really wanted to learn Empathy, they can't. It's too late. Their brain has moved on and any learning of Empathy they did would be mechanical, like learning a foreign language. Any Vampire that tells you that they understand how you feel is lying.

The big difference between toddlers and adult Vampires is that toddlers don't disguise their lack of Empathy and Vampires do. The Vampire knows full well that not having Empathy is considered to be bad, so they have developed "cold empathy". What that refers to is the passing off of intellectual understanding of the emotions of others as feeling the emotions of others. Some Vampires are so good at this that they are almost undetectable, which makes them incredibly dangerous because not only do they know they do not have the required ability to relate emotionally to others, they are actively trying to pass themselves off as a person who does. And they know it. They know.

So what does all this add up to? Given that the Vampire is driven by Fear, Shame, Rage and Envy and has no capacity for Empathy, what you've got here is an individual with an emotional reality that is not even close to what you or I would call "normal". It most certainly isn't healthy.

The Vampires emotional reality is one in which they respond to their Fears, hide their Shame, defend themselves with Rage and Envy those around them. The behaviours that follow from this are toxic, abusive and dangerous and highly destructive. The Vampire knows this full well and they simply do not care. In other words, the mind of the Vampire is a mess. And another word for mess? Disorder. That's entirely why the term is used. The personality of the Vampire is a Disorder. As I said before, while technically they have a personality disorder, their disordered personality is actually who they are. And who they are is driven by basic, destructive emotions designed to fill an emotional void that can never be filled and they don't care who they hurt to fill it.

In concluding this chapter, I'll share a little of my own experience. When I first started writing this book, I conceived of the Vampire as somehow different from humanity, like another species. Many Survivors do that while we come to terms with what just happened. I know better now.

Vampires are people, but they are people who have bits of their brain missing and other bits in their brain where they shouldn't be. They have nothing where Empathy should be. They have Envy where there should be nothing. They have Shame and Rage where there should be guilt and anger. They have Fear where there should be nothing. I believe there is a formula for making a Vampire and it goes like this: Take a human brain and bring it to maturity. Now take out the Empathy and replace it with Fears, Shame and Rage and you're done. Frankensteinian as that may sound, that is the mind of the Modern Vampire. I never said it would be fun.

Phew! That's a lot to take in, isn't it? How about we have an Interlude?

Interlude 2

"The seaweed is always greener in somebody else's lake" – Sebastian, "The Little Mermaid"

Hello again, dear Survivor!

There is this feeling we all get when we finally understand what the Vampire really is. It goes a bit like this: "Fuck! I've been dealing with an emotional child all this time? Not that I didn't realise in my gut that they were massively immature and impossible to communicate with, but an actual emotional child? Holy Shitballs!"

It's not your fault, dear Survivor. You didn't know that at the time. You didn't create the Vampire; you just got involved with them. And let's face it, you'd have to be pretty messed up to make something like that, right? In fact, you'd have to be a Vampire. Knowing what you know now, would you get involved again? Are you still thinking about breaking No Contact? If the answer to either of those is "Yes", try reading that chapter again please.

Many of you are now reaching for the good old "Mug of Guilt" to have a big drink from. Put that down please. None of this is anything to do with you. Vampires swan about the place hunting for Narcissistic supply and they don't give a fat rat's ass who they have to hurt to get it. Are you responsible for that? No! So don't drink the Guilt Tea. Put the mug down. The bit that used to make me really angry from my own experience is when I thought of how nice I was to the Vampire parents of my Vampire partners. I actually bought them Christmas presents! I would've been better off just handing them my heart and my brain and saying "Thanks for your Daughter! Great job!"

Anyway, I'm about to address another one of those burning questions we all have once we get away from the Vampire, so here goes:

Will the Vampire be happy in their new relationship?

Nope. Absolutely not. No chance. Probability: Zero.

The Vampire is a miserable bastard; every single one of them. Remember what a bundle of joy they were with you? Remember all the Silent Treatments, all the accusations, all the guilt trips, all the constant never feeling good enough, all the walking on eggshells, all the depression and feelings of worthlessness? Yeah? Do you think they did that because they were happy? Last time I looked happy people didn't do that because they're HAPPY. You know who does that? Miserable people, that's who does that. Honestly, when was the last time you remember your Vampire actually being honest-to-goodness happy? It's never going to happen.

Oh, I know they LOOK happy. There they are, with their stupid smiley face all over social media, being all cosy with their new source of Narcissistic supply doing all that "soul-mate" shit. I know they LOOK happy, they're just not. They never will be. They are incapable of being happy. Think about it. I just spent an entire chapter explaining how their mind works. Having a mind like that and being utterly incapable of feeling even vaguely normal unless you're getting Narcissistic supply from someone is not exactly a recipe for happiness, is it? To the Vampire, Happy is just a Dwarf.

And here's how I know: They are Egocentric. They are not happy with their new supply, they are excited. They've got a new toy and that's making them feel good about themselves. Just like you did, remember? Didn't last, did it? And it won't last this time either. Once that new source of Narcissistic supply does something stupid (like being human), the Vampire will notice, and then everything they did to you will begin with them. Why? Because Vampires are incapable of change. Not only that, they are disordered and the only way they know how to exist is through the abuse of others, and that goes for everyone. There is no such thing as a Target that can make a Vampire happy because Vampires are never, ever happy. They are miserable, disordered individuals who abuse people. Case closed.

But for those of you who still need convincing, I'm going to go through the only 2 scenarios that could be happening, just so we can eliminate the idea that the Vampire might be happy:

The new source of Narcissistic supply is another normal person like you.

This is very common. It was almost certainly what happened to you, so you know how it goes. It goes like this:

1) The Vampire draws the Target into the relationship using the False Self and Mirroring to do so.

2) The new source of Narcissistic supply turns out not to be able to provide for all the Vampires emotional needs, because no-one on the planet can. The Vampire therefore sets about abusing them, just like they did with you.

3) Either the new source of Narcissistic supply sorts themselves out and leaves or they get discarded, just like you.

That's it. There is no "Happy Ever After". The Vampire will NOT be happy. They will do the same shit they did with you and they will destroy the next relationship just like they did with you. They won't want you to know that of course. They won't want anyone to know. They will want to play the Victim and walk away blaming the Target, just like they tried to do to you. Rinse and Repeat. Anything anyone tells you to the contrary is a lie, especially if that's the Vampire themselves or one of their Flying Monkeys.

The new source of Narcissistic supply is another Vampire.

This is also pretty common. Vampires sometimes mistake each other for decent sources of Narcissistic supply because they've managed to fool each other with their respective False Selves. It's like two TV's facing each other with big expensive movies playing but then they both find that the only thing on after that is endless re-runs of the same Amateur Golf competition. It goes like this:

1) The Vampires draw each other into the relationship using the False Self and Mirroring to do so.

2) The shit hits the fan. Instead of getting a decent source of Narcissistic supply, they've each ended up with an emotional cripple who does nothing but try to destroy their Self Respect, not that there was much there in the first place. And that's BOTH of them doing that. Endless provoking of each other's Shame, so Rage all over the place, Fear and Envy are constant companions. Everyday life is a toxic mess of lying, cheating, accusations, drama and constant chaos. And the weirdest part is that they have to find a way to HIDE that from the rest of the world in order to preserve their False Selves. Behind closed doors though? Absolute Shit Show.

3) Oh yeah, a Discard will happen. I don't care who Discards who. Neither should you.

Again, there's no "Happy Ever After". The Vampire has just made themselves a bed of explosives and they are going have to sleep in it. But it is total misery and they will tear each other to pieces because there simply isn't anyone providing the Narcissistic supply. All that's happening is they are cannibalising each other.

Once again, they will hide that from the world for fear of looking bad, gather their respective Flying Monkeys and create deluded stories for themselves that their False Selves can live with. Don't buy it, dear Survivor, because just like everything else the Vampire says, it's a lie.

So there we are, dear Survivor. I hope that's served to cheer you up a tad. These Interludes are supposed to lighten us all up. If it hasn't helped you yet, why not have a friend read it to you in a funny voice? Chapter 3 next. See you on the other side.

Chapter 3

The Vampire's Attack Cycle

In this chapter, I'd like to take a look at how the Vampire attacks their Target, and I'm using the work "attack" for a very good reason. The Vampire would have their Target believe that their attentions and intentions are love. They're not, and the Vampire knows that.

Oh, they may have deluded themselves into thinking they're in love with the Target, they're just not because they can't feel love. More often than not, they're not deluded anyway. They know exactly what they're doing. The purpose of any and all people in the life of the Vampire is to provide the necessary Narcissistic supply to maintain their False Self. I use the word "attack" because that is what it is. The Vampire assaults the Target with the express intention of draining them of all resources and Narcissistic supply without remorse, without empathy and definitely without love.

That is predation, and predators attack their Targets, they don't love them. Understanding the Attack Cycle is essential in coming to terms with how the Vampire operates and once we understand the nature of the Attack Cycle, much of the behaviour of the Vampire become very clear indeed. Before we get underway, I'm going to point out a couple of important elements of the Attack Cycle:

It never ends.

Once a Vampire has located a potential source of Narcissistic supply, they will initiate the Attack Cycle. How far that proceeds depends on a number of factors as we'll see in a little while, but they will initiate an attack on any potential source of Narcissistic supply. Once the Attack Cycle has been initiated, they will not stop. They may pause for a while but since the Vampire feels entitled to pick up the attack again whenever they feel like it, they will attempt to continue the cycle whenever the opportunity presents itself.

What that results in is an attack that never ends. The more unfortunate Targets will go through the Attack Cycle many times, the luckier and more canny ones only once but all Targets go through it and the only thing that stops the Vampire from doing it is when they are forced to stop. They never stop voluntarily.

It always follows the same pattern

The Attack Cycle is predictable. It always follows the same sequence for reasons that will be explained in a bit and it never, ever changes sequence. If it wasn't so awful, it would be laughable. Understanding the pattern of the Attack Cycle is invaluable in dealing with the Vampire because it allows Survivors to predict what will happen next and prepare for it. It also allows Survivors to recognise the signs of a Vampire that is attempting to initiate the Attack Cycle and avoid them.

The Attack Cycle exists in 4 distinct Stages:

1) The Seduction, Idealisation or Love Bombing Stage (or just "Idealisation")

2) The Devaluation Stage

3) The Discard Stage

4) The Hoover Stage

The Seduction, Idealisation or Love Bombing Stage (Idealisation)

When a Vampire has located a Target that they believe will serve as a good source of Narcissistic supply, they will initiate the Attack Cycle on that Target. This will take the form of highly focussed attention. The Vampire will engage the Target with a high (usually excessively high) level of praise, flattery, flirting, compliments, gift giving, messages, phone calls, personal contact etc. This can take many forms, but the Target will definitely be aware that the Vampire is focussing their attention on them.

There is a name for what is going on here: "Love

Bombing". It's taken from research on cults and is just as applicable to the early attentions of the Vampire. The object of the exercise when Love Bombing is being employed is to overwhelm the Target. Since the Vampire is incapable of conducting "normal" relationships, the usual practice of gradually getting to know the other person over a long period of time is beyond their ability. Therefore, the Vampire will try to "rush" the early stages because they lack the necessary emotional stamina to engage in normal relating.

It is during this Stage that the Vampire is doing several things. Firstly, they are learning what the Target wants, likes, dislikes, aspires to, values, desires and needs. This information will be used by the Vampire later on the Attack Cycle to harm the Target. The Vampire is also learning the Target's vulnerabilities. Again, this will be used later in the Attack Cycle to harm the Target.

Second, the Vampire is figuring out how best to secure the Target by "Mirroring" them. Mirroring is the process by which the Vampire works out how they need to behave in order to secure an emotional connection to the Target. The Vampire knows that they cannot simply approach the Target and explain that they are full of feelings of Shame, Fear, Rage, Envy and Self-loathing and that they want the Target to make them feel better. Instead, the Vampire hides behind their mask of the False Self while they engage in Mirroring the Target.

Through careful observation of the characteristics, behaviours and traits of the Target, the Vampire adopts those same characteristics, behaviours and traits because they know that the Target will respond positively to them if the Target believes that they and the Vampire are similar. In this way, they seek to create a "bond" with the Target in which they believe that they have found someone with whom they have a great deal in common, who is just like them and who seems to be genuinely attracted to them.

Third, the Vampire is assessing the Target's suitability as a source of Narcissistic supply. If the Target appears to have people pleaser traits, low Self Rr]espect, to be empathic, to be kind, to be compassionate and to have character flaws that indicate that they can be made to feel ashamed of themselves easily, the Vampire will consider the Target to be a viable source of Narcissistic supply.

The behaviours of the Vampire in the Idealisation stage of the Attack Cycle will be entirely focussed on ensuring that the Target becomes infatuated or obsessed with them. This stage can continue for some time, especially if the Target is difficult to work out, difficult to Mirror, or has not exhibited sufficient weaknesses for the Vampire to exploit at a later date.

Remember that the Vampire does not see people as people, they only see them as sources of Narcissistic supply. Therefore, in the Idealisation Stage, the Vampire is not creating a "bond" with the Target in order to create a healthy relationship. The Vampire has no interest in having a healthy relationship with the Target. They want to secure, enslave and feed off the Target as a source of Narcissistic supply.
In the mind of the Vampire, the Target is currently being idealised. The Vampire really believes that the Target is to be admired and is strongly attracted to them.

Targets who have fallen prey to a Vampire can at least take some solace in knowing that they were extremely attractive to them during this Stage of the Attack Cycle. Not because of who the Target is, of course, but because they represented an excellent source of Narcissistic supply. Further, the Target would have possessed attributes, both physical and emotional that were highly attractive to the Vampire, and therefore also to "normal" people. The Vampire does not waste their time trying to secure poor sources of Narcissistic supply because that involves too much effort for too little return. Physically or emotionally unattractive people are poor sources of Narcissistic supply to the Vampire, and will not be bothered with. Therefore, the more effort the Vampire expends in the Idealisation Stage, the more the Target can consider themselves to be an attractive person in general, not just to Vampires.

This Stage of the Attack Cycle will continue until such time as the Vampire feels confident that they have "hooked" the Target and that the Target will now serve as a source of Narcissistic supply that can be controlled and manipulated. That is not the same as simply starting an "official" relationship. This Stage continues until the Vampire feels safe that they have established control of the Target, which might mean living together, marriage, engagement, pregnancy or simply that the Vampire feels secure.

This Stage of the Attack Cycle requires very high levels of effort on the part of the Vampire. In this Stage, they are operating against their natural state of Shame, Fear, Rage, Envy and Self-loathing and they cannot keep up the effort for long. If the Target requires more effort to secure than the

Vampire is willing to expend at this Stage, they will disengage from the Target and seek other sources of Narcissistic supply elsewhere.

In simple terms, Vampires are sprinters, not marathon runners. They want to rush intimacy in this first stage, fast-forwarding the relationship at every opportunity because they simply cannot maintain this facade for long. It is very common for early marriage proposals to occur in the Idealisation Stage, as are proposals to move in together, have children and any other event that will serve to bring the Target to a high level of commitment in the relationship in the shortest possible time.

Rushing intimacy and fast-forwarding the relationship are major Red Flags of the Vampire. Normal, healthy people take time to get to know one another and build respect, trust and love over time. Vampires don't do that. Instead, they do everything in their power to convince the Target that they have met their soul-mate and try to rush them into a commitment so that they can move to the next stage of the Attack Cycle: The Devaluation Stage

Spotting and dealing with the Idealisation Stage

Many Survivors report that they never saw the attack coming. They were swept up in the whirlwind of attention they got from the Vampire and thought they had finally met "the one". It's entirely unsurprising that this happens so often. Society conditions us to accept that these things can happen, that a bond of love can form incredibly quickly and that two people can be completely compatible straight off the bat. The truth is that life isn't really like that. In reality, these bonds of love and intimacy do exist and people really do achieve that feeling of having a "soul-mate" but the important difference is that healthy bonds form over time, not instantaneously. It is a major warning sign that the relationship feels too good to be true. If it feels that way, it almost certainly is too good to be true and the person providing that sense is almost certainly a Vampire.

Healthy relationships can form bonds of love that far exceed anything the Vampire might inspire in the Idealisation Stage but they take time and they follow a healthy pattern, not a Vampires Attack Cycle. When two healthy people get to know each other, the first thing that needs to happen is to build mutual respect. Once that's been done, trust tends to follow when both partners demonstrate through their actions that they are consistently reliable and that they "walk the talk". In other words, their words and their actions match. When trust has been built, love can follow if there is an emotional and physical attraction and the establishment of love can lead to intimacy.

When put like that, it becomes clear that intimacy cannot be achieved without the other 3, and that each stage relies on successfully achieving stability at the previous ones. The Vampire cannot build respect because they don't respect anyone, including themselves. They cannot build trust because their entire existence is based on a lie. They cannot build love because they are incapable of doing so and they cannot build intimacy because they will never, ever expose their True Selves.

Therefore, what the Vampire is trying to do in the Idealisation Stage is to "short-circuit" the healthy process of building a relationship in order to get the Target locked in. They know full well that they can't do any of the healthy stuff required for a real relationship and, what's more, they need their fix of Narcissistic supply much more quickly than would be offered if they followed a healthy relationship pattern, so they use the Attack Cycle instead.

The best possible advice for anyone who thinks they may be subject to the Idealisation Stage of the Attack Cycle of a Vampire is this: SLOW THE FUCK DOWN. If you are dealing with a healthy person, they will not want to rush your relationship and they will respect your decision to take things slowly. A Vampire will not. They are incapable of doing so because they are motivated by securing Narcissistic supply. Slowing down effectively denies the Vampire access to Narcissistic supply, and they hate that. A healthy person will stick around, a Vampire won't or they will keep trying to rush the relationship.

Remember, the Vampire is a sprinter, not a marathon runner. They cannot maintain the effort required to secure the Target for long and, when challenged to do so, will simply give up and seek supply elsewhere.

Another key skill in discerning whether you are dealing with a Vampire is to learn the use of the word "No". It is threatening to the Vampire because it means that you are stating and defending a boundary. Vampires hate the word "No" because it means they are not going to get their way. They live to turn No's into Yes's and if you stand by your

"No", they will push at first, and then give up because the Vampire looks for easy Targets who don't state and defend their boundaries.

In practical terms, if you suspect that you may be dealing with a Vampire, simply say "No" a few times when they ask for something. If they propose a date to a particular place, say "No", just once. If they want to fast-forward the relationship, say "No". If they ever do anything that makes you feel uncomfortable, say "No". Healthy people will respect your boundaries and your right to defend them. They will stick around. The Vampire won't. Use the word "No". It is powerful, it works and nothing is more effective at repelling Vampires than stating and defending boundaries.

Overall, once it's been confirmed that you're in the Idealisation Stage, get out. Stop the relationship in its tracks, go "No Contact" with the Vampire and get on with your life. DO NOT engage further with the Vampire because to do so would simply show them that your boundaries are weak and they love that.

There will be a chapter on "No Contact" later, so plenty of help there but for now, the best and only advice in dealing with a Vampire that is Idealising you is to get the hell away and stay the hell away from them.

The Devaluation Stage

Following a successful Idealisation Stage, the Vampire will proceed to the Devaluation Stage of the Attack Cycle. They may return to the Idealisation Stage if they feel that doing so would be effective in controlling the Target, only to proceed to the Devaluation stage again, but in most cases, once the Devaluation Stage has been initiated, the Vampire will remain there until they proceed to the Discard Stage.

The purpose of the Devaluation Stage of the Attack Cycle is to systematically break down the self-respect of the Target in order to ensure that they remain in the relationship and are increasingly dependent on the Vampire for their sense of Self Respect. By engaging in Devaluation (and occasional returns to Idealisation), the Vampire seeks to create a dependency in the Target on them. In this way, the objective of the Vampire is to render the Target addicted to them so that the Target feels unable to leave the relationship and they can continue to feed off the Target's Narcissistic supply. Once the Target has been "hooked" into a relationship with them, the objectives of the Vampire are to ensure that the Target:

a) Does not leave the relationship,
b) Never figures out what the Vampire really is, and
c) Becomes entirely dependent on the Vampire for their sense of Self Respect.

Getting the Target into the Devaluation Stage of the relationship was the Vampires objective from the start. This is because the effort required in the Idealisation Stage is very high for the Vampire. They would much rather move to the Devaluation Stage as quickly as possible and remain there for as long as possible before moving to the Discard Stage. If the Vampire is forced to return to the Idealisation Stage more often than they feels warrants the expenditure of energy required to do so, they will in most cases move to the Discard

Stage instead. However, it is worth noting that a Target that demands that requires the Vampire to return to the Idealisation stage more often than they want to will be treated even more cruelly during the Devaluation Stage as punishment for making the Vampire work harder than they intended to.

The Vampire will spend their time in the Devaluation Stage working on undermining and destroying the self-respect of the Target and they will do it consistently and ceaselessly. They do this for a number of reasons. Most of those reasons are connected to their Fears but it is well worth noting that many Vampires actually enjoy hurting their Target and therefore it is not uncommon for their behaviours in the Devaluation Stage to be driven by pure sadism.

As an example of Devaluation to stave off Fear, let's look at the Fear of Abandonment. Devaluation serves to reassure the Vampire that the Target's Self Respect is lower than their own. Since the Vampire is full of Shame and Self-loathing, they perceive the Target as a threat until they can assure themselves that they occupy a higher position in these characteristics than them. The Vampire is terrified that the Target will abandon them, leaving them without a source of Narcissistic supply and requiring them to seek out another and so by rendering the Targets Self Respect lower than their own, the Vampire assures themselves that the Target will not leave.

Devaluation also serves to assuage the other Fears of the Vampire. By attacking the Target's Self-Respect, the Vampire intends to dominate and control them. If successful, this allows the Vampire to avoid the fear of losing control of the Target, and therefore their own emotions. The Vampire manages to avoid the fear of loss of resources by rendering the Target incapable of leaving the relationship and willing to sacrifice any and all resources to the Vampire for fear of losing their approval. By destroying the Self Respect of the Target, the Vampire places themselves in a superior position in all interactions with them and thereby allows the Vampire to avoid the fear of feeling or appearing inadequate or inferior.

Finally, by controlling the narrative of the relationship and controlling the Targets access to a support network, the Vampire manages to avoid the fear of public exposure.
All the behaviours the Vampire engages in when in the Devaluation Stage are designed to break the will of the Target, destroy their Self Respect and render them addicted to the Vampire.

The range of weapons and tactics the Vampire uses is vast, so vast that the subjects occupy two chapters in this Field Manual. Every weapon and tactic will be explained later in terms of how it serves the Vampire during Devaluation, but for now it should be noted that nothing the Vampire does in the Devaluation Stage is designed to benefit the Target in any way at all. Anything the Vampire does that benefits the Target either represents a veiled attack for the purpose of manipulating the Target or was an accident.

The Vampire is completely aware that if they engage in abusive behaviours it will have the desired effect of destroying the Targets Self Respect. They also know that if they occasionally offer rewards in the form of love and affection, the Target will stick around and endure their abuse. Because both of these things are true, what occurs is a cycle of abuse in which the Vampire switches from Idealisation to Devaluation and back again. It's what lies at the heart of the "Jekyll and Hyde" nature of the Vampires personality.

The cycle between Idealisation and Devaluation shifts over time, starting with predominantly Idealisation with small amounts of Devaluation as the Vampire probes the Target to find out how much abuse the Target is willing to tolerate towards predominantly Devaluation with small amount of Idealisation offered to keep the Target hooked into the relationship. During this process, the Target is being subjected to a sustained attack on their Self Respect and will inevitably buckle under the pressure. In a later chapter, I'll be describing how the cycle of Idealisation and Devaluation lead to the creation of an addiction in the Target, but for now it is enough to know that is exactly what occurs, that it is exactly what the Vampire wants and that they do it deliberately.

Spotting and dealing with the Devaluation Stage

The transition from Idealisation to Devaluation is gradual and subtle. The Vampire does not simply "flip a switch" and go from full Idealisation to full Devaluation. Not at the start anyway. Later in the relationship, this is often exactly what happens but that is only when the Vampire feels confident that they can do so and get away with it. In the beginning, the Idealisation - Devaluation balance will be heavily in favour of Idealisation. From time to time, the Vampire will engage in the use of weapons and tactics associated with Devaluation to see how the Target responds.

If the attack is successful, it will be repeated. It's not a case of if; it is a case of when.

Over time, more and more severe attacks will be launched, each one pushing the Targets boundaries further until they are accepting abuse that they would never have conceived they could accept. By the time the relationship comes to an end, the Target will find that they have tolerated things they never thought possible.

This does not happen overnight, it happens a little at a time. Narcissistic abuse is insidious. The Vampire picks away at the Target's Self Respect over time, finding the Target's weaknesses and exploiting them, creating a narrative around the relationship that the Target is the "crazy" one, isolating the Target and covertly (and overtly) tearing their Self Respect to pieces.

So, how can the Devaluation Stage be spotted and dealt with? Spotting whether you're in an abusive relationship is often difficult because of the insidious nature of Narcissistic abuse. Targets are often in denial about the abuse and justify it to themselves as a survival technique. However, some of the behaviours of the Vampire in Devaluation are:

Humiliating or embarrassing you.
Constant put-downs.
Hypercriticism.
Refusing to communicate.
Ignoring or excluding you.
Extramarital affairs.
Provocative behavior with the opposite sex, or same sex.

Use of sarcasm and unpleasant tone of voice.
Unreasonable jealousy.
Extreme moodiness.
Mean jokes or constantly making fun of you.
Saying "I love you but..."
Saying things like "If you don't _____, I will_____."
Domination and control.
Withdrawal of affection.
Guilt trips.
Making everything your fault.
Isolating you from friends and family.
Using money to control you.
Constant calling or texting when you are not with him/her.
Threatening to commit suicide if you leave.

In addition, one of the really big signs that someone is in an abusive relationship is that they do things like Google the phrase "Am I being abused?", or "Is my partner abusive?", or "What is a Narcissist?". The bottom line with that is that if someone feels the need to search online for whether they are being abused or not, they almost certainly are. People in normal healthy relationships never, repeat NEVER have to ask those questions. If you're having to ask, the probability is extremely high that you are being abused.

As with the Idealisation Stage, once it's been confirmed that you're in the Devaluation Stage, get out. Stop the relationship in its tracks, go "No Contact" with the Vampire and get on with your life. DO NOT engage further with the Vampire. Which is, of course, incredibly difficult if not impossible in some circumstances.

Many, many Targets find themselves married, have children and other commitments when they figure out they are in the Devaluation Stage and that creates any number of complications. Again, there will be a chapter on "No contact" as well as other techniques for dealing with leaving a Vampire but for now, if you can, get out and stay out.

The Discard Stage

The Vampire does not see people as people. They only see people as a source of Narcissistic supply. Once the Vampire has decided that the current Target has ceased to be a good source of Narcissistic supply, they will move to the Discard Stage of the Attack Cycle and end the relationship. For many Survivors of the Attack Cycle, this Stage is the most painful and confusing. The Vampire frequently gives no warning that they are about to Discard the Target, and many Survivors report that they never saw it coming. This is deliberate and premeditated on the part of the Vampire because, contrary to what most people believe, in the Vampire's mind, it is not the end of the relationship, it is just another Stage in the Attack Cycle. There are several reasons why the Vampire moves to the Discard Stage of the Attack Cycle:

1) They have located an alternative Target that promises to be what they consider to be a better source of on-going Narcissistic supply. In this case, the current Target will be discarded and the Vampire will immediately enter a new relationship with the new Target. This new Target will be in the Idealisation stage of the Attack Cycle with the Vampire and, if they do not escape, will move to the Devaluation stage

as soon as the Vampire feels confident that they can do so.

2) The Target has figured out that there is something wrong in the relationship and has taken steps to work on their Self Respect. This is usually the result of engaging a therapeutic professional, who is working with the Target to repair the damage that is being done by the Vampire. The Vampire hates that. It means that the Target is becoming harder to control and represents a constant threat to the Vampires Fears. The Vampire will move to the Discard Stage of the Attack Cycle in order to escape what they perceive as a threat to their Narcissistic supply and / or to avoid their Fears.

    The Vampire also frequently engages in "fake Discards", in which the end of the relationship is threatened but not carried out. They may even Discard for short periods of time like days or even hours, sometimes longer. This is an attempt to smash the Targets Self Respect and bring them back under the Vampires control. In such cases, when the Vampire believes their control has been reasserted, the Discard will be abandoned and they will attempt to move back into the Attack Cycle as if nothing had happened.

3) The Target has become aware of what the Vampire really is and has actively turned off the Narcissistic supply. The Vampire finds themselves unable to gain Narcissistic supply from the Target and is slowly collapsing in on themselves as they can no longer stave off their feelings of Shame. In many cases, the Vampire must now either locate an alternative Target, or engage an existing Target that they were Triangulating (more on that later) as their main source of Narcissistic supply.

4) The Vampire has Devalued the Target to the point that they are no longer capable of providing Narcissistic supply. This may be due to physical or mental breakdown. Again, the Vampire will immediately enter a new relationship with a new Target that they have been Triangulating. This new Target will be in the Idealisation Stage of the Attack Cycle with the Vampire and, if they do not escape, will move to the Devalue Stage of the Attack Cycle as soon as the Vampire feels confident that they can do so.

5) The Target has turned the tables on the Vampire. Unknown to the Vampire, the Target has been making steady, covert progress in rebuilding their Self-Respect and is equipped with the knowledge and skills not only to escape the Vampire but potentially expose them to the world for what they really are. The Target has done excellent work on their Self Respect, and is now immune to all of the Vampires attacks. Not only that, but if they choose, they could make others aware of what the Vampire really is, which threatens their False Self. In this case, the Vampire will move to the Discard Stage of the Attack Cycle in order to escape someone who has become such a threat to them that they can no longer expect to survive around them.

The Discard stage of the Attack Cycle is brutal. In Discarding the Target, the Vampire is attempting to inflict as much psychological and emotional damage on the Target as possible. The objective is simple: to incapacitate the Target so that they remain controlled in the Vampires absence. Therefore, the Discard will be as far from a healthy breakup as is imaginable. In healthy breakups, there are reasons and those reasons make sense. Both partners still care for each other, even if the love has gone and both want the breakup to cause as little damage as possible. Both partners are open and honest with each other, take responsibility for their part in the failure of the relationship and seek to find the mutual benefit in the breakup. Crucially, blame for the breakup is avoided wherever possible. Breakups are hard, and are no-one's idea of a good time. In healthy ones, both partners help the other to get through it with compassion and empathy.

None of those things will be present in a Discard because it is not a breakup; it is an attack.

Whether overtly or covertly, the Vampire will blame the Target for the breakup, playing the Victim wherever possible. This is designed to create Shame in the Target and leave them with the entire weight of the breakup. Whatever reasons the Vampire gives for the Discard (if any are given) will not make sense and the Target will experience enormous confusion as a result. The Vampire will lie throughout the Discard, denying the existence of a new Target but either overtly or covertly entering the Idealisation Stage with the new Target immediately. The Vampire will show little or no regard for the welfare of the Target and will provide no support for them during the Discard or afterwards. Far from wanting to help the Target through the discard and showing compassion and empathy, the Vampire actively enjoys the Discard, taking sadistic pleasure in the Targets suffering and basking in the Narcissistic supply their cruelty creates.

Again, the Discard is not a breakup. It is a massive, all-out attack on the Target that is designed to utterly devastate them. For the Vampire, this is a win-win situation again. Their sadistic cruelty is rewarded with enormous amounts of Narcissistic supply, they get to unleash all their Rage on the Target, vomit out all their feelings of Shame, and there is a very high likelihood that the Target will be so wiped out by the attack that they will remain in their crushed state until such time as the Vampire chooses to return to gain more Narcissistic supply.

In all cases, when the Vampire moves to the Discard Stage of the Attack Cycle, they do not consider the relationship with the Target to be over. All that has happened is a temporary cessation of hostilities. Depending on the Vampires goal for the Discard, this may be hours, days, weeks, months or even years. If the Vampire believes that they can gain further Narcissistic supply from the Target, they will move to the next Stage of the Attack Cycle: The Hoover Stage.

Spotting and dealing with the Discard Stage

Because of the devastating and confusing nature of the Discard, the majority of Targets do not realise what is going on because they are too busy trying to make sense of something that makes no sense and attempting to keep their emotional and psychological reality together. However, that is exactly how the Discard can be recognised. A healthy breakup is emotionally and psychologically challenging because it represents a fundamental change in the life of both partners. But healthy breakups make sense and are characterised by mutual compassion and kindness.

The emotional and psychological landscape of a healthy breakup is kind and supportive and a sense of rationality and responsibility runs through all the emotional turmoil that is an inevitable feature. In a healthy breakup, both partners walk away with their Self Respect a little damaged, but intact.

A Discard, on the other hand, feels completely different. It feels devastating, makes no sense, is characterised by emotional reasoning and is devoid of any sense of reason. Blame is a central feature and the Vampire will place themselves in the role of Victim throughout. The Target will feel entirely responsible for the Discard and have their Self Respect shattered. Rather than knowing that the breakup was right and necessary, the Target will have little to no sense of what happened or why. Above all, the overwhelming sense the Target will be left with is Shame and shattered Self Respect.

So how to deal? Not easy, but it can be done. The first thing to do either during or after a potential Discard is to examine how you feel. If the feelings are that you are to blame, that you are confused about the reasons, that you feel Shame and you feel loss of Self Respect, what just occurred was not a breakup; it was a Discard.

Once the Discard has been recognised for what it is: disengage. If the Discard is happening now, let it happen. Do not engage with the Vampire, accept whatever "reasons" they offer for the Discard and get away from them as quickly as possible. If the Discard is over, accept it for what it is. In either case, go "No Contact" immediately. If there are practical ties to the Vampire, go "Grey Rock" instead.

A Discard is a blessing, because it means that the Vampire has voluntarily ceased attacking, however temporarily. The key thing now is to make sure it stays that way.

The Discard Stage is at one and the same time the worst and best Stage of the Attack Cycle for the Target. It is the worst because it is devastating, but it is the best because it is the point at which the Target can become a Survivor. This is exactly what the Vampire fears; that the Target will realise that they now have the power to become a Survivor and dictate the terms of their own life from this point forward. The choice to become a Survivor is made in the next Stage of the Attack Cycle, the Hoover Stage.

The Hoover Stage

The Vampire is an insane predator; they never stop attacking the Target. If the Vampire believes that they can gain Narcissistic supply from the Target, they will move to the next Stage of the Attack Cycle: The Hoover Stage. The Vampire also does not see people as people, they only see them as sources of Narcissistic supply. The Hoover Stage of the Vampire's Attack Cycle is designed to "suck" the Target back in to engaging with them again and providing them with Narcissistic supply.

A Hoover tactic is literally anything that the Vampire does that involves the Target after the Discard Stage of the Attack Cycle or after the Target has ended the relationship. Some of these tactics are passive, others are active. This is why the range of techniques used by the Vampire in the Hoover

Stage of the Attack Cycle is so vast, but they are all employed with one goal in mind: to "suck" the Target into engaging with the Vampire and providing them with Narcissistic supply.

It would be possible to go through all the potential forms of attack the Vampire may elect to use in the Hoover Stage here but they are the same ones the Vampire used in the Idealisation Stage and the Devalue Stage. The only difference is that there may be some "tailor-made" ones to suit the particular circumstances of the Discard or however the Target ended the relationship. Here and now I would like to cut through all that and say this:

Every interaction between the Target and the Vampire following either a Discard or the termination of the relationship by the Target is a potential Hoover.

<u>Never</u> underestimate the Vampire and their ability to attempt a Hoover. Like a crocodile that stores meat under logs to be consumed later, the Vampire stores people to be attacked later for Narcissistic supply. The only way to ensure that the Attack Cycle ends is to end it yourself; the Vampire never will.

There are two reasons why the Hoover Stage of the Attack Cycle is so dangerous for the Target. The first is that the Target usually doesn't know that it is an Attack Stage. Most Targets believe that the Attack Cycle has ended after the Discard Stage. It hasn't, because the Vampire never stops attacking their Target. The second reason is that the Hoover Stage, if successful, leads directly to either the Idealisation

Stage or the Devaluation Stage and continues the Attack Cycle.

If a Vampire is successful in employing a Hoover tactic, they will return to one of these two Stages, and then another Discard, and each time that happens it will be worse for the Target because they will have shown the Vampire exactly what works. Once the Vampire knows this, they will exploit that knowledge remorselessly. The Vampire does not know how to stop attacking the Target, and they don't want to stop. They only know that they need Narcissistic supply and they use all Stages of the Attack Cycle to get it.

In most cases, the Vampire will be the one to engage in a Hoover tactic. However, it is possible for the Target to accidentally trigger one by contacting the Vampire after the Discard Stage of the Attack Cycle, or after ending the relationship. Once the Vampire has moved to the Hoover Stage of the Attack Cycle, No Contact is vital in ensuring that the Target does not offer the Vampire the opportunity to engage in a Hoover tactic because the Vampire <u>will</u> take it.

Spotting and dealing with the Hoover Stage

The Hoover Stage is easy to spot because the Vampire is absent. Whether that absence was caused by a Discard, or by the Target's own actions, the Vampire is no longer a part of the Targets life, and there is no relationship between them. However, the Hoover Stage should be recognised for what it is: another Stage in the Attack Cycle. The Vampire will always seek to attack the Target if they are given the opportunity to do so. Therefore, if there is no need to contact the Vampire, then No Contact should be implemented immediately.

There is a great deal of information later in the Field Manual on how to do this, so I won't dwell on it here but for now, by far and away the best technique available to the Target in this Stage is immediate and sustained No Contact. If you'd like, please go have a look at that now. It's in Chapter 12. Any contact with the Vampire will result in a continuation of the Attack Cycle. It really is that simple. Anyone who wants the Attack Cycle to end must end it themselves because the Vampire never will.

In cases where No Contact is not possible, the technique Grey Rock should be employed. Again, there's loads of information on that later in the Field Manual, so I won't dwell here and you are most welcome to go to Chapter 12 and read up on it now if you'd like. For now, Grey Rock involves cutting off the Narcissistic supply to the Vampire every time you have to deal with them. It means that they get as little emotional response from the Target as possible, preferably none. In other words, as much emotional response as a Grey Rock would give.

The Hoover Stage should also be recognised as a golden opportunity for the Target to choose to become a Survivor. The Vampire is now absent, and therefore has no input on how this Stage of the Attack Cycle runs, which means that this is the Stage of the Attack Cycle that can exist solely on the Survivors terms. Yes, it is part of the Vampires Attack Cycle, but it is also when they are at their weakest, and this weakness should be exploited to the full. The brutality of the Discard was designed specifically to distract the Target from the fact that the Vampire is now exposed and is risking losing Narcissistic supply from Target permanently, which is why it is critical to realise that the Hoover Stage for the Vampire is actually the Escape Stage for the Survivor. I'll say that again:

The Hoover Stage is the Escape Stage for the Survivor.

The Survivor can now dictate whether the Vampire is allowed back into their life and they can elect to employ No Contact and/or Grey Rock and end the Attack Cycle for good. The Survivor now has full control in deciding how they want to proceed with their life and in doing so the Vampire has absolutely no influence other than that given to them by the Survivor. In other words, the Survivor now has all the power and is now dictating the terms. The Vampire has no power and can dictate nothing.

The Survivor is well advised at this point to seek as much support as possible, specifically from trained therapeutic professionals. Chapter 11 looks at how that can be done, so please go and have a look at that now too if you'd like. For now, the Escape Stage allows the Survivor to begin working on their Self Respect, rebuilding their life, re-establishing their social connections and re-discovering who they truly are. Friends, family and anyone and everyone sympathetic to the Survivor can now become assets in making sure the Survivor does not allow the Vampire to continue the Attack Cycle.

And there we are. Once the Attack Cycle is understood, dealing with it becomes much easier. The key thing to remember is that the cycle will continue for as long as it is allowed to do so. The Attack Cycle will never be broken by the Vampire because it does not serve their interests to do so. It must be broken by the Target by electing to become a Survivor. Doing so involves taking back the power they always had but the Vampire did not want them to know they had. Once the Survivor realises that they have the power to take control of their lives, the Vampire can no longer engage in the Attack Cycle and the Survivor is free.

And now, let's have an Interlude, shall we?

Interlude 3

"The past can hurt. But the way I see it, you can either run from it or learn from it." – Rafiki, "The Lion King"

Hello again, dear Survivor!

Ah, the good old Attack Cycle. This is another of those cases where you just can't explain it to someone who hasn't been there. Anyone who has will be all too familiar with the Hoover. What really fucks me off is that our society normalises that shit. "Oh, they're back together. That's great" people say while the Target gets abused some more. "Maybe they can make it work this time" they say while the Target gets Gaslighted some more. "Getting back together" is a crock of shit. Always has been, always will be.

There, I said it. I feel better. Look, if you break up, it's because you both knew what breaking up meant. It meant the end of the relationship, which is a really big deal. It's a one-way street to "Separate-Future-Ville". If both of you knew what that meant, and you both valued the relationship, then that decision would have been worth ploughing your whole world into, because so was the relationship, right? That's why breakups kill, but you know both know that when it's right, it's right.

You know who doesn't do that? Vampires.

If two people break up, there must have been a reason. Has that reason been resolved? No? Then why the fuck are you back together? Of course we know the reason, dear Survivor. It's because the relationship featured a Vampire and that bastard has Hoovered once again. In all likelihood, the Target was blaming themselves for the breakup thanks to the Vampire's Gaslighting, so they go back for more. Seriously, normal grownups don't do that shit. They just don't. When normal adults break up, that's it. Done and done. You're great, I'm great, here are our reasons for not being together, and those reasons make actual sense. Yes, it hurts. Will it kill you? No. And in large part, that's because you know that the other person wants you to be happy and that's what you both agreed when you parted.

There's a song by Thomas Dolby that says it all. It's called "I love you, Goodbye". Give it a listen and I dare you not to cry. Don't watch the video, though - it's mostly about hats for some reason.

Not so with the Vampire. Their reasons for breaking up never make sense, because they will always try to make sure that the Target is never, ever at ease with the breakup. What they want is to break up without giving reasons that make sense because that way they keep the door open for a Hoover. What they want is to make sure that the Target never gets to a place where they are happy, because they never want the Target to be happy under any circumstances, and the discard is just another opportunity to make that happen. These bastards will try to resurrect a relationship no matter how dead it is. They put the romance into Necromancer.

If there's one thing you can count on, it's that the Vampire will Hoover. It breaks my heart that so many Targets go back. It means that they're not finished with the abuse, that they still believe they deserve it in some way, that the Vampire somehow isn't a Vampire, and that the relationship is still important. And that's why the Hoover works.

Now, I'm not here to tell Survivors what to do with their lives, but if I had my way, whenever a Vampire Discarded a Target, they would be required to hand over an official "DisCARD" that gave the Survivor the legal right to prosecute the Vampire whenever they bothered them again. Imagine a world in which the DisCARD could be handed to a passing policeman and the Vampire would be arrested on the spot, just for attempting a Hoover. Now that, my friends, is a future worth investing in. Let's see if we can make that happen.

Anyway, here's the answer to the third of the burning questions.

Even if that new relationship fails, is there someone out there with whom they can be happy?

I think you already know the answer to this one. It's the same as for question 2, and for exactly the same reasons. Just for the hell of it, I'll give that answer again:

Nope. Absolutely not. No chance. Probability: Zero.

The Vampire will follow the same boring, predictable Attack Cycle over and over again. They basically start out with the assumption that the relationship will fail miserably and then go about proving themselves right. The only thing that stands between them and the demise of the relationship is the optimism and hard work of the Target.

I read some research recently that claimed that the best partner for a Vampire is another one. Maybe that's true. It sure ain't one of us. I'd like to think it is true, actually because if it is, it does a couple of really handy things for the rest of us. First, it goes some way to keeping two of these bastards off the street at the same time. Second, it contains the misery of two of them in the same relationship, rather than two separate ones.

You see, there's this amazing thing that happens when two Vampires get together. Not only do they utterly destroy each other, they also have a really hard time stopping. They act out all nicey-nice to the outside world but do their best to kill each other at home and they can't stop! Neither of them wants to stand up and say they made a mistake! Why? Because that would cause...let's all say it together, shall we? ...Shame!

Instead, they have to come up with all these creative reasons why they are the Victim in the relationship they themselves are selling as perfect! The mental gymnastics involved with that is just staggering! The resulting drama when each one's supporters get involved is like West Side Story, but with Flying Monkeys. West Side Flying Monkeys. Not a bad name for a band, actually.

So: No. There is no-one out there with whom they can be happy. I realise that you're probably only thinking of that because you're also thinking of their new relationship and how you've read or been told that will fail (including by me), so the next natural question is "what about the one after that?" Well yeah, the one after that will be the exact same thing. Same choice: Decent person or Vampire, same outcomes, over and over again until they die. Old folks' homes all over the world are rammed with ageing Vampires. I'm not kidding. Ask anyone who works in one. That's pretty much where they all end up because they can't have a relationship they don't destroy.

It's either that, or they end up living with some poor unfortunate family member who has to listen to them going on all day about their operations, or their bowel problems, or how the neighbours hate them, or what an asshole you were all those years ago (because they never forget), or how their hairdresser would be nice if they weren't so stupid, or how they could have been successful it wasn't for Sagittarius popping up in Saturn, or how much they wish their brother hadn't married that bitch, or whatever random negative thought occurs to them at that point in time. Eerily like they were when they were with you, actually. Remember? They just sit around making vengeance soup all day and giving the kids dirty looks for daring to be happy.

So don't you worry about it, dear Survivor. Karma never loses an address. The person you need to worry about now is you. You are the most important person in your life. You are amazing, and brilliant, and full of potential. You could keep focusing on what's going to happen to the Vampire but I already know, and now so do you. This would be an excellent time to start giving all that attention to the most wonderful person you know: You. Deal?

OK. Onward into Chapter 4. See you on the other side.

Chapter 4

The Weapons of the Vampire

In this chapter, I'd like to look at some of the Vampires' arsenal of weapons that they employ to attack the Target in the hope that it will ring some bells for Targets and Survivors and help dispel any notion that Vampires behaviour is somehow "normal", because it really isn't.

As we saw in the last chapter, the Vampire is always attacking the Target in order to dominate and control them for the purpose of securing Narcissistic supply. In doing so, the Vampire has an uncanny ability to turn pretty much anything into a weapon to use in their attacks. Any form of interaction with a Vampire can be considered an attack because that is what Vampires do. If what they're doing doesn't look like an attack, it just means the attack hasn't been spotted, not that it isn't happening.

There is simply no such thing as a peaceful interaction with a Vampire and even though they may appear to be being

"Nice" at any given point, that appearance is simply a set-up for another attack, and therefore part of that attack. What follows here is an outline of some of the more common weapons in no particular order. It is not an exhaustive list and Targets and Survivors would do well to remember that any interaction with a Vampire is not an opportunity for an attack by the Vampire, it is an attack.

Praise & Compliments

Normal, healthy people use praise and compliments honestly. They praise and compliment others freely, but are aware of boundaries in doing so, never seek to use praise and compliments to create division between people and always ensure that their partner is held above all others in their esteem when using praise and compliments. In other words, they are used positively and to recognise others while maintaining and building the primacy of their partner in the relationship.

Where normal, healthy people praise and compliment their partner frequently, the Vampire does not. The Vampire actively withholds praise and compliments from the Target, replacing them with criticism and insults while praising and complimenting others instead in order to undermine the Targets Self Respect. By doing so, the Vampire is attempting to create a narrative in which anyone they choose is placed in higher esteem than the Target, who they actively degrade through insults and criticism.

In almost all cases, by using praise and compliments, the Vampire is attempting to create a Drama Triangle (more on that later). They will praise and compliment a person they know the Target does not like in order to provoke the Target to create an emotional response, which provides the Vampire with Narcissistic supply. They will praise a person they know the Target aspires to be like in order to make the Target feel insecure. They will praise and compliment a person who they know has hurt the Target to hurt the Target further in order to reduce the Targets Self Respect. They will praise and compliment a third party on their positive qualities in order to make the Target feel insecure in the relationship and undermine their Self Respect. They will praise and compliment one or more of their own supporters (see Flying Monkeys) in order to lure the Target into engaging with them, allowing them the opportunity to enforce their version of reality on the Target.

Whenever the Vampire uses praise and compliments toward another person when in contact with the Target, they are attacking the Target. When it comes to the Target themselves, in the Idealisation Stage of the Attack Cycle, praise and compliments are used to secure the Target. In all subsequent Stages of the Attack Cycle, praise and compliments are used to attack the Targets Self Respect. If the Vampire is praising or complimenting others in the presence of the Target, they are attacking the Target. It is as simple as that.

Insults & Criticism

Normal, healthy people do not use insults or criticism. They do not insult or criticise others and they never insult or criticise their intimate partner. The Vampire will use insults and criticism as a weapon. The Vampire will use insults and criticism directly against the Target while simultaneously using praise and compliments towards others of their choosing in an attempt to destroy the Targets Self Respect.

As with praise and compliments, in almost all cases, insults and criticism are used by the Vampire to create a Drama Triangle. They will insult or criticise the Target directly in an attempt to reduce the Targets Self Respect. They will insult or criticise the Target's friends and family and colleagues, which is designed to undermine the Targets faith in them and is an attempt to get the Target to isolate from them. They will insult or criticise people they knows the Target likes. This is an attempt to undermine the Target, have them adopt the Vampires preferences instead and cause the Target to question their own judgement. In the Idealisation Stage, they will insult or criticise the Targets current partner if they have one. This is an attempt to undermine the Target by questioning their judgement and values, to create division in the relationship and establish whether the Target is able to be manipulated. At the same time, they will insult or criticise their own partner if they have one (which they almost certainly have) and their previous partners. This is designed to elicit sympathy from the Target and allow the Vampire to employ the tactic of Victimhood.

Targets and Survivors are well advised to pay attention to those that the Vampire does not insult or criticise. The Vampire will only insult or criticise the Targets friends and family and colleagues, not their own, unless they are trying to employ the tactic of Victimhood. The Vampire will only insult or criticise those who have value to the Target, not those who have value to the Vampire. The Vampire will insult or criticise those they cannot control, and therefore anyone the Vampire does not insult or criticise is a prime candidate for being a Flying Monkey.

Knowledge

The Vampire will take whatever knowledge the Target has and use it as a weapon. They will learn what the Target knows and then use that knowledge as their own. When discussing something with others, they will claim that they know more than them. Using very little knowledge on a subject, they will behave as if they are an expert. The Vampire is an interminable know-it-all. They pretend to know more than everyone around them because they have to appear to be superior.

They will take a very small amount of knowledge on a subject, assume that others know nothing about the topic and then talk like they have a PhD. The Vampire is never wrong in their mind and if others disagree with them, they will sulk, steamroll, criticise, insult and undermine them in an attempt to have the upper hand in all conversations. For the Vampire, discussions are just like anything else: An attack. And they will always seek to win, which means they never really have discussions, they have arguments. If the argument isn't going their way, the Vampire will resort to emotional tactics to gain the upper hand.

Money

In normal, healthy intimate relationships, both partners know "where the money is". Secrecy about shared money is absent, its use is mutually agreed and neither partner has greater control over it than the other. It is also the case that the use of money controlled entirely by each partner is treated with respect, is never considered to be mutually controlled and is never considered to be the resource of the other partner. Discussions about shared money are open and honest and it is used for the mutual benefit of both partners. The use of individually controlled money to benefit the other partner is broadly reciprocal and is never used as a weapon to inflict guilt or shame in the other partner. Where loans of money exist between partners, the terms of the loan are clearly agreed on and honoured by both partners.

None of this applies to the Vampire. The easiest way to sum up how the Vampire views money in the relationship with the Target is the phrase "What's Mine is Mine and What's Yours is Mine". Matters of money when dealing with the Vampire are never, ever transparent. In the mind of the Vampire, money, whether shared, their own, or the Targets is a resource that should be used to prioritise the Vampire.

A huge warning sign is that the Target will not know "where the money is". The Vampire is highly secretive about any money that they possess and will lie to either inflate or reduce the amount of money they have in the mind of the Target. Any mutual agreements about the use of shared money will be broken by the Vampire if they choose to do so, and the Vampire will consider that they have greater control over shared money than the Target.

Wherever possible, the Vampire will seek to have sole control over shared money so that they can use shared money as a resource for themselves. When it comes to individually controlled money, the Vampire will lie about how much they have, or do not have. They will expect the Target to use their money for mutual benefit and will avoid using their own for the same reason wherever possible. They do not respect the Target's right to use their own money for their own benefit and will criticise the Target for doing so. In essence, the Vampire considers the Targets money to be their money and will seek to access use of the Target's money using whatever tactics are effective.

Discussions about shared money will be subject to whatever tactics the Vampire finds effective in securing those resources for themselves. The goal of the Vampire in discussions about money is to confuse, undermine and dominate the Target so that the Target allows them to access the shared money being discussed as they see fit. The use of individually controlled money is never reciprocal in dealing with a Vampire.

They will employ a range of tactics to get the Target to spend their own money for mutual gain and they will avoid doing the same wherever possible. The Vampire will lie about reciprocity. If it has been agreed that the Target will spend their own money now for mutual benefit and the Vampire will return the gesture at a later date, they will not do so. They will lie about the agreement and will employ whatever tactics they find effective to avoid being challenged on the matter.

The Vampire will use money as a weapon to inflict feelings of Shame on the Target. They will claim that they have no money in order to elicit pity from the Target so that they provide money for them. They will refer to money that is "coming" in order to have the Target spend their own money in the short term but will never repay the favour. They will lie about having financial difficulties in an effort to elicit money from the Target, make the Target feel guilty about spending their own money on themselves, or gain access to shared money for their own purposes.

Where a loan exists between the Vampire and the Target, the loan will not be repaid. If the terms of the loan have been agreed, they will deny this and attempt to redefine the terms, especially if nothing exists in writing. They will lie and employ other tactics to elicit sympathy from the Target in order to avoid paying back the loan. In all cases, when a loan has been agreed between the Target and the Vampire, they will employ whatever tactics prove effective in order to avoid paying back as much as possible of the loan. The goal of the Vampire in all loan agreements is to never pay back the loan.

Sex

In normal, healthy, intimate relationships sex is a pleasurable activity in which both partners gain satisfaction, are sensitive to each other's needs and preferences, do not seek to prioritise their own pleasure over that of their partner and both partners are invested in preserving a mutual bond between them. Sex occurs based on intimacy, mutual love and affection, and both partners have a positive attitude towards it, their own sexuality and the sexuality of their partner.

If one or both partners experience difficulties with sex, the partnership functions to overcome that with kindness, love and understanding. If new sexual activities are engaged in, they are mutually agreed on and supported by both partners. Coercion of one partner by the other is absent. If monogamy has been mutually agreed, both partners feel confident that the relationship will remain monogamous and neither seeks sexual partners outside of the relationship. Neither partner seeks to prioritise their own sexual needs, to minimise their partner's sexual needs or to use sex to manipulate, control or dominate their partner. In normal, healthy intimate relationships, feelings of Shame or inadequacy related to sex are entirely absent.

None of this applies to the Vampire. The Vampire always uses sex as a weapon. The purpose of sex for the Vampire is to obtain Narcissistic supply, to dominate and to control the Target. The Vampire has absolutely no concern for the sexual satisfaction of the Target. If they appear to be concerned, it is simply because they know that a lack of satisfaction in the Target could be a criticism of themselves. They have no concern for establishing and maintaining a mutual sexual bond with the Target, and see such a bond as meaningless.

The Vampire sees their sexual "performance" as a means of obtaining Narcissistic supply, and concern themselves with using their sexuality to stave off feelings of Shame. This means that the Vampire is highly insecure and sensitive to criticism of their sexuality, and they will engage in a range of tactics against the Target to defend themselves against such criticism. For the Vampire, sex has no connection to intimacy, love or affection, since they are incapable of experiencing these things. In addition, the Vampire does not have a positive attitude to sex, their own sexuality or the sexuality of the Target. Any positivity that appears to exist simply reflects their understanding that revealing their negativity could lead to criticism. Therefore, they conceal their negativity and create an illusion of positivity in order to protect themselves from criticism. In many cases, they do this to a very high degree, often "overcompensating" for their negativity.

     The Vampire will always blame sexual difficulties on the Target. They will never take responsibility for any part of the issue. In order to avoid criticism, the Vampire will engage in any tactic they find effective to absolve themselves of any involvement in any sexual difficulties that either they or the Target are experiencing. In this way, they attempt to have the Target carry the entire weight of any issues in order to reduce the Targets Self Respect, confidence and sense of security while simultaneously protecting themselves from criticism. This is entirely deliberate. New sexual activities will not be mutually agreed on. If the activity is proposed by the Target, the Vampire will criticise the Target, and seek to make them feel Shame for suggesting it. If the activity is proposed by the Vampire, they will engage in tactics to force the activity on the Target.

     Coercion of the Target by the Vampire is very common. They will coerce the Target into sexual activity regardless of the feelings or expressions of the Target. This is not only done to gratify the needs of the Vampire, it is used to induce feelings of Shame in the Target, as well as undermine the

Target's Self Respect. It is not uncommon for the Vampire to coerce the Target into sexual activity against their will and attempt to Shame the Target for doing so at a later point. In essence, any and all Shame carried by the Vampire will be projected onto the Target which serves the purpose of undermining the Targets Self Respect while protecting the Vampire from their own feelings of Shame.

Sexual relationships with Vampires are never functional, intimate or loving. They are dysfunctional, and serve only to attack the Targets Self Respect. Wherever possible, sex will be used to hurt the Target, both physically and emotionally and as a means for the Vampire to dominate and control the Target. Withholding of sex is very common, particularly if the Target has openly expressed their sexual needs. This is directly connected to the way the Vampire withholds from providing for the Targets emotional needs and is a way of undermining the Targets Self Respect and establishing dominance over the Target. Not only this, the Vampire will also criticise the Target for expressing their sexual needs in an attempt to induce feelings of Shame in the Target and undermine their Self Respect.

Monogamy has absolutely no meaning for the Vampire. They see sex as a means of obtaining Narcissistic supply, and if they are not obtaining Narcissistic supply through sex with the Target, they will seek it through others outside the relationship. The Vampire knows exactly what they are doing in all such cases; they simply do not care because their need for Narcissistic supply exceeds any and all needs of the Target, or the relationship.

The Vampire not only prioritises their sexual needs over those of the Target, they believe that the Target exists only to serve their sexual needs, just as they believe that the Target exists only to serve their emotional needs. They know that the Target has sexual needs, they simply don't care. The Vampire uses sex to manipulate, control and dominate the Target at all times, and they will engage in a vast array of tactics in order to achieve this. In sexual relationships with a Vampire, feelings of Shame and/or inadequacy are not only common, they are <u>guaranteed</u> to occur.

Sleep and Rest

Sleep and rest are vital to good mental and physical health. In normal, healthy relationships both partners respect the sleep and rest needs of the other. Sleep disorders or disturbances of sleep and rest experienced by either partner are addressed by both partners. Neither partner prioritises their own needs for sleep and rest over those of the other, and mutual arrangements are made in order to ensure that both partners needs for sleep and rest are met. Neither partner deliberately disturbs the sleep and rest of the other, minimises them or dismisses them. Both partners are sensitive to the physical and mental health of the other and each encourages the other to sleep and rest when required.

None of this applies to the Vampire, because they do not care about the mental and physical health of the Target. They pay no attention to the sleep and rest needs of the Target and actively seek to disturb the Target when they are sleeping or resting. The Vampire offers no assistance if the Target is experiencing a sleep disorder or disturbance. Wherever possible, they will use such disorders or disturbances as a weapon against the Target through criticism and/or deliberate creation of circumstances that make the condition worse, further criticising the Target to undermine their Self Respect.

They will deliberately prioritise their own needs for sleep and rest at the expense of those of the Target, often creating needs that do not exist in order to do so. The Vampire will never agree to mutual arrangements for sleep and rest. They will instead seek to control when, where and in what way the Target has access to sleep and rest. This often involves exerting control over the areas and resources of the environment that offer access to sleep and rest.

The Vampire will deliberately disturb the sleep and rest of the Target. If the Target is engaging in sleep and rest, they will wake the Target and/or engage the Target in activities that do not allow them to sleep and rest. If the Target attempts to express their needs for sleep and rest, the Vampire will criticise, minimise, dismiss and undermine those needs. The Vampire actively seeks to use sleep and rest to attack the mental and physical health of the Target. If they notice that sleep and rest would benefit the Target, they will engage whatever tactics are effective to ensure that they are denied.

Hobbies & Interests

In normal, healthy relationships, one or both partners often engage in hobbies and interests outside of the relationship. These are very important for bringing a sense of individuality to each partner, as well as serving as a source of Self Respect for each partner as they achieve goals and engage in activities that bring a sense of accomplishment. In addition, these hobbies and interests may serve as a means by which partners can show an interest in each other's lives without active engagement, which allows them to demonstrate their love and affection for their partner.

Many healthy partnerships engage in mutual hobbies, which serve to deepen the bond between them and provide a means by which they can demonstrate their love and affection for each other. In normal healthy relationships, the right of each partner to engage in hobbies and interests outside the relationship is respected, and neither partner prioritises their hobbies and interests over those of their partner, or the needs of the relationship. If the hobby or interest is not shared by one partner, they respect the right of the other partner to engage in it, they actively encourage their partner's enjoyment of it and they do not seek to denigrate it, or deny their partner access to it. If the hobby or interest is shared, each partner seeks mutual enjoyment of it, does not seek to capitalise it at the expense of their partner and actively encourages their partner's enjoyment of it.

None of this applies to the Vampire. If the Target engages in a hobby or interest outside the relationship, the Vampire will use it as a weapon against the Target. The Vampire has no interest in allowing the Target to develop a sense of individuality outside of the relationship because this threatens their ability to control them. They also seek to use the hobby or interest as a weapon to reduce the Targets Self Respect.

They have no interest in using hobbies and interests as

a means of demonstrating love and affection for the Target because they are incapable of experiencing these emotions. In the mind of the Vampire, anything that reduces the Targets ability to provide them with Narcissistic supply is perceived as a threat, and so they will engage in a range of tactics to attack the Targets hobbies and interests in an attempt to have the Target stop engaging with them and focus instead on providing the Vampire with Narcissistic supply.

In some cases, the Vampire will initially engage in the hobby or interest of the Target in order to set up attacks on them. They will deliberately lose interest in it and suggest or demand that they and the Target cease engaging in it. They will denigrate it and criticise the Target for engaging in it. They will engage in tactics by which they express that the hobby or interest is somehow harmful to them, the Target or the relationship.

In all cases, they will create drama and conflict around the Hobby or Interest in an attempt to make it difficult, if not impossible, for the Target to engage in it. All of these and any other tactics engaged in by the Vampire serve one purpose: to have the Target stop engaging in the hobby or interest and focus instead on providing the Vampire with Narcissistic supply. In other cases, the Vampire will take on the hobby or interest of the Target and seek to take it over. They will deliberately become more committed to it, or better at it in an attempt to achieve two things. First, to undermine the Target's sense of accomplishment and thus their Self Respect; second, in an attempt to have the Target abandon the hobby or interest, allowing the Vampire more of the Target's time to force the them into providing them with Narcissistic supply.

Aspirations

In normal, healthy relationships each partner has aspirations for the future. These may be related to their career, interests, relationships or any number of other areas of their lives. In normal, healthy relationships both partners treat each other's aspirations with respect, support their partner in achieving them, and recognise the positive contribution of aspirations to their partner's Self Respect. Each partner is aware of the other's aspirations and actively seeks ways that they can support their partner in achieving them. They never minimise, denigrate, ignore or demean their partner's aspirations. They never prioritise their own aspirations over those of their partner and they never seek to undermine the aspirations of their partner. If the aspiration is shared by both partners, each partner seeks to achieve it in ways that have been mutually agreed and to the mutual benefit of each partner and the relationship.

None of this applies to the Vampire. They will use any and all aspirations the Target has as a weapon against them. The Vampire does not want the Target to have aspirations because any change or improvement the Target makes to their own lives represents a threat to the Vampires control of them. A Target with aspirations will almost certainly make improvements to their Self Respect as they achieve their aspirations and this represents a threat to the Vampire, since their objective is to ensure that the Targets sense of Self Respect must be kept lower than their own at all times. Therefore, it is critical to the Vampire that they destroy any and all aspirations the Target has.

The Vampire will show no interest in the Target's aspirations. If the Target expresses their aspirations, they will ignore them. If the Target actively engages in achieving their aspirations, the Vampire will engage in an array of tactics in an attempt to sabotage them. The Vampire will instead prioritise their own aspirations above those of the Target at all times. They will engage in whatever tactics are effective in ensuring that the Target abandons their own aspirations and instead focuses on supporting them to achieve their own, while simultaneously providing them with Narcissistic supply.

If the aspiration is mutually held, the Vampire will engage in tactics designed to allow them to achieve the aspiration, while simultaneously denying the Target the ability to achieve it. Where aspirations are concerned, the Vampire recognises only their own. At best, they simply do not care about the aspirations of the Target and, at worst; they perceive the aspirations of the Target as a threat and will do everything in their power to destroy them in order to ensure that the Target focuses on providing them with Narcissistic supply.

The Vampire will criticise the Target for engaging in activities designed to help them achieve their aspirations, minimise the Targets achievements, claim any achievements as their own, and create drama around the aspiration and the Targets activities in achieving them in order to make it difficult, if not impossible for the Target to engage in them and focus instead on providing the Vampire with Narcissistic supply.

Holidays

In the context of the Modern Vampire's weapons, Holidays refer to all forms of dedicated time set aside for a purpose other than everyday activities. They include birthdays, anniversaries, Christmas and other religious holidays, and vacations. In normal, healthy relationships, holidays are positive events because they represent an opportunity to celebrate with friends and family. They are an escape from everyday life and allow people to rest, play and enjoy themselves. Normal, healthy people enjoy holidays and seek to maximise the enjoyment of the people they are with. They do not seek discord or to capitalise the holiday for their own ends. They do not seek to spoil the holiday, or bring other people down by their actions. Overall, normal healthy people use holidays as a way of expressing their love and affection for each other, to enjoy the company of others and to engage in activities that are mutually rewarding.

None of this applies to the Vampire. For the Vampire, holidays serve as means of gaining Narcissistic Supply and attacking the Target. If the holiday is centred on another person, the Vampire will attempt to manipulate the situation so that they become the centre of attention. If the Vampire does to feel that they are receiving sufficient Narcissistic supply from the holiday, they will engage in any number of tactics to gain it. It is very common for the Vampire to create a "scene", or other drama so that attention is placed on them, even if the holiday is actually focussed on them. Many Targets find that they have to work harder during holidays to provide the Vampire with Narcissistic supply, especially if the holiday is geared towards another person. The experience for many

Targets is that the Vampire attempts to "spoil" the holiday at some point through their behaviour. Often, the Vampire will attempt to isolate the Target during a holiday in order to minimise the Targets contact with other people and to have the Target focus on providing them with Narcissistic supply.

Employment

In normal, healthy relationships both partners support each other's employment and the partnership serves to support the employment of each partner. Any issues or challenges that arise with one partner's employment are dealt with by both partners. Opportunities that arise for one partner to further themselves in their employment are supported by both partners. Changes to employment are discussed by both partners and agreed within the context of the relationship.

Agreements that are made between partners regarding one or both partners' employment are honoured and both partners feel that they have the other partners support. In normal, healthy relationships, a partners' employment is never undermined, criticised or demeaned. Neither partner attempts to sabotage the other's employment and neither partner attempts to cause circumstances, or support circumstances that would damage the other's employment.

None of this applies to the Vampire. To the Vampire, employment, whether their own or the Targets serve only as a means of securing either Narcissistic supply or financial resources. If the Vampire is employed in a position that does not provide Narcissistic supply, or if the effort required to secure it outweighs the Narcissistic supply, the Vampire will sabotage the position, attempt to create conflict at the workplace in order to secure Narcissistic supply, or quit the position altogether.

This often means that the Vampire is frequently unemployed or underemployed, because their criterion for staying in a position of employment is to secure Narcissistic supply. If the Target is employed in a position which will allow them to gain Narcissistic supply, directly or indirectly, the Vampire will attempt to associate with the Target's employment wherever possible.

If an opportunity arises for the Target to further their position of employment, the Vampire will not support them. This is because furthering their position will lead to an increase in the Target's Self Respect, which they will do everything in their power to destroy. Further, if the Target does not take the opportunity, the Vampire will criticise them for not doing so. This is also an attempt to undermine the Target's Self Respect.

If an agreement has been made between the Target and the Vampire that the Target will be supported in a change of employment, the Vampire will not honour it. The Vampire is only interested in gaining Narcissistic supply, and if the effort required to support the Target outweighs the Narcissistic supply gained, the Vampire will not engage in providing support. Further, the lack of support from the Vampire will be used as a means of undermining the Targets Self Respect when the Target struggles to tackle the change alone.

The Vampire will criticise the Targets employment,

earning capacity, and prospects. This is an attempt to undermine the Target's Self Respect and ensure that the Target does not focus on their employment, instead focussing on supplying the Vampire with Narcissistic supply. In addition, the Vampire will sabotage the Target's ability to function in their employment. By employing various tactics, they will undermine the Target's ability to meet employment success criteria. This is an attempt to undermine the Self Respect of the Target, which could lead to the Target losing their employment which offers the Vampire the opportunity to secure more of the Target's time in order to extract Narcissistic supply from them.

Children

The subject of children in relationships with a Vampire is extremely sensitive and complex. This Field Manual cannot hope to be anywhere near comprehensive enough to cover all the complexities involved. All that can be done here is to point out how the Vampire sees children: as a weapon.
In normal, healthy relationships children are seen as a priority by both partners. The relationship functions to ensure that children receive positive parenting, love, affection, the teaching of boundaries, guidance, praise and skills and knowledge about the world that will allow them to grow into healthy adults.

If a decision is made to have children, the decision is mutual and appropriate plans are put in place to provide for the welfare of the child. If a pregnancy occurs that was unplanned, both partners discuss the best course of action and the decision is honoured by both partners.

In normal, healthy relationships children are not seen as an extension of the parents and are encouraged to individuate and become their own person. Their achievements are celebrated and encouraged, their bad behaviour is challenged in ways that challenge the behaviour but do not imply that the child themselves are bad, and encourages the development of empathy. Parents model behaviour to their children that allow the child to observe how normal, healthy relationships function. The Child's fears and concerns are addressed in ways that encourage the child to overcome them in healthy ways that support the development of Self Respect.

Parents are aware that their children should learn to develop and protect healthy boundaries that will protect them as they grow and the child is taught the use of the word "No" in appropriate ways in order to enforce those boundaries as they grow.

Overall, in normal, healthy relationships the Parent and Child dynamic is recognised as something that exists to benefit the child, not the parent. Both partners discuss the child's needs and mutually agree strategies to ensure that those needs are met in healthy ways. Both partners support each other in parenting and function as a team to provide for the developing child's needs.

None of this applies to the Vampire. The Vampire uses children as a weapon. To the Vampire, children serve several purposes: First, as a source of Narcissistic supply; second, as a means of securing the Target and keeping them in the relationship to serve as a source of Narcissistic supply; third, to serve as a means of securing Narcissistic supply from third parties. The Vampire is incapable of providing parenting to a child because they <u>are</u> a child.

The Vampire has no interest in providing for the needs of a child. If the effort required exceeds the Narcissistic supply gained from doing so, they will not do it. The Vampire is incapable of providing love, affection, the teaching of boundaries, guidance, praise and skills and knowledge about the reality of the world because they do not possess these things.

Decisions made between the Target and the Vampire about having children will not be honoured. Instead, the Vampire will lie about whether they want children or not in order to secure the Target. If they believe that having children will secure the Target, they will commit to having children, but they will not honour any parenting agreement subsequently since that was not their intention.

In relationships with the Vampire, pregnancy is used as a weapon. The male Vampire will deliberately get the Target pregnant and the female Vampire will deliberately get pregnant if either believes that their goal of securing the Target would be served by doing so. If the Vampire knows that the Target wants to have children but they do not, they will deliberately deny the Target pregnancy in order to reduce the Target's Self Respect. Further, they will blame the Target for the lack of pregnancy, reducing the Target's Self Respect further.

Any failure of conception will be used as an opportunity by the Vampire to blame the Target in order to reduce the Target's Self Respect. In relationships with Vampires, unplanned pregnancies are common, and mutual decisions about the appropriate course of action will not be honoured by the Vampire unless their need for Narcissistic supply will be met by doing so.

The Vampire sees children as an extension of themselves. They do not want the child to individuate and become their own person; they want the child to serve them as a source of Narcissistic supply. The achievement of the child will be celebrated and encouraged only if it serves to supply the Vampire with Narcissistic supply.

Bad behaviour in the part of the child will not be addressed in terms of the behaviour. Instead, the Vampire will address the child in a way that makes the child believe that they are a bad person. This is designed to induce feelings of Shame in the child in order to destroy their Self Respect and make them more susceptible to further tactics employed by the Vampire.

The Vampire is incapable of encouraging empathy in their children because they do not possess empathy. The Vampire is incapable of modeling healthy behaviour and relationships to their children because they are incapable of doing so. The child's fears and concerns are addressed by the Vampire in ways that serve to reduce the child's Self Respect in order to leave the child vulnerable to further tactics employed by the Vampire.

The Vampire does not want their children to develop healthy boundaries because that would limit their ability to use their tactics on the child, and the healthy use of the word "No" is never taught to the child by the Vampire because this would be self-sabotaging for the Vampire since it would be teaching the child one of the most important skills in repelling them. The dynamic between the Vampire and the child is seen as one which exists to benefit only the Vampire.

If parenting strategies are discussed between the Target and the Vampire, they will not be honoured if they benefit the child or the Target more than the Vampire. There is no "team" that exists between the Target and the Vampire in providing for the needs of their children. Instead, the Target will find themselves alone in parenting both the child and the Vampire.

Friends & Family

In normal, healthy relationships friends and family are valued as source of love, affection and support for each partner. Each partner treats the other's friends and family with respect and encourages their partner to engage with them regularly. Any concern that either partner has about the behaviour of the other partner's friends and family are expressed in terms of the welfare of the other partner and is based on objective evidence. Neither partner insults, criticises or denigrates the other partner's friends and family. Wherever possible, each partner seeks the involvement of the other partner's friends and family in group gatherings and they never seek to prioritise the involvement of their own friends and family over those of their partner.

None of this applies to the Vampire. To the Vampire, the Targets friends and family are a threat to their control of the Target. Because they know that the Targets friends and family are a source of love, affection and support for the Target, the Vampire will engage a variety of tactics to ensure that the Target becomes isolated from them. This serves several purposes: First, to ensure that the Target does not have a support network that might identify the Vampire for what they are; Second, to ensure that the Vampire can exert their version of reality on the Target without other versions of reality being available to them; Third, to reduce the Target's Self Respect so that the Target becomes more vulnerable to the Vampire's tactics to control and dominate them so that they serve as a source of Narcissistic supply.

The Vampire will actively discourage the Target from engaging with their friends and family. They will express concerns about the Targets friends and family that have nothing to do with the welfare of the Target and are not based on objective evidence. Often, they will express concerns that the Targets friends and family are harmful to the Target, the Vampire themselves, or the relationship. Overwhelmingly, Survivors report that their Vampires' attitude to their friends and family was indifferent at best, or actively hostile at worst, never positive. The Vampire will insult, criticise and denigrate the Targets friends and family in order to undermine the Target's judgement and values, further reducing the Target's Self Respect. In arranging group gatherings, the Vampire will prioritise their own friends and family over those of the Target. Wherever possible, the Vampire will engage tactics to exclude the Target's friends and family from group gatherings.

The Vampire will use any potentially negative

information they have about the Targets friends and family to criticise them, and the Target for associating with them, in an attempt to create Shame in the Target and undermine their Self Respect. Any of the Targets friends and family that can be recruited as Flying Monkeys will be recruited, and if the Vampire cannot do this, they will seek to marginalise those individuals in an attempt to ensure the isolation if the Target.

Flying Monkeys

Flying Monkeys is a term used to refer to those people in the social circle of the Vampire that serve them as agents. Some Flying Monkeys are aware that they are in this role while others are unaware but all Flying Monkeys are being manipulated by the Vampire in order to achieve their goals. Flying Monkeys are relatively easy to identify because they believe the Vampires version of reality concerning the relationship with the Target, which is always the direct opposite of the actual reality.

Unknown to the Target, the Vampire will have been recruiting Flying Monkeys since the start of the relationship, and many will already have been in place before that time because the Vampire is constantly recruiting Flying Monkeys and will have gathered many by the time they meet the Target.

To the Vampire, new additions to their social circle resulting from their engagement with the Target present them with the opportunity to recruit more Flying Monkeys. Those that they cannot recruit will be perceived as a threat to the Vampire since not only are they are a potential source of love, affection and support for the Target, they also represent a threat to them of revealing them for what they really are. Therefore, any individual that the Vampire does not believe they can recruit as a Flying Monkey will be subject to an array of tactics in order to have the Target isolate from them. In the mind of the Vampire, individuals in their social circle can be divided into two groups: Flying Monkeys and Threats. They will seek to maximise the number of Flying Monkeys and minimise the number of Threats.

Once they have recruited a Flying Monkey, the Vampire will continue to ensure that they use them so that they are perceived as the Victim in the relationship with the Target and that the Target is perceived as the abuser. This is, of course, the direct opposite of the actual reality of the situation but, by recruiting Flying Monkeys, the Vampire protects themselves from the actual reality. In addition, the Vampire will attempt to exert the influence of their Flying Monkeys on the Target as soon as possible in order to undermine the Targets version of reality. Flying Monkeys are often employed by the Vampire in the Hoover Stage of the Attack Cycle, as they will use them to contact the Target and attempt to Hoover by proxy.

Many Flying Monkeys are Vampires in their own right. This explains why some Flying Monkeys enjoy the company of the Vampire, because each supports the others world view. Therefore, when a Flying Monkey has been identified, they should be considered to be a Vampire. While they may not be, they will be serving the Vampires agenda, and therefore represent a threat to the Target. Flying Monkeys that are also Vampires will actively engage in carrying out the Vampires requests because doing so provides them with Narcissistic supply.

Flying Monkeys can be extremely dangerous to the Target because the Target may mistakenly reach out to one when they begin to suspect what the Vampire really is. This will result in the Flying Monkey not only exerting the Vampires version of reality on the Target; they will also report what the Target has said to the Vampire. Not only this, the Flying Monkey may begin a smear campaign against the Target in order to portray the Target as the crazy one in the relationship. If the Vampire has already started such a smear campaign, the Flying Monkey almost certainly will contribute to it, using the Target's attempt to reach out for support against them.

If the Target has been successfully isolated from their support group by the Vampire, they will find themselves in the awful position of having either no support group at all, or a group that consists entirely of Flying Monkeys. This explains why many Targets do not escape from their abuser because every time they attempt to do so, the Flying Monkeys return them to the Vampire and pass information about them to the Vampire, also contributing to whatever smear campaign exists in the process.

The Vampires family, along with any and all members of the social circle of the Vampire had when they met it are prime suspects for being Flying Monkeys, along with any subsequent friends made by the Vampire alone since that time. In addition, any mutual friends the Target and Vampire have made are also suspects for being Flying Monkeys.

When examining their own friends and family for evidence of being a Flying Monkey, a prime indicator for the Target is whether or not the Vampire has attempted to isolate the Target from that individual. If the Vampire has attempted to, or has succeeded in isolating the Target from an individual, that individual is probably not a Flying Monkey because the Vampire will always attempt to isolate the Target from any individual that they cannot recruit as a Flying Monkey.

Food

In normal, healthy relationships food is understood for what it is: a resource that is vital to the mental and physical health of both partners. Food is purchased on a mutually agreed basis, usually with mutually controlled money, for the mutual benefit of both partners and with a mutually agreed division of labour to do so. Where food purchase is achieved by use of individually controlled money, the arrangement is broadly reciprocal. Neither partner has unequal access to food, neither has control over who eats what and when, neither partner has the power to dictate the food distribution in the household.

Any special food requirements due either to preference, medical requirement or food content are known and respected by each partner and neither partner seeks to force their own food preference on the other. Partners do not seek to control food as a resource in any way and any discussion about food is respectful and considerate. Changes to one or both partner's patterns of food consumption are respected and any additional expense incurred is mutually agreed.

None of this applies to the Vampire. To the Vampire, food is a resource that can and will be employed as a weapon against the Target. The Vampire has no concern for the mental and physical health of the Target. If they have any knowledge of the impact of food on the mental and physical health of the Target, they will use that knowledge to attack the Target using an array of tactics.

The Vampire will seek to secure food as a resource using the Target's money where possible, mutually controlled funds if necessary and their own money as a last resort. In securing food, they will seek to have the Target do so whenever possible.

The Vampire will seek to dictate the terms of how food is used in the household. They will at all times consider food to be a resource that they control, or dictate the terms of use of. They will place their food preferences before those of the Target and, in some cases, force the Target to consume food they know the Target does not like either because they do, and don't care about the Target, or because they know that this causes the Target to suffer and therefore reduce the Target's Self Respect.

The Vampire, if they can control the cooking of food, will disregard the preferences of the Target and prioritise their own, dictating the terms of which foods are consumed, on which days and at which times. This is an attempt to exert control over resources, and therefore the Target. If the Vampire does not want to control the cooking of food, they will exert control over the cooking of it by criticising the Target when they attempt to do so. This is an attempt to reduce the Targets Self Respect. Any food prepared by the Vampire will be considered to be beyond criticism, and anything other than gratitude on the part of the Target will be perceived as criticism by the Vampire. Any food prepared by the Target will be considered by the Modern Vampire to be worthy of criticism in an attempt to reduce the Self Respect of the Target.

Any particular food requirements the Target has will either be disrespected or ignored by the Vampire. If those food requirements are due to political or social preference, the Vampire will criticise the Target for holding them. If those food requirements are due to a medical condition, the Vampire will either deliberately ignore the requirement and lie about ignoring it, or criticise the Target for having the requirement. In some cases, the Vampire will deliberately attempt to provide food to the Target that they know goes against the Targets political or social preferences because they simply do not care and, in some cases, they will deliberately attempt to provide food to the Target that they know will endanger the health of the Target. This serves three purposes: First, to undermine the physical health of the Target; Second, to provoke the Target into a confrontation about food, which will provide the Vampire with Narcissistic supply; and Third, to simply torture the Target and undermine their Self Respect.

As I said at the start of this chapter, all interactions between the Target and the Vampire are an attack on the Target. The weapons outlined here are not the only ones in the Vampires arsenal, since everything that the Vampire can use as a weapon will be used as a weapon. In identifying potential weapons, there are two broad categories: People and

Resources.

If the Target finds themselves in an interaction with the Vampire, and therefore under attack, any people and any resources available to the Vampire are potential weapons that the Vampire may use to attack them. The overall picture is that the Vampire will always seek to dominate and control the Target using whatever is effective in doing so. The best and only advice in dealing with the weapons of the Vampire is to end the Attack Cycle and deny them the opportunity to use them. The Vampire is incapable of launching an attack on a Target if the Target has ended the attack cycle. The extent to which the Vampire will continue to attack the Target therefore is the extent to which they and the Target share access to people and resources. If it is possible to establish No Contact, this is ultimately effective in denying the Vampire weapons with which to attack the Target. If it is not possible, it is advisable to take stock of shared people and resources and consider them all to be potential weapons.

Right, well that was a long one. Anyone fancy an Interlude?

Interlude 4

"That's not a knife!" – Mick Dundee, "Crocodile Dundee"

Hello again, dear Survivor!

    Well, weapons, eh? Who knew Modern Vampires could be so inventive? Personally, I'd settle for a blunt object if it came to subduing a burglar, but the Vampire? They'd criticise the burglar's career choice.

    I'm not kidding when I say that everything is a weapon. They will use anything and everything to hurt you. I shit you not. I had a pet used against me as a weapon once. Not in the Monty Python-load-it-into-a-catapult kind of way but in a trying-to-Shame-me kind of way. When I finally told my last Vampire where to go, she changed her profile picture on Facebook to a photo of the dog to show me what a terrible person I was abandoning such a cute fluffy creature. That, and to just plain taunt me. They know no boundaries, dear

Survivor. None at all.

I thought I'd take this opportunity to talk for a bit about why I use the term "Vampire" to refer to these individuals. Some people will always question this because the natural inclination is to think of the Vampire as a person who needs help. They are not. Individuals who qualify as Vampires are disordered, dangerous, and abusive and they <u>refuse</u> to change.

Now, I have enormous sympathy for people who suffer but that only goes as far as the point at which they start trying to make other people pay for their suffering and if they also refuse to change that, I believe we need a new word for those individuals because "person" or "people" just don't fit the bill. People can choose to change; an individual person can choose to change. Individuals who choose not to change are fine with me right up to the point at which their behaviour causes harm to others. At that point, if they are harming others and they are refusing to change, I believe that they have forfeited their right to call themselves a "person", or collectively "people". Further, if they are hurting others and enjoying it, and they refuse to change, then as far as I'm concerned we need a new word for that, and I've chosen to use the word "Vampire", because it fits.

So yes, I use the term Vampire, and I do it with good reason. We have names for other predators, so why not Vampires? We don't go about the place mistaking other predators for people, so what's different about Vampires? "Nancy" might be a nice name, but if Nancy is a crocodile, it's still going to chew your face off it gets half a chance. You could put a dress on Nancy if you like (once you've sedated it). You could put shoes on it, if that's your thing. You could give Nancy a job title. You could give Nancy a PhD for all I care. Nancy is a crocodile, and a Vampire is a Vampire. I don't care what they call themselves, what they look like, what they wear, what awards they have, what they do for a living, what their portfolio is or anything else. They are a Vampire and they will attack you because that's what predators do, and Vampires are predators, just like crocodiles. Do we refer to crocodiles as people? Of course we don't. No-one in their right mind would do that. Ever see a professional crocodile hugger? Ever hear of anyone having a relationship with a crocodile? Didn't think so. I'm sure I don't have to ask you why that is, do I?

Anyway, that's the rant over. Let's get to the next burning question.

How can the Vampire move on so quickly as if I never mattered?

I'm not going to pull my punch here, dear Survivor. It's because you only mattered to the Vampire in terms of how you made them feel about themselves. They never cared about you. But, there are really good reasons why that's a good thing, so read on...

In Chapter 2, I talked about how the Vampire is an emotional child, and that they can only relate to others in terms of how they make them feel about themselves because they are Egocentric, remember? Well think about it for a moment. You made them feel amazing, because you are amazing. You represented something that made them feel amazing about themselves. You were a source of everything they cannot supply for themselves: Love, Compassion and Empathy. The whole nine yards. Basically, you were the surrogate for all of the emotional needs they cannot supply for themselves and what an incredible job you did of it too! You kept on doing that long after it made sense to stop, and you kept on giving and giving and giving to an individual that will eternally take and take and take. That makes you one of the strongest human beings on the planet!

Take a moment to think about that. You have the capacity to love in adversity, to care when it hurts, to give when you're empty and maintain it all in the spirit of a relationship that is bigger than both of the people within it. That, dear Survivor, is priceless and never let anyone tell you otherwise. So, why did the Vampire move on so quickly as if you never mattered? That's actually very easy to answer, and it's not your fault. You were too good for them. Let's all say that together, shall we?

You. Were. Too. Good. For. Them.

That's the simple truth. No, it's not directly answering the question but bear with me, I'm getting there. The Vampire looked at you as a source of things they had absolutely no chance of providing for themselves. Therefore, they had to either provide for themselves, which they have zero chance of doing, or look to you to do that job forever, which you could stop doing at any time. In either case, they were screwed. If they tried to do for themselves, they would fail. If you left, they would implode through lack of Narcissistic supply.

So, there you were, being everything they could not do for themselves all day, every day.

Now, something must have shifted or you wouldn't be a Survivor. You'd still be a Target. If you are still a Target, this applies to you as well. The Vampire had to look at you, all day, every day and say to themselves "What will I do if I lose this?" The answer from their perspective is simple: I'm screwed. So, they will seek out other individuals that could serve as on-going sources of Narcissistic supply. How and when they found them is immaterial. They found them because they had to. The risk of losing you was too high for them not to. So, there the new source of Narcissistic supply is, already drawn into the Attack cycle just like you were, oh-so-pleased with the attention they are getting and believing that all their birthdays have come at once. And then the change came. In all probability, you did something to bring it about.

You stopped providing Narcissistic supply. Maybe that was because you were tired of all the bullshit, and started to challenge the Vampire. Maybe that was because you were just plain tired and had decided that you couldn't give any more, which is awesome because it means you were putting yourself first. Maybe you have become an active challenge because you had actively turned off the Narcissistic supply. Whatever the circumstance, it was always YOU that made it happen, which makes you the powerful one here.

Once you had taken action, the Vampire had to escape. They were totally screwed if they stayed because the supply had been turned off, so away they went. Straight to the new source of Narcissistic supply. Did that look like they moved on like you never mattered? Of course it did, otherwise you wouldn't be asking the question. Is that actually what happened? Hell NO.

What actually happened is that the Vampire was forced to move on to the new source of Narcissistic supply because the last one (that's you) was too good for them. They couldn't hang on to you because you had shaken them loose. They were looking at someone utterly fucking amazing that they couldn't feed off any more, so of course they fled! What you were doing was making them feel ashamed of themselves every single day because you never stopped being amazing, and they had lost control of you. I shit you not. They had to look at you every single day and know that they were a piece of shit that could not control the wonderful person they were trying to feed off. They had to do that every day. Every. Single. Day.

And that's why they appeared to move on so fast. Take a moment to put yourself in their shoes (I know, that's disgusting - feel free to shower afterwards). If you had to choose the shit-box car because your luxury car had locked the doors and driven itself over the horizon, wouldn't you try to convince yourself that the shit-box car was cool, especially if the luxury car was watching? I realise that this has all gone a bit Disney, but I think you take my point.

The simple reason the Vampire appeared to move on so fast is that they had to. You were always too good for them, and they always knew that. The new source of Narcissistic supply is just that: a new source of Narcissistic supply and the same story will be repeated with them as it was with you. Is the Vampire happy? No, and I've answered that question before. The best thing you can do right now, dear Survivor is realise that the new source of Narcissistic supply is where you used to be and get the fuck out of Dodge. Get away and stay away from the Vampire.

And here's the last thought I'll leave you with. You know how you provided all that supply to the Vampire? You know how you could love in adversity, care when it hurts, and give when you're empty and maintain it all in the spirit of a relationship that is bigger than both of the people within it? You know who really deserves that? <u>You do</u>. The person you need to be in a relationship with now is you. When you give all the love, care and attention to yourself that you used to give to the Vampire, you will be happier and more at peace than you could ever imagine. If you can't quite believe that yet, please take it on trust for now. I know it because I've been there. I didn't believe it either at first but it is absolutely 100% true. I promise.

And now, it's time for Chapter 5. See you on the other side.

Chapter 5

The Tactics of the Vampire

In this chapter, I'd like to take a look at some of the tactics that the Vampire employs. As with Chapter 4, I hope this will ring some bells with Targets and Survivors and serve as a reminder that the Vampires behaviours are not even close to "normal" behaviour. All of the Vampires tactics are driven by their disordered nature, all of them are designed to impose the false reality of their False Self, and all of them are designed to control and dominate the Target with the intention of feeding off them for Narcissistic supply.

Every single tactic employed by the Vampire is highly, highly abusive and extended exposure to them is extremely dangerous to the Targets mental and physical health. Healthy people just don't do the things I describe here; only Vampires do. Therefore, if you are currently the Target of a Vampire, or suspect that you are, and you recognise any of these tactics in your relationship, please take steps to remove yourself safely from the relationship. Chapter 11 will help with that. If you're a Survivor, this should help you understand more about what the Vampire does and what you've been through.

Gaslighting

In normal, healthy relationships the mind of each partner is their own sovereign territory. Each partner's thoughts and beliefs are respected by the other partner, and any and all variations from absolute confidence in each partner's thoughts and beliefs are discussed openly, with compassion and respect and for the partner expressing them. Under no circumstances does one partner seek to question the reality of the other, and under no circumstances does one partner seek to enforce their version of reality on the other.

None of this applies to the Vampire, and Gaslighting is the primary means by which they control their Targets mind. Gaslighting is a deliberate, malicious and sustained attack on the mind of the Target. It is designed to undermine the Target's (true) sense of reality, and replace it with the (false) reality of the Vampire. It is often thought of as a form of brainwashing, but this is not the case. Brainwashing is obvious. Gaslighting is covert, subtle and is carried out in ways that allow the Vampire employing it "plausible deniability", which is the most insidious part of this disgusting practice. Where brainwashing seeks to replace the Target's current beliefs about reality with those of the brainwasher directly and by force, Gaslighting seeks to replace the Target's current beliefs about reality with those of the Vampire covertly and by stealth.

The Vampire carries out Gaslighting deliberately and they will never stop Gaslighting their Target. They do this because they are attempting to defend themselves against actual reality because that is the place where they will encounter the truth about what they really are. Since they deliberately and knowingly engage in tactics that inflict pain and psychological harm on the Target on a daily basis, every single day represents the potential for the Vampire to have to introspect on what they are and take responsibility for their actions.

Since the Vampire simply cannot face the reality of what they are, they must Gaslight their Target for two reasons: First, to assure themselves that their (false) reality is true, and therefore their behaviours are justified; Second, to gain the agreement of the Target that their (false) reality is true. In other words, if the Vampire does not Gaslight the Target, they must face reality. A Vampire that is unable to Gaslight their Target will begin to implode as they face more and more situations in which the truth of what they really are is the only possibility left to them. Because Gaslighting is a self-preservation mechanism for the Vampire, contradicting the narrative they create through Gaslighting is akin to trapping any other predator: they will defend themselves at all costs, and are therefore can become extremely dangerous. Directly contradicting them is not the best course of action therefore and by far the better course is to escape them and thereby deny them the ability to Gaslight. The Vampire cannot Gaslight a Target that is not there.

The Vampire Gaslights using several techniques relentlessly and continually. Below are some of the techniques employed in Gaslighting. There are more, as many in fact as the Vampire considers necessary to impose their (false) reality on the Target.

1) They lie constantly

2) They deny they have said things that the Target knows they said, even if the Target has evidence

3) They criticise individuals that support the Target that they cannot recruit as Flying Monkeys

4) They lie about the negative "opinions" of the Target held by others outside the relationship

5) They say one thing and do another. Their actions do not match their words

6) They deny or minimise their actions

7) They project. They accuse the Target of having feelings they themselves have and of doing things they themselves have done

8) They question the Target's memory for events, actively deny events, or claim that the Target is "making it up"

9) They pick a small flaw in the Target (real or imagined) and make that the cause of all relationship problems

10) They blame the Target for their own actions

11) They create conflict for no reason, and blame the Target for the conflict

12) They constantly criticise and insult the Target

13) They provoke the Target to anger in order to make them appear crazy

14) They accuse the Target of being "too sensitive"

15) They threaten the Target with leaving the relationship

16) They claim that the Target would never find another relationship if they leave

17) They threaten the Target with potential consequences for them attempting to leave the relationship, such as threats of suicide

18) They claim that other people are liars, particularly those close to the Target and the Target themselves

19) They demonstrate indifference to the suffering of the Target, particularly if they have caused it

20) They blame the Target for all issues in the relationship and claim that the Target is "crazy"

Regardless of the technique or tactic employed to Gaslight the Target, there are several signs of Gaslighting that the overwhelming majority of Survivors report after escaping their abuser. There are many more, but if ANY of the below are present in the Target, there is a high probability that they are being Gaslighted:

1) Constant confusion and unease

2) Second guessing themselves

3) Apologising frequently, often for no reason

4) Making excuses for the Vampire's behaviour

5) Believing that they are too sensitive

6) Feeling like the "crazy" on in the relationship, or feeling "crazy" in general

7) Withholding information from friends and family about what happens in the relationship

8) Self-medicating with drugs or alcohol

9) Having problems making simple decisions

10) Feeling overwhelmed by everyday life

11) Feeling that they are a different person to who they were before the relationship

12) Feeling that they can't do anything right

13) Feeling inadequate

14) Overpraising the Vampire to others

15) Justifying the Vampires behaviour to themselves and others

16) Denying that there are problems in the relationship to themselves and others

17) Feeling dread when going home

18) Sleeping too much, or too little

19) Feelings of depression

20) Constant anxiety

At the heart of Gaslighting is the process of creating an environment in which the Target is blamed for having an "issue" that causes the "problems" in the relationship, whether those problems are real, or have been invented by the Vampire. The Vampire will enlarge the "issue" out of all proportion and attempt to create a narrative in which the "issue" is far worse than it actually is.

The objective of Gaslighting is to deflect from the actual, objective truth: That the Vampire is the source of all problems in the relationship. The Vampire will alternate between accusing the Target directly for the having the "issue" and behaving in ways that appear to support the Target in overcoming the "issue". In all cases, the Vampire will attempt to ensure that the "issue" is the cause of any and all problems (real and imagined), and will create enormous conflict if the Target ever attempts to defend themselves, or point out another source of the problem at hand.

In the mind of the Vampire, the Target and their "issue" has already been identified as the source of all problems (real and imagined). If the "issue" is resolved clearly and with consistent evidence, the Vampire will select (or invent) another one to take its place. For example, a Target that enjoys a glass of wine at the end of the day might be accused by the Vampire of being an alcoholic. If the Target then stops drinking entirely, the Vampire will switch to making the (imagined) post-drinking behaviours of the Target the new "issue". This constant focus on the Target's "issue" serves the purpose of absolving the Vampire of all responsibility for problems in the relationship when, in fact, they are the only source. This allows them to avoid feelings of Shame, justify their actions to themselves, destroy the Target's Self Respect, justify smear campaigns and brings a sense of peace to the Vampire that they will never experience if they are not Gaslighting. And they absolutely know that they are doing it.

Gaslighting is not something the Vampire does by accident; it is something they do knowingly and deliberately. In many cases, they enjoy doing it not just because it brings a sense of relief from having to face their True Self but because they enjoy watching the suffering of the Target as they struggle to come to terms with the dissonance between objective reality and the false reality of the Vampire. Gaslighting is sadistic, because so are Vampires.

The mind of the Vampire is so twisted that they will also engage in a process known in the psychological community as "projection". This process involves the complete conviction in their mind that they are the Victim in the relationship, and they constantly seek others to play the role of the "Bad Guy" (see Chapter 6 on the" Drama Triangle"), primarily the Target.

During Gaslighting, the Vampire will constantly claim that not only is the Target the source of the problems in the relationship, but also that they (the Vampire) are the Victim of the Targets behaviours. They deny any and all negative qualities in themselves to protect themselves from Shame, and instead attempt to either find, or induce those qualities in the Target. If they succeed in doing so, they will attack the Target remorselessly for possessing the very negative qualities or behaviours they possess but cannot face for fear of feelings of Shame. The resulting drama provides them not only with Narcissistic supply; it allows them to avoid the feelings of Shame that accompany possessing those negative qualities and behaviours. This success of accomplishing projection compels the Vampire to carry out the process again and again and again.

Projection means that the Target is not perceived by the Vampire as a person at all. Instead, they perceive the Target as a "screen" on which they project all their negative qualities so that they can attack them, which makes the Target simply an object to be abused. An example would be the Vampire "needling" the Target until the Target displays signs of verbal aggression. The Vampire will then take the Victim position, claim that the Target is being abusive and feed off the Narcissistic supply that follows as they accuse the Target of being all the horrible things that they, in fact, are.

In this way, the Vampire pushes their negative qualities onto the Target, forcing the Target to accept them as their own. This serves two purposes: To allow the Vampire to deny that they have negative qualities, and to attack the Target so that they provide Narcissistic supply. In all cases, it serves to reinforce the Vampires (false) reality: That the Target is the abuser and the Vampire is the Victim.

This disgusting and despicable practice is carried out subtly, deliberately, remorselessly and will continue until the Target escapes or is Discarded. This is why so many Survivors report that they don't know who they are when they have escaped or been Discarded; their identity has been stolen, and they have been forced to accept an identity they do not recognise.

FOG (Fear, Obligation, Guilt)

Gaslighting creates FOG. In normal, healthy relationships, feelings of Fear, Obligation and Guilt are entirely absent. Neither partner is bound to the relationship for any other reason than the mutual bond of love, affection and mutual concern for the other's welfare.

In the relationship with the Target, the Vampire uses Gaslighting to create an atmosphere of Fear, Obligation and Guilt (FOG). FOG is essential to the survival of the Vampire in their relationships because it is the means by which they seek to ensure that the Target does not leave the relationship.

Healthy relationships do not feature FOG at all, since they contain two adults. Healthy adults do not experience Fear, Obligation and Guilt in their own lives, and therefore do not bring those feelings into relationships. Only Vampires do that.

Therefore, throughout this next section, it should be made clear that if the Target is feeling any of these things, the Vampire is to blame. It is the Gaslighting employed by the Vampire, combined with Victim playing, projection and projective identification that creates FOG. By far the simplest way to detect whether FOG is present is for the Target or Survivor to examine their own feelings. If they are experiencing FOG, it is because the Vampire is inducing those feelings with their behaviour. It is <u>not</u> the Target or Survivors doing.

These are some of the signs of the <u>Fear</u> element of FOG:

1) Fear that the Target is unlovable, and so will not find love with anyone other than the Vampire

2) Fear of what the Vampire may attempt to do to themselves or the Target if they attempt to leave the relationship

3) Fear for the welfare of any children involved

4) Fear of loss of resources if the Target leaves the relationship

5) Fear of a smear campaign against the Target if they leave

6) Fear of being alone after the Target leaves the relationship

7) Fear of having to start life over again

8) Fear of whatever the Vampire has identified the Target

already fears outside the relationship that they will attempt to magnify in the mind of the Target

These are some of the signs of the <u>Obligation</u> element of FOG:

1) Obligation to the commitment the Target made to the relationship

2) Obligation to the commitment the Target made to the Vampire

3) Obligation to any financial commitment made by the Target

4) Obligation to any future commitment made by the Target

5) Obligation to any children that exist in the family

6) Obligation to "what the relationship has been through"

7) Obligation to any commitment the Target made to helping the Vampire

8) Obligation to whatever arbitrary idea the Vampire creates (real or imagined)

These are some of the signs of the <u>Guilt</u> element of FOG:

1) Guilt about what the Target has done to the Vampire (which only ever exists in the mind of the Vampire)

2) Guilt about what the Vampire has done for the Target

(which only ever exists in the mind of the Vampire)

3) Guilt about what would happen to the Vampire if the Target abandons it (which only ever exists in the mind of the Vampire)

4) Guilt about what would happen to any children in the family if the Target leaves (which only ever exists in the mind of the Vampire)

5) Guilt about breaking any commitments made by the Target (see Obligation)

6) Guilt about what others will think of the Target for leaving the Vampire
7) Guilt about whatever arbitrary idea the Vampire creates (real or imagined)

If any of the above is present in the relationship, the Target is experiencing FOG that has been induced through Gaslighting. The best course of action is to safely remove themselves from the relationship.

Future faking

In normal, healthy relationships plans made for the future are based on honesty, mutual respect and concern for each partner and the relationship. Plans for the purchase of property are made in realistic terms, appropriate financial commitments are made by both partners in mutual agreement and are revisited regularly. Plans for marriage are made seriously, with mutual respect for both partners attitude to marriage and financial commitments are made by both partners in the same way as plans for the purchase of property. Any other future plans are made in similar ways to the first two mentioned here and at no time are changes made by either partner without discussion. For plans regarding children, see the section "children" in the chapter on weapons. Overall, the approach taken by both partners is respectful, realistic and honours the commitment made.

None of this applies to the Vampire, who routinely engages in lies about their commitment to the future of the relationship. This is referred to as "Future Faking". The Vampire regards the future of the relationship as something that they can dictate, and they will not honour any agreement they make about the future if it does not serve their needs for control, domination and Narcissistic supply. For the Vampire, future plans are meaningless unless they provide an opportunity to further enslave the Target and/or provide them with a source of Narcissistic supply.

The Vampire will assess the needs, wants, desires and aspirations of the Target in the Idealisation Stage of the Attack Cycle and lie about their commitment to those things in order to secure the Target. They will then continue to lie about those commitments throughout the relationship. No commitment made by the Vampire exceeds their need for Narcissistic supply, and if the effort required to follow through on a commitment is greater than the Narcissistic supply it will provide, the Vampire will not follow through.

However, while they have no intention of following through with a commitment, the Vampire will continue to lie about that commitment all the time they need to in order to retain the Target as a source of Narcissistic supply. Therefore, the Target may find that they have made all financial and other commitments necessary to bring about the future plan only to find that the Vampire has done nothing, or that they have discarded the Target despite whatever future plans were in place up to and including the day of the discard.

Trauma bonding

In normal, healthy relationships the bond that exists between partners is based on mutual trust, love, affection, intimacy and mutual concern for each partner's welfare. The behaviour and personality of each partner is stable across time and neither partner seeks to "rush" a bond between them. Neither partner attempts to create unnecessary drama between them and neither partner seeks conflict. Each partners needs for their own time and space is respected and neither partner seeks to capitalise the time and space of the other. Neither partner seeks to manipulate the behaviour of the other through their own actions, and neither partner is dependent on the other for their sense of worth or validation.

None of this applies to the Vampire because they are incapable of experiencing trust, love, affection and intimacy and have absolutely no concern for the Target's welfare. Because they are disordered, the personality of the Vampire is never stable. In the Idealisation Stage of the Attack Cycle, they will try to rush the relationship, often moving very fast and occupying far too much of the Target's time and space. Survivors often report a "whirlwind" romance followed by the most traumatic and damaging relationship of their lives.

What the Vampire attempts to do at all times in the relationship is to create a Trauma Bond. This is very similar to an addiction, and at the level of brain chemistry, it functions exactly the same way as an addiction (see chapter 8). In the Idealistion Stage of the Attack Cycle, they will "Love Bomb" the Target. This is designed to overwhelm the Target and convince them that they have met their "soul mate". None of the behaviours during this Stage are the true behaviours of the Vampire. Rather, they are "Mirroring" the Target. They reflect all of the Target's positive qualities back to them in an attempt to lure the Target into the relationship.

This is the first part of the trauma bond because the Vampire will show glimpses of this false behaviour infrequently during the rest of the relationship in order to keep the Target "hooked". The intensity of the positive attention from the Vampire creates an idealised version of them in the Target's mind that they intend to lure the Target with for the rest of the relationship.

When they move to the Devaluation Stage of the Attack Cycle, the Vampire will begin to employ their range of tactics and weapons to attack the Target. From this point forward, they will alternate between their abusive True Self and their idealised False Self in order to maintain and strengthen the Trauma Bond. This deliberately creates confusion in the mind of the Target, and the reason why this occurs is actually biological. The damage done to the brain of the Target will be examined in chapter 8, but for now the alternating between "Dr. Jeckyl" and "Mr. Hyde" that the majority of survivors report about their Vampire has the following impact:

1) When things are "good", the "reward centre" of the Target's brain is flooded with neurochemicals. In a non-abused, normal brain, these neurochemicals operate in the "reward centres" of the brain and increases in them are perfectly natural in response to rewarding experiences. So, when the Vampire is being "Dr Jeckyl", the reward centre of the Target's brain floods with these neurochemicals and they feel happy.

2) When things are "bad" and the Vampire is being "Mr. Hyde" the "reward centre" of the Target's brain drains of neurochemicals. In addition, the Target's brain responds to the stress with an activation of the fight/flight response, causing a release of adrenaline and inducing feelings of anxiety. Again, these are quite normal responses to both negative experiences and emergencies in a non-abused brain.

The process of alternating between Dr Jeckyl and Mr Hyde causes the Target's brain to alternate wildly between hugely high levels of neurochemicals, and wildly low levels of the same, combined with high levels of Adrenaline. Over time, this causes the Target to become addicted to the behaviour of the Vampire. Analysis of the brain chemistry of people addicted to Heroin, and the brain chemistry of the Survivors of abuse has revealed that they are exactly the same.

The net effect of Trauma Bonding is that the Target is addicted to the Vampire's behaviour. Just like an addict seeking their drug, the Target spends their time seeking the positive behaviours of the Vampire in order to experience the feelings of the "high" that increased levels of the relevant brain chemicals brings. In between these "highs", the Target suffers withdrawal, and experiences feelings of craving, which motivates them to engage in behaviours they believe will cause the Vampire to behave in ways that will provide the "high" they are now addicted to.

Trauma Bonding is therefore a deliberate tactic employed by the Vampire in order to render the Target addicted to their behaviour. Once the Target is "hooked", they will behave however they wish to in order to manipulate the Target's behaviour to serve their needs for Narcissistic supply. Needless to say, Trauma Bonding is a disgusting and despicable practice.

Although the Vampire does not know the biological mechanics of Trauma Bonding, they do know the impact of it on the Target's behaviours, and therefore they use it to serve their needs for Narcissistic supply. The Vampire is doing this deliberately and has absolutely no concern for the damaging effects this practice has on the Target.

Lies

Lies damage relationships, because they undermine trust. One of the fundamental qualities of normal, healthy relationships is that both partners understand this simple idea. While people do, of course engage in creative ways to say things that might hurt their partner's feelings, healthy relationships are characterised by an atmosphere in which the truth is held as something that is valued by both partners and each knows that the other would not deliberately lie to them in order to serve their own ends.

None of this applies to the Vampire because they are a

compulsive liar. They will lie about their intentions, activities, feelings, achievements, commitments and anything else besides if they believe that doing so would serve one or both of two purposes: First, to secure Narcissistic supply, and second; to dominate and control the Target.

The lies of the Vampire may not be direct contradictions of the truth. They will also lie by omission, leaving out important pieces of information that are relevant to the question at hand. They will engage in lying by influence, answering questions with statements that may be true but are unrelated to the question. The Vampire will evade directly answering questions, offer Word Salad (see later) answers, deflect, project, distort and engage many other tactics to avoid telling the truth if doing so would potentially cause them to feel Shame. If cornered with evidence and are unable to lie, they will respond with Rage.

The Vampire will also lie directly to the Target about them. They will distort the truth about the Target in ways that either inflate or deflate their characteristics or achievements depending on whether it is trying to manipulate the Target or attack their self-esteem. Because the Vampire is so adept at lying, the best advice is to pay no attention at all to <u>anything</u> they say. Instead, pay attention to what they <u>do</u>. The truth about what the Vampire is will always be revealed in their action, never their words. Attempting to track, monitor, discover or disprove the Vampire's lies is a futile exercise. They will lie about lying and will stop at nothing to direct blame from themselves to another person, particularly the Target.

Conflict creation

Normal, healthy relationships do not contain conflict. If disagreements arise, they are dealt with in a mature way and, if conflict is the outcome, both partners know that they should walk away, gain some perspective, do their best to understand the other's point of view, and return to the discussion later to resolve the issue. Both partners know that if conflict is a recurrent theme in the relationship then something is wrong and they will seek help from a counselling professional to help them overcome this.

None of this applies to the Vampire because they thrive on conflict. They are entirely unable to exist without the drama that conflict provides because it represents a source of Narcissistic supply. If the Vampire cannot obtain positive supply, they will create conflict in order to obtain negative supply. Since most Targets do not need conflict in this way, they are constantly forced into drama and conflict that they did not cause, do not want, and gain nothing from. Only the Vampire finds reward in conflict and they will provoke it whenever or wherever they think appropriate if doing so will provide them with Narcissistic supply. This explains why, once they have escaped their abuser, the overwhelming majority of Survivors report that the relationship was plagued by chaos, drama and conflict.

The Vampire does not simply create conflict for no reason. They do so to validate their own existence. If they do not receive Narcissistic supply from their Target, they will begin to introspect, which will inevitably lead to feelings of Shame. If they are alone at these times, they will seek out sources of Narcissistic supply in order to stave off feelings of Shame. If they are in the company of the Target, and the Target is not providing positive Narcissistic supply, they will provoke the Target into providing negative Narcissistic supply by causing conflict. Therefore, in the same way that they are compelled to Gaslight, they are compelled to create conflict.

The Vampire will often create conflict in order to escape a situation. If they believe that they are about to be challenged, they will create conflict. If they believe that evidence of their wrongdoing is about to be presented, they will create conflict. But they will also create conflict in order to allow them to leave the home and pursue other sources of Narcissistic supply.

It is extremely common for the Vampire to create conflict, leave the home in the middle of it and meet with another source of Narcissistic supply they have been grooming. In this way, they achieve several things: First, they create conflict, which provides them with Narcissistic supply; second, it allows them to further Gaslight the Target and third, it allows them to escape to pursue the other source of Narcissistic supply. If patterns like this occur in the conflict creation, the Vampire is almost certainly carrying on an affair.

Mirroring

Mirroring is a tactic that is mostly employed by the Vampire in the Idealisation Stage of the Attack Cycle. Once they have located a Target, they engage Mirroring to ensnare the Target and convince them that they possess the same traits, qualities, likes, dislikes, values and personality quirks that the Target does. In many cases, Survivors report that their first few encounters with their Vampire involved the Vampire looking at them and listening to them intensely to an unnerving extent. For many Survivors, this was interpreted as genuine interest, but the reality is that the Vampire was actively engaged in Mirroring.

The process of Mirroring requires the Vampire to gather as much information about the Target as possible in order to know what they must become in order to secure them as a source of Narcissistic supply. Once they believe that they have sufficient information about the Target, they will begin to behave the way the Target does. They will reflect back to the Target the traits, qualities, likes, dislikes, values and personality quirks they have observed.

Survivors report that they believed that they had met their "soul mate", "twin flame", or other such titles because the Vampire appeared to have so much in common with them that the attraction was undeniable. This is entirely deliberate on the part of the Vampire, and is a calculated and premeditated means by which they seek to secure the Target in order to have them commit to a relationship.

Mirroring is the primary means by which the Vampire secures all sources of Narcissistic supply. This can serve as an "early warning sign" that the Vampire is Triangulating (see Triangulation). If the Target finds that the Vampire is adopting the traits, characteristics and so on of another person, they are Mirroring that person, and therefore perceives them to be a potential source of Narcissistic supply.

Blame-shifting

Normal, healthy people will accept responsibility for the outcomes of their actions, both positive and negative. The Vampire is incapable of accepting responsibility for the negative outcomes of their actions because to do so would trigger feelings of Shame. Blame-shifting is a tactic that the Vampire employs in order to preserve themselves from feelings of Shame.

They can never accept responsibility for any negative consequence that arises from their behaviours, so they will always seek an external source to explain to themselves and others why they engaged in the behaviour in the first place. In most cases, that external source will be the Target but may include whatever person they feel they may plausibly shift blame to. This explains why so many Survivors report hearing phrases such as "you made me", "I wouldn't have to...... if you didn't.....", and "If you only.....I wouldn't...." and so on once they escape their abuser.

Accusations

Accusations about an intimate partners behaviour are not a feature of normal, healthy relationships because they indicate that there is a lack of trust and/or a lack of accountability in the relationship. The Vampire uses accusations constantly. They will accuse the Target of possessing the negative traits they possess to avoid feeling Shame. They will accuse the Target of behaviours that they are carrying out for the same reason. They will accuse the Target of doing things the Target has not done, or behaving in ways they do not, having characteristics they do not have or lacking characteristics they do have. They will accuse the Target of acting in ways that hurt them. They will accuse the Target of not doing things they want them to do, or doing things they don't want them to do.

The Golden Rule when dealing with the Vampire's accusations is that the Vampire is projecting, and therefore the accusation is actually being made at them, the Vampire. The simplest way of understanding any and all accusations the Vampire makes against the Target is this: They are all false. Normal, healthy people do not make accusations; they make gentle, kind and considerate observations. Accusations are always a means of Projection (see Projection), Blame shifting, DARVO (see DARVO) and/or Splitting and all are designed to move the focus from the Vampire to the Target, especially if they are being challenged.

Splitting

Splitting is a very primitive psychological defense mechanism that the Vampire uses to protect themselves from feelings of Shame. It is a form of Black and White thinking that leads them to cast the Target as the Bad Guy, and themselves as the Victim, and they will use Splitting and Accusations together in arguments.

Where normal, healthy people understand that their partner has good and bad qualities that exist even when there is disagreement; the Vampire exists in a world of absolutes. The Target is either all good or all bad. If they feel threatened, they will cast the Target as all bad and engage in Splitting so that they can play the Victim. This will lead them to use statements like "You always....", "You never......", I always......", "I never....", and so on. It is an all or nothing method of thinking and speaking that the Vampire uses to protect themselves while attacking the Target. In normal, healthy relationships Splitting is not a feature of conversation because it is clearly nonsense. No-one is always or never anything, and both partners accept each other's good and bad points.

Isolation

In normal, healthy relationships both partners have active networks of friends and family that they engage with regularly, and are encouraged to do so by their partner. Neither partner seeks to remove the other from these networks, nor seeks to drive these networks away or close them down. None of this applies to the Vampire. As stated before, people outside the relationship are seen by the Vampire as falling into two groups: potential Flying Monkeys and potential Threats. They will seek to drive away any potential Threats and/or have the Target isolate themselves from them.

The Vampire knows that they cannot carry out their manipulation, domination and control of the Target if there are Threats present. They will therefore engage in a number of tactics to isolate the Target. They will capitalise the Target's time, criticise the Threat, criticise the Target for associating with the Threat, insult the Threat, and claim that the Threat is somehow hurting the Target, the relationship and/or the Vampire themselves. Above all, they will use Gaslighting to induce the Target to abandon their association with the

Threat.

In addition to attempting to isolate the Target from what they perceive as Threats, the Vampire will also attempt to isolate the Target from sources of financial support. The objective in both cases is to create a situation in which the Target is entirely dependent on the Vampire. They will undermine the Targets ability to work in an attempt to get them fired. They will attempt to control all finances. They will Gaslight the Target to have them believe that they will take care of their financial needs (which they will not) and/or they will Future Fake regarding finances.

The overwhelming majority of Survivors report that they lost contact with friends and family during their relationship with a Vampire, sometimes never being able to re-establish them. In many cases, the Gaslighted Target will actively turn against their friends and family because they believe the Gaslighting, or to appease the Vampire. This often leaves friends and family confused and hurt, but any attempt to reconnect with the Target will be met with the tactics of the Vampire in an attempt to remove the Threat from the Target, or the Target from the Threat. Many Survivors also report that they lost property, jobs, careers, savings and access to financial support of all kinds because the Vampire they were with succeeded in isolating them from sources of financial support.

Cheating

In normal, healthy relationships where monogamy has been agreed between partners, monogamy remains the basis for the relationship until either the relationship ends or the arrangement is renegotiated mutually between partners. Most intimate relationships are based on monogamy and this is more often than not implied when the relationship starts, but not all are like this, and there is no hard and fast rule that dictates how two people conduct their relationship. However, the sign of a healthy one is that both partners are entirely happy with whatever arrangement has been made. In a monogamous relationship, neither partner seeks outside sources of intimacy, both are committed to protecting the monogamy of the relationship, and both maintain a healthy boundary around the relationship, which functions to maintain the monogamous bond between them.

None of this applies to the Vampire because they have no concept of monogamy on a practical level. They will not maintain a boundary around the relationship, and will routinely become intimate with others regardless of anything they say to the contrary. For the Vampire, Narcissistic supply takes precedence over all other concerns, including the relationship and especially the needs of the Target. If they believe that they can secure Narcissistic supply from cheating, they will do so and will show no remorse and no regret. Any regret they do show if they are caught will be regret that they have been caught, and they will engage in any number of tactics to excuse what they have done.

For normal, healthy people who have entered a monogamous relationship, cheating is regarded as a "deal breaker". It means that the relationship has now ended, and each partner must go their own way. The Vampire does not understand this. They believe that any cheating on their part should be understood by the Target, and they will seek to blame the Target for it. If this fails, they will engage in pity plays and begging to re-secure the Target and continue the relationship, and the cheating. The Vampire has absolutely no concept of boundaries in relationships. It is extremely common for a Vampire to engage in many emotional and sexual affairs with prospective new Targets before they discard the current Target.

Hoovering

Hoovering has mainly been addressed in the chapter on the Attack Cycle, but is included here because it is a tactic that the Vampire will employ on people other than the Target during the course of a relationship. In a similar way to Cheating, they will attempt to Hoover previous Targets for the purposes of an affair or for use in Triangulation (see Triangulation). This can happen at any time, but is most common when the Target is resisting the Vampires attempts at Gaslighting, is indicating that they are doubting whether to stay in the relationship or simply because the Vampire's senses a threat to their control.

The Vampire has no concept of people other than as sources of Narcissistic supply, and therefore has no issue with Hoovering previous Targets, regardless of their current situation. If they can succeed in doing so, then either a Triangulation will occur, they will engage in cheating with the previous Target, or they will Discard the current Target in favour of the previous one. The re-emergence of a previous Target in the life of the Vampire is never a coincidence, despite what they say to the contrary. They will have

Hoovered this individual and are actively trying to engage in one of the outcomes above.

Projection

Projection is a very primitive psychological defense mechanism that the Vampire employs to protect themselves from Shame and to attack the Target. Normal, healthy people accept that they are not perfect, that sometimes their actions are less than they would like and that they are capable of behaving in ways they may feel guilty about. However, guilt is about something a person has done. Shame is about something a person is.

The Vampire cannot tell the difference between the two and therefore, if they feel guilty about something they have done, they immediately feel Shame about who they are. Projection allows them to push all of their negative qualities and actions away from themselves and onto the Target so that they do not have to experience Shame.

In practice, this results in the Vampire constantly claiming that the Target is in some way shameful and they will attempt to induce feelings of Shame in the Target. They will accuse, blame-shift, threaten, guilt trip, give silent treatments and use any number of other tactics that prove effective in order to make the Target feel Shame so that they do not have to. In particular, they will claim that the Target possesses their own negative traits, characteristics and behaviours. This will occur constantly, relentlessly and without remorse.

If the Target attempts to fight back against Projection, the Vampire will escalate the conflict until the Target backs down. At some point, this leads to a choice on the part of the Target: either accept the Projection, or leave the relationship. Since they will never cease Projecting, all relationships with a Vampire will feature high levels of projection for which the only alternative to accepting each and every one is to leave the relationship.

Threats

In normal, healthy relationships threats are entirely absent because they represent an attempt by one partner to force their will on the other. Threats are exceptionally dangerous in all interactions between people because they induce a stress response in the person being threatened. If the threats are on-going, they serve as a cause of on-going stress that will damage the psychological and physical health of the person being threatened.

The Vampire routinely uses threats against the Target. These may be explicit or implicit, but in any case are very common and are used precisely for the reasons outlined above: to impose their will on the Target, to cause on-going stress to the Target and to undermine their Self Respect

The Vampire will threaten the Target in a number of different ways. They will threaten the future of the relationship, they will threaten the removal of resources, they will threaten their involvement in activities, and they will threaten whatever the Target values. If phrases that contain "If you......then I....." are used at any time, the Vampire is making a threat. In other words, if they make statements that amount to conditions that must be met on the part of the Target for them to do or not do something, they are making a threat.

If the Vampire **EVER** threatens physical or sexual violence **OF ANY KIND**, the Target **MUST** leave the relationship immediately and never return. Threats of this nature inevitably lead to actual violence.

DARVO

DARVO stands for Deny, Attack and Reverse Victim Order. It is a tactic regularly employed by the Vampire whenever they are confronted with their negative actions or the consequences of them in an attempt not only to absolve themselves of responsibility, but also to portray themselves as the Victim of an attack by the Target. First, they will deny any wrong doing and then attack the Target for bringing the accusation. In doing so, they are attempting to occupy the Victim position in a Drama Triangle (see chapter 6 on the Drama Triangle).

If the Vampire is employing DARVO as a tactic, it means that they feel that they are "in a corner" because the tactics of Lying and Blame-shifting have failed. They often employ DARVO when confronted with hard evidence of their wrong doing and this tactic will lead to an escalation of conflict if they cannot complete the DARVO. A Vampire that is engaging in DARVO feels threatened and will not cease the conflict until either the Target removes the threat or the Vampire leaves the situation. If a Vampire is engaging in

DARVO and cannot leave the situation, they have now become extremely dangerous. It is often safer for the Target to distance themselves from a Vampire using DARVO and simply leave the situation and preferably the relationship.

Word salad

Word salad is used to refer to the use of language in such a way that no intelligible sense can be made from it. In Word Salad, listeners are confused by a constant stream of grammatically incorrect, logically nonsensical and contradictory sentences that make no sense individually or together. Users of Word Salad are often disordered individuals who cannot make sense of their own internal world and are simply saying the first thing that comes to mind whether it makes sense or not. Extended use of word salad in speech will leave the listener with no real sense of what has been said, only that the speaker is trying to express something.

The Vampire uses word salad frequently and deliberately in order to confuse the Target and undermine their ability to communicate clearly with them. They will frequently engage word salad to evade questions and/or explanations of their actions. It is very common for Survivors to report that, when trying to have a conversation with a Vampire they encountered, they began to feel tired and confused because the conversations quickly made no sense, that so many ideas were being brought forward in the Word Salad by the Vampire that they could not keep up and that the original topic got lost in the confusion. This is, of course, the intention of the Vampire when using Word Salad.

A prime indicator that the Vampire is using Word Salad is that the Target no longer feels that they are in the conversation and that if the Vampire stops talking, the conversation will have moved on beyond the original question. If the Target feels that they have to constantly keep coming back to the same point over and over again, the Vampire is engaging in the use of Word Salad. Once they have started engaging in Word Salad, the entire effort to keep the conversation on the original topic will lie with the Target and the Vampire needs do nothing except engage in more Word Salad, which takes significantly less effort. Therefore, if a Vampire is engaging in the use of Word Salad, it is far better to walk away from the conversation and preferably the relationship. Normal, healthy people do not engage in Word Salad, and Vampires cannot be reasoned with.

Idealisation

Idealisation is an extension of Splitting and reflects the Black and White thinking of the Vampire. Idealisation involves seeing another person as "all good" and the Vampire will seek to become as close to that person as possible, spending as much time with them as possible and talking about them in very positive terms to the Target (in order to attack their Self Respect) and others, particularly Flying Monkeys. This is almost without exception because that person will serve as a source of Narcissistic supply, so they will often use Idealisation in combination with Triangulation and Cheating. Idealisation of the Target is frequently used in the Idealisation Stage of the Attack Cycle to secure the Target but is included here because it is a tactic that the Vampire will employ on people other than the Target during the course of a relationship.

The Vampire Idealises those who they believe will serve as good sources of Narcissistic supply. A good "early warning" sign of Cheating and Triangulation is that the Vampire is openly Idealising an individual and expresses their Idealisation of them to the Target. Therefore, if the Vampire is Idealising another person, Triangulation is definitely occurring, and Cheating may be occurring also.

Silent treatment

The phrase "Silent Treatment" is fairly common and refers to the deliberate practice of ignoring another person. It is a form of psychological punishment that is intended to devalue the person receiving it by implying that they are unworthy of the attention of the person carrying it out. In normal, healthy relationships the Silent Treatment is never used because of its psychologically damaging effects. If one partner is unhappy with the other, they express their issue openly and respectfully. If one partner needs time away from the other in order to reflect on their feelings about a disagreement, they express this openly and respectfully and both partners respect each other's need for physical and psychological space.

In normal, healthy relationships if one partner is preoccupied and appears not to be listening to the other, this can be challenged and the preoccupied partner will either cease their preoccupation and listen or arrange a time to talk and stick to the commitment to do so. Neither partner deliberately ignores the other, or attempts to make them feel uncomfortable around them by ceasing to engage with them. In addition, neither partner seeks to control communication between them in order to exert power and control.

None of this applies to the Vampire because they want the Target to feel devalued and ignored and seeks to psychologically harm them. The Silent Treatment is the hallmark of the Vampire. It involves deliberately ignoring the Target, avoiding them in the home, not entering into conversation when invited to do so, turning away from offers of affection, involving themselves in activities that exclude the Target while in their company for extended periods of time, pretending that they did not hear the Target when they speak to them and a host of other behaviours that are specifically designed to make the Target feel unworthy of their attention. Many Vampires are so adept at the Silent Treatment that they can keep it applied to the Target for hours or even days at a time.

The psychological effect of the Silent Treatment is profound. The cessation of response from the Vampire causes the Target to wonder why they are behaving the way they are. This often results in many Targets wondering what they have done to cause the Vampire to withdraw in this way and this is exactly what they want. Any attempt to open communication with them during a Silent Treatment is futile, as they will maintain the Silent Treatment for as long as they feel necessary to cause maximum harm to the Target's Self Respect. For as long as the Target is suffering and still trying to open communication with them, the Vampire will maintain the Silent Treatment.

All the power in the relationship lies with the Vampire during a Silent Treatment because in order to break it, the Target must do all the work, while they need to do nothing at all. The objectives of the Vampire during a Silent Treatment are: to do as much damage as possible to the Target's Self Respect; to establish control over the communication in the relationship; to create an atmosphere of FOG; to dominate the Target and to punish the Target for whatever behaviour they imagine they want to punish them for.

This despicable, disgusting and insidious practice is designed to make the Target feel as though they have done something wrong and force them into a position of complete powerlessness. This is due to one simple fact: the Target cares about the Vampire and the relationship and the Vampire does not. Given this, during a Silent Treatment, they are actually demonstrating how little they care about the Target and the relationship and is one of the few times during the relationship when they are actually being honest.

Passive-aggression

In normal, healthy relationships communication between partners is open, honest and respectful. When one partner is angry with or hurt by the behaviour of the other, they express their feelings calmly and firmly. Overt anger is rarely, if ever, present and partners do not hide their anger or hurt behind other expressions of emotion. In other words, each partner takes ownership of their feelings and is capable of dealing with them in healthy ways that do not involve indirect and negative expressions through their words or behaviour.

None of this applies to the Vampire. Passive Aggression is, in fact, a hallmark of the way in which they deal with their negative emotions. Passive aggression is a non-verbal way of expressing anger and hurt that manifests in negative behaviour. When the Vampire feels angry or hurt by someone, they will not tell them directly because they have no way of regulating their emotions. They will shut off communication, give angry looks at the Target, engage in obstructive behaviour, sulk, or engage in Stonewalling, which is a form of Silent Treatment.

They will also agree to go along with a plan only to either not do the agreed thing at all, or sabotage the plan. All of these behaviours are designed to attack the Target in ways that do not openly express anger. Any Passive Aggressive behaviour is designed to punish the Target for something the Vampire believes they should have done, or not done. Because the imagined "failure" on the part of the Target is never explained to them, the Passive Aggressive behaviour of the Vampire places all the power in their hands and removes it from the Target.

In fact, Passive Aggression is more harmful than open expressions of emotion because the Target is never really sure what is going on, and this undermines their sense of Self Respect, which is exactly what the Vampire wants. Essentially, Passive Aggression is a means of exerting power and control through a lack of action and therefore requires the Vampire to do nothing in order to make the Target feel powerless and worthless. Because it takes so little effort, and results in so much power, control and Narcissistic supply as the Target tries to find out what is wrong, it is the favoured form of expression the Vampire has at their disposal.

Passive Aggression is designed to communicate that something is wrong with the Target's behaviour without pointing out what it is. It is a deliberate attempt to undermine the Self Respect of the Target in order to dominate, control and punish them. It plays out in a number of ways, but always features: Ignoring the Target; Evasion of problems; Obstruction of plans; Withholding attention; Procrastination; Ambiguity (deliberate vagueness); "Forgetting" commitments; using Excuses and Sulking.

Targets will end up feeling that they are "Walking on eggshells" around the Vampire and will also experience feelings of Loneliness; Self-Blame; Sadness and the knowledge that something is "up" but not knowing what it is. There is only one effective response in dealing with Passive Aggressive behaviour: Leave the situation. If confronted on what is "wrong", the most common answer from the Vampire is "nothing", which continues the issue. The Target will have no more understanding and the Vampire will have gained more Narcissistic supply. Alternatively, the response may be criticism of the Target, accusations, threats, or any number of other tactics.

Therefore, confronting Passive Aggressive behaviour is futile at best and damaging at worst because it provides the Vampire with opportunities to attack the Target. By far the best response is to leave the situation, and preferably the relationship.

Triangulation

Normal, healthy relationships between two people only contain two people. They are a partnership bonded by mutual love, affection, respect and trust. Neither partner seeks outside sources of these things and both partners actively create a boundary around the relationship to keep others who seek to invade it out.

This does not apply to the Vampire. In their mind, the Target is (usually) their main source of Narcissistic supply but rather than being reassured by a relationship bond, they are scared by one. To the Vampire, the Target actually represents a threat because they could potentially remove their source of Narcissistic supply at any time by leaving the relationship. This triggers the Vampires fear of Abandonment, which is why they are constantly attempting to enslave the Targets mind and destroy their Self Respect.

However, this is never enough for the Vampire. They are compelled to seek outside sources of Narcissistic supply that serve as "backup" to the main source, the Target. In the event that their attacks fail to enslave the Target, they will have other sources that they can attack in order to secure Narcissistic supply. Therefore, they are always seeking out other potential Targets and most, if not all Vampires will have identified these individuals very quickly (if they were not in place at the start of the relationship with the Target) and will attempt to keep them in the Idealisation Stage of the Attack Cycle for as long as possible in case they need to secure them as the new Target and is not uncommon for Vampires to have multiple other potential Targets lined up outside the relationship.

This process is known as Triangulation because it places 3 people in the relationship, not 2. It should be clear therefore, that the Vampire has no regard whatsoever for having a boundary around the relationship since, in their mind, the Target is interchangeable whenever they believe they need to do so. This always leads to the "Drama Triangle" (chapter 6).

Triangulation is not always covert. The Vampire may draw the Target's attention to their Triangulations if they believe that it would serve to upset the Target, cause pain and confusion and result in them working harder to meet their needs for Narcissistic supply. Any and all people, real and imagined, will be used by the Vampire if they believe that doing so will be effective. People that they know may be referred to as being somehow superior to the Target, even if this is a lie and in some cases such people may not even exist. Their previous Targets will be referred to as somehow superior to the Target, even if this is not true. They will talk openly about the attentions of another person, even if this is a lie. They will exaggerate the nature of a relationship with another person, making it sound threatening to the relationship. They will talk openly about the positive qualities of a mutual friend or acquaintance, implying or pointing out their superiority to the Target.

In any and all such cases, the objective of the Vampire is the same: To destabilize the Target's sense of Self Respect and security in the relationship. Triangulation is a means by which the Vampire constantly places the relationship in a position of being threatened if the Target does not take action of some kind to re-secure it. Needless to say, this practice is disgusting, despicable and enormously abusive. Over time, it renders the Target completely insecure in themselves and the relationship, which is exactly what the Vampire wants.

Some Triangulations however, are covert. The Vampire may deliberately avoid talking about a potential Target that they are Triangulating because they do not want the Target to know about their existence. In most cases, these individuals will be the next Target in the mind of the Vampire, which explains why they appear to move on into a new relationship so quickly after a Discard. In reality, the new Target will have been covertly Triangulated for some time and will have been kept in the Idealisation Stage of the Attack Cycle until the Vampire was ready, or was forced to switch Targets. Triangulation is a hallmark of the Vampire, and it impossible for any relationship with one to exist without Triangulation.

Smear Campaigns

Related to triangulation, and an extension of DARVO, Smear Campaigns are an active attempt by the Vampire to portray themselves in a positive light in the relationship and to portray the Target as the aggressor or "crazy person". A Smear Campaign is an on-going tactic that the Vampire uses in which they talk secretly about the Target in ways that have listeners believe that the Target is a bad person and that the Vampire is the innocent party, or long-suffering partner. The Vampire will take every opportunity to elicit Narcissistic supply from Flying Monkeys by claiming behind the Target's back that the Target is abusive, an addict, difficult, argumentative, violent, neglectful or whatever they feel they needs to say in order to play themselves off as the victim in an abusive relationship.

They will use Smear Campaigns to undermine the Target's Self Respect by sowing lies about their behaviour, provoke them to an emotional response in front of Flying Monkeys to perpetuate the illusion that the Vampire is the Victim and the Target is the abuser. They will deliberately create conflict in the home, allowing them to leave so that they can perpetuate the Smear Campaign with other potential Targets they are Triangulating.

Smear Campaigns begin as soon as the Devaluation Stage of the Attack Cycle does, so the Target will be the subject of a Smear Campaign far longer than they know, and will have been long before they realise after the relationship has ended. In effect, a Smear Campaign is designed to reverse the positions of the Vampire and the Target in the minds of others, particularly Flying Monkeys.

The Vampire will amplify the Smear Campaign after the relationship has ended in order to place themselves in the position of innocent victim of abuse that was forced to escape, and the Target as the abuser they were escaping. Targets often do not realise the extent of the Smear Campaign that has been launched against them, hence they often experience cold and distant behaviour from Flying Monkeys or strangers, further undermining their Self Respect.

Victimhood

The Victim position in the "Drama Triangle" (chapter 6) is the most powerful of the 3 positions, and the Vampire will seek to occupy it constantly. In normal, healthy relationships neither partner claims to be the Victim of the others behaviours, because it implies that the other partner is deliberately trying to hurt them, which contradicts their bond of mutual love, affection, respect and trust. Any attempt to claim Victimhood would therefore be a betrayal of the relationship bond and enormously damaging to the relationship.

This is precisely why the Vampire adopts the Victim position. It is a form of attack which betrays the bond that the Target is attempting to build, harms the Target and undermines the relationship. All of this is deliberate and designed to dominate the Target, control their behaviours, destroy their Self Respect and gather as much Narcissistic supply as possible from the Targets attempts to return the relationship to "normality" which, of course, will never happen.

By adopting the position of Victim, the Vampire places themselves in a position where they can claim that whatever is happening either in the relationship or from outside sources is happening to them. This means that nothing can be happening to the Target (even though it invariably is), the needs of the Target do not matter (even though they are actively being attacked) and, significantly, nothing can be done by the Target to remove the Vampire from the Victim position without being perceived as an attack (even though the Target is actually the legitimate Victim). Therefore, once the Vampire has secured the Victim position, they will never let go of it.

Victimhood is inevitable in all relationships with a Vampire without exception. A prime indicator that they are using this tactic is that the Target will feel that they can never do anything right. They may gain some Self Respect if they are working to please the Vampire but, if they cease to do so even for a short time, or even if the Vampire deliberately undermines their efforts to force them to do more, they will lose that Self Respect very quickly. This results in the "emotional rollercoaster" that the vast majority of Survivors report characterised their relationship with a Vampire. There is only one strategy for dealing with this: Leave the relationship

Devaluation

Devaluation is a tactic that is most commonly employed in the Devaluation Stage of the Attack Cycle but it is mentioned here because the Vampire may employ it against others outside the relationship. If they perceive an individual to be a Threat, the Vampire will devalue them. They will use a host of tactics to reduce that individual's value to them and the Target in an effort to push the Threat as far away as possible. Any or all of their tactics will be employed for this purpose, so Devaluation may best be thought of as a process rather than a tactic. If a Vampire has Devalued an individual, they will continue to do so all the time they consider them to be a Threat. If that individual begins to try to win the favour of the Vampire in response to being Devalued, they will employ tactics in order to convert the Threat into a Flying Monkey.

As a final word on the subject of tactics, the best solution to all of them is to leave the relationship. Anyone on the receiving end of any of the tactics laid out here is being attacked, and that attack will not cease until the Target or Survivor has removed themselves from the relationship, and the Vampire. As discussed in the chapter on the Attack Cycle, the Vampire will never cease attacking the Target and therefore the Target must end the Attack Cycle, and all its associated tactics by ending the relationship and going No Contact or employing Grey Rock.

And after all that, time for an Interlude, yes?

Interlude 5

"Never interrupt your enemy when he is making a mistake" – Napoleon Bonaparte

Hello again, dear Survivor!

Oh dear, Tactics. What a bunch of remorseless bastards these Vampires are, huh? Every single thing they do is a tactic, all day every day. How exhausting is that? For those of us who don't have to suck the souls out of our nearest and dearest just so we can get into the shower in the morning, there is a lot to be said for not being a Vampire.

Like being able to enjoy a sunrise without wondering if anyone is looking at us while we do it. Or being able to eat cereal and enjoying the experience without having to worry about how we're going to post about it on Instagram so that all our Flying Monkeys will know we didn't die in the night through lack of having tedious non-intimate sex with our long suffering Target again. Or being able to say "Hello" to a stranger as we pass just because we can without freaking out because they didn't recognize the new article of clothing we're wearing that we bought with the express purpose of impressing strangers that we carefully selected for their ability to recognise new articles of clothing,

Or being able to get through a day of work that ends in a lovely date night without having to find 50,000 ways of fucking the whole day up so that we could make our partner pay for having the audacity for loving us in the first place and therefore deserving our absence and/or difficulty and/or hostility and/or silent treatment for simply existing and/or daring to demand that we live up to our promises and/or being a mammal, the bitch/bastard. How dare they demand that we self-sabotage to such an elaborate extent, and why don't they appear to hate themselves enough yet? Note to self: Destroy Target.

I'm serious, folks. We have it easy by comparison. We get to do all the good stuff, and we don't even have to try. I know you know what I'm talking about. We get to go on exponentially joyous riffs with our friends where the comedy just flows and none of us can ever remember why we were even laughing in the first place. You know why? Because we don't fucking care! The point is that we are laughing, and that's what we all want for each other.

You know what a Vampire is thinking at those times? They're thinking all sorts of fucked up things. For example: "Did I cause this?", "Am I as funny as that person?", "Did anyone hear that joke I just made?", "Is Person X looking at me?", "Am I looking sexy while I tell this anecdote?" They are totally paranoid when it comes to having fun. If they're the centre of attention, that's fun to them. If they're not, they do all these weird gymnastics so that they are. It's especially weird when they get together. It's like some bizarre form of Roman gladiatorial contest where they have convinced themselves that the last Vampire standing gets to watch all the other Vampires burn to death or something.

How much hard work is that? It's no wonder they get so sour during celebrations, is it? Vampires would compete for whose blood it really was at the last supper...

But we can save ourselves. And so we should. And so we shall, because we can feel something the Vampire never will: Joy. Joy, dear Survivor, is what marks us apart from the Vampire. It is what defines us as Survivors, binds us as a community, gives us the will to reach out to others and, ultimately, will set each and every one of us free. When we give Joy to each other and ourselves, we can truly say that we are alive. Joy is the sunlight that the Vampire cannot stand, but is always drawn to.

When we feel genuine Joy, and can protect that within ourselves it makes us attractive to all people. But importantly, we will be able to hold that Joy within us and only share it with others who can also generate their own. When we truly feel that we deserve our own Joy, we will cease trying to give it to individuals that cannot generate their own and must therefore feed off the Joy of others. You see, we cannot simply will ourselves to feel Joy. We must act in ways that produce Joy.

That's a tall order, I know. Especially if you are still a Target, or have recently become a Survivor. But it is possible. I shall leave you with a simple and Joyful message:

You, dear Survivor, are a Joyful person. If you weren't, you wouldn't be a Survivor.

And now, another of the burning questions:

Does my Vampire miss me?

I'm not famous for pulling my punches, dear Survivor. This is one of those moments that will contribute to that reputation.

No. They don't miss you, because they can't. The Vampire does not exist as a real person. They are an emotionally dead thing walking around in a shell of a human body. The idea of missing someone is a concept that only applies to Targets and Survivors, because we know a real live person when we see one. We can genuinely miss someone we have lost, because we know the difference between alive and dead. We even mistake the living dead for real people because we want to believe that a Vampire can be a live person, which is testament to our optimism. They're just not live people, and that's the point. You are asking an emotionally dead thing to miss you. Do the dead miss the living? Nope. They just move on once they've drained all your emotions and try to feed off someone else. However, as always there are really good reasons why that's a good thing, so read on...

The reason you're asking this question is almost certainly because a part of you misses the Vampire, and you want that feeling to be reciprocated. What you may not realise yet is that there is someone you miss more than you miss the Vampire. You miss You. That feeling you're having? Wanting to know if the Vampire misses you? That's you aching to be with You. You've probably been aching to be with You all your life. It doesn't matter whether the Vampire misses you. The Vampire never mattered. You did.

Oh, my dear Survivor, I know. I know how much it hurts. Really I do, because I've been there. But please take this one on faith. If I have taught you anything at all, and you believe anything I've said so far, then please take this one on trust, even if you can't feel it yet. Take a deep breath and then say this to yourself out loud:

"I love me, and I miss being with me".

You were always in a relationship with yourself. Yep. Sounds weird, right? It's abso-fucking-lutely true though. Think about it. Who did all the work? Who did all the forgiving? Who did all the hoping? Who put up with all the bullshit? Who did all the loving? Who did all the encouraging? Who did all the support? Who paid the emotional price? Who made the other the centre of their world? Who would have given anything for the other? Who cried? Who lost sleep? Who gave and gave and gave until it hurt and then gave some more? That was you, wasn't it? And who wanted to get all that returned in kind? That was you too, wasn't it?

What if the person on the receiving end of all that you gave had given it back in equal measure? You would have been blissfully happy every single day, wouldn't you? That would have been all your Birthdays and Christmases all come at once every day, wouldn't it? Well, you know what was always in the way of that happening? The fucking Vampire. The Vampire took all you had to give and gave nothing back. They took all your love, affection, compassion, attention, encouragement, support, understanding, your money and every other resource you had. And what did they give back? Fucking nothing.

Now turn that around. Instead of the Vampire being on the receiving end of everything you gave, put yourself there. What would you give to the person who gave you everything? Thought so. See? The person that should always have been on the other side of you was You. The person you really miss is You.

Oh, I get it, dear Survivor. I really do. Right now, you may not be able to even consider being in a relationship with someone like you, let alone yourself. But I promise you it is possible. I know because I've done it. Is it easy? No. Is it possible? Abso-fucking-lutely! And it's a damn sight easier than being in a relationship with a fucking Vampire! Once you get back into a relationship with you and you treat yourself the way you treated the Vampire, you'll see that whether the Vampire misses you is totally irrelevant. In fact, you won't want them to miss you because that might mean they try to come back and disrupt the best relationship you ever had: Your relationship with you.

The greatest gift the Vampire can bestow, dear Survivor, is their absence. That gives you the opportunity to have the greatest relationship experience of your life: the one you have with yourself. The question was actually phrased wrong. It should have said: "Do I miss me?" The answer to which is: "Yes, now go and fall in love with yourself." My dear Survivor, it can and will be done. And when you do it, I promise you that you will know the greatest love of your life.

Take your own hand and move into Chapter 6. See you on the other side.

Chapter 6

Drama and the "Drama Triangle"

In an ideal world, conflict and drama is not a feature of relationships. Even the healthiest relationships sometimes encounter conflict, but the defining feature of healthy relationships is that such conflict is dealt with by the two mature adults in it and peace, not drama is the goal of the relationship in general and therefore what characterises it.

Relationships with the Vampire always have drama as the defining characteristic. Survivors overwhelmingly report that things were never peaceful in their relationship with the Vampire and that they lived in an environment in which they were always "waiting for the other shoe to drop". In other words, the sense they had was that conflict and drama were always just a moment away.

There is very good reason for this. Peace in a relationship is profoundly disturbing to the Vampire because these are the moments in which they are not receiving Narcissistic supply, and without it, they begin to starve. Where normal, healthy people enjoy the peace and comfort of intimacy that healthy relationships bring, the Vampire experiences this as a threat to their very existence because, unless they are receiving constant Narcissistic supply, they are forced to be with themselves (even in company) and this will lead to their natural emotional state: Shame. The Vampire will do anything to avoid being left alone with themselves and, when given the opportunity to create conflict and drama to achieve this, they will take it every time.

Given the connection between drama and Narcissistic supply, there are two main reasons why the Vampire creates drama.

1) Boredom. Normal, healthy people experience boredom as a state of "nothing to do". They are restful, but not seeking sleep and so they look for things to occupy them. They are happy to be with their own thoughts, but don't experience that as a bad thing and are generally happy with themselves. Introspection is just something that healthy people do.

The Vampire experiences Boredom very differently. To the Vampire, boredom is experienced as a lack of Narcissistic supply, and introspection will always lead to feelings of Shame. In other words, without external sources of supply, the Vampire is left alone with their own assessment of what they are, which is always terrible. The experience is that of a crushing void in which the only opinion of the Vampire is their own: Worthless and Shameful. Since the Vampire is incapable of providing themselves with a source of positive Self Respect, boredom represents a state in which they are presented with a choice: either face their own self-assessment, which would lead to feelings of Shame, or seek external sources of Narcissistic supply. Therefore, boredom, when experienced by a healthy person is a state of "nothing to do", but the Vampire experiences boredom as a state of "nothing to be".

2) Hypersensitivity to criticism. For healthy people, criticism is experienced as being about something they have done. Healthy people are able to separate what they have done from who they are. They respond by examining the facts and assessing the truth of the criticism. If they find that the criticism is true, they respond by making a choice about whether they want to change their behaviour or not. If they find that the criticism is false, they ignore it.

The Vampire experiences criticism very differently, because they are an emotional reasoner. To the Vampire, criticism is not about what they have done, it is about who they are. Where healthy people experience reason in response to criticism, the Vampire experiences emotion. Therefore, when presented with criticism, rather than respond rationally, the Vampire responds emotionally, and the primary emotion of the Vampire is, of course, Shame.

Once emotional reasoning kicks in, the Vampire will be completely obsessed with protecting themselves from feelings of Shame, and therefore will do everything in their power to avoid whatever they perceive to be attacking them at that point in time. By creating drama, the Vampire can distance themselves from feelings of Shame and seek to create a situation which will distract from what they have done. It's a bit like a kid whose just been caught with their hand in the cookie jar, but on Shame steroids. Setting fire to the whole house is better than owning up to the theft.

It's well worth remembering that the Vampires sensitivity to criticism is extreme, and completely irrational. Anything that comes from the outside world that does not support the Vampires False Self will be perceived as criticism, which means that it is impossible to have any interaction with the Vampire based on objective reality. The only interactions that the Vampire will tolerate without feeling criticised are those in which the False Self is supported, regardless of how far at odds the False Self is with objective reality. This is why it is so exhausting trying to reason with a Vampire. The vast majority of Survivors report that trying to explain reality to the Vampire was like trying to talk to a child, and that's because that's exactly what the Vampire is: a child that cannot deal with reality.

The Vampire will also use Drama to distract the Target from what they really are, and what they are doing for the same reason. If they perceive a challenge to their False Self because the Target is using logic and reason to approach them, they will feel threatened. They are completely incapable of using reason and logic to explain their behaviour because they and their behaviours are entirely irrational and illogical. The Vampire will respond by creating Drama if they feel that the Target is approaching seeing them for what they really are and is using reason to explore that.

The use of Drama in these cases allows the Vampire to distract the Target from their enquiries and protect themselves from the feelings of Shame that would inevitably follow should the Target succeed in exposing them and/or their behaviours. Therefore criticism, when experienced by a healthy person is a state of "something I've done", but the Vampire experiences criticism (real or imagined) as a state of "something I am".

In essence, then, there are two primary reasons why the Vampire creates drama: either they are bored, and are therefore in danger of experiencing their own Shame, or they are experiencing criticism (real or imagined), and are therefore in danger of experiencing their own Shame. Yes, it really is a simple as that. If the Vampire is creating drama, it is for one of these two reasons.

The only time the Vampire will not create drama is when they are receiving positive Narcissistic supply. If the Vampire is content with the positive supply they are receiving, they will be inert. However, as soon as the positive supply is withdrawn, or not available, they will create drama for one, or both of these reasons. This explains why the overwhelming majority of Survivors report that being with a Vampire felt like a full time job, and why they felt fearful of what they might do next.

The Drama Triangle

The Drama Triangle refers to the work of Stephen Karpman (1968). The whole purpose of the Drama triangle is to explain the thinking and behaviours of individuals when they interact with each other. It is best thought of as "roles" that people adopt when they talk with each other and negotiate how to resolve conflict.

In healthy relationships, the Drama Triangle can be used in this way. However, the hallmark of a healthy relationship is that interactions are based on mutual love and respect and therefore the positions in the Drama Triangle, while they may apply and can change according to the conflict at hand, are not used by one or other partner as a main means of interaction and do not represent permanent positions in the relationship's on-going interactions. This is because the Drama Triangle explains conflict, not harmony, and healthy relationships seek harmony first. In healthy relationships, conflict is dealt with by mature adults who are not seeking to create drama for their own purposes. If they encounter drama in their relationship, healthy people seek to resolve it in ways that are mutually beneficial and the goal is always to return to harmony.

None of this applies to the Vampire because they cannot live without drama. For the reasons given above, the Vampire must create drama in order to survive. Therefore, a relationship without constant drama is impossible with a Vampire. The Vampire will seek to occupy positions in the Drama Triangle for the purpose of creating conflict and will seek to force others to occupy positions to perpetuate that conflict.

In the Drama Triangle, there are three positions:

1) The Victim
2) The Rescuer
3) The Persecutor

The Victim

The Victim position is one of helplessness. The person occupying the position of the Victim can be seen as the person who is being attacked by the Persecutor and needs to be saved by the Rescuer.

The Rescuer

The Rescuer position is one of saving the Victim. The person occupying the position of the Rescuer can be seen as the person who is stepping in to save the Victim from the Persecutor.

The Persecutor

The Persecutor position is one of attacking the Victim. The person occupying the position of the Persecutor can be seen as the "Bad Guy", or Villain that the Victim needs to be saved from by the Rescuer.

The Vampire and the Drama Triangle

Whenever the Vampire experiences boredom or perceives criticism, they will initiate drama and attempt to force those around them to engage in that drama. There are many ways in which the Vampire will do this, and some are given here. However, unless the Vampire is receiving sufficient positive Narcissistic supply, they will always seek to create drama and force others into a Drama Triangle to facilitate that Drama.

The Vampire and the Victim Position

Within the Drama Triangle, the Vampire will always attempt to occupy the Victim position. This is because it is the position that requires the minimum amount of effort for the maximum amount of Narcissistic supply provided. Individuals in the Rescuer position will provide positive Narcissistic supply in the form of sympathy, praise, cajoling, affection and so on. Individuals in the Persecutor position will provide negative Narcissistic supply in the form of insults, accusations, anger, frustration and so on. In both cases, the attention of each position is focussed on that of the Victim and therefore, in either case, the Vampire in the Victim position needs to do very little in order for this position to be highly effective in gathering Narcissistic supply. For the Vampire, it is a case of "light the fuse, stand back, and enjoy".

This does not mean that the Vampire will always begin the drama they initiate from the Victim position. They may do so from either of the other two. However, as soon as a drama has been provoked, they will attempt to occupy the Victim position as soon as possible, and for as long as possible during the ensuing drama.

For the Target, this is why the behaviour of the Vampire is so crazy making. Once drama has been created, the Victim position requires the Vampire to do nothing because the position is passive. The other positions are active, either offering positive supply (the rescuer) or negative supply (the persecutor). In other words, the vampire can use the drama to provoke the Target into occupying one of these two roles, and then do nothing while the Target proceeds to do all the work in providing Narcissistic supply. The Target has been cast in a role they didn't ask for, don't want but also don't know how to escape.

The overwhelming majority of Survivors report this kind of crazy-making behaviour from the Vampire. In addition, because they were consistently forced into an active position (Rescuer or Persecutor) during all drama with their abuser they also report that they believe that they were to blame for many of the conflicts because they were the one doing all the work in the drama while the Vampire did next to nothing. This aspect of the Vampire's manipulations is highly abusive, deliberate and contributes in all cases to their on-going campaign of Gaslighting the Target, portraying them as the "Bad Guy" in the relationship, and themselves as the Victim.

The Drama Triangle in action.

In practice, the Drama Triangle needs someone to start it. In some cases, this may be the Target, such as by opening a conversation about an issue they want to resolve, in which case the Vampire will seize the opportunity to occupy the Victim position. In most cases however, it will be started by the Vampire themselves for the purposes of gaining Narcissistic supply.

If the Vampire begins a Drama Triangle from the Persecutor position, they will attack the Target in some way. This is likely to take the form of criticism, or passive aggression. As soon as the Target responds to the attack by defending themselves, the Vampire will immediately adopt the Victim position and accuse the Target of attacking them. They will minimise their own attack and magnify the response of the Target to make it appear that the roles of abuser and Target are reversed. This is a classic DARVO move and is extremely common.

If the Vampire begins a Drama Triangle from the Rescuer position, they will appear to be concerned about the Target in some way. However, this concern is actually a veiled attack because they will show concern only for the Target in terms of the "issue" they are using during Gaslighting. Therefore, any concern they do show is simply drawing attention back to the thing they are actually using to attack the Target. They will continue to "needle" the Target regarding the "issue" until the Target responds by either defending themselves or asking the Vampire to stop. The moment either of these two things happens, the Vampire will immediately adopt the Victim position and claim that they were "only trying to help", "just showing concern" or "wanting the best" for the Target. All of these are lies, of course. What the Vampire was actually doing was trying to provoke the Target to attack them so that they could adopt the Victim position and soak up the ensuing Narcissistic supply.

If the Vampire begins a Drama Triangle from the Victim position, they will open the Drama with a complaint, Passive Aggression, or silence and the Silent Treatment is often used to achieve this. By complaining, the Vampire is placing themselves in the Victim position and is imagining a Persecutor. That may be the Target if the Vampire is attempting to place the Target in the role of Persecutor, or someone outside the relationship if the Vampire is trying to place the Target in the role of Rescuer. By engaging in Passive Aggression, the Vampire may issue a "backhand compliment" to the Target in an attempt to provoke them and place them in the Persecutor position.

By engaging in the Silent Treatment, the Vampire is offering a choice to the Target of either occupying the Rescuer position by trying to figure out what's wrong, or occupying the Persecutor position by challenging the Vampire on their behaviour. In either case, the Vampire has already occupied the Victim position and needs to do nothing at all to initiate the Drama. Instead, they simply have to wait for the Target to plausibly occupy either role and then soak up the Narcissistic supply that ensues.

All Survivors report that they experienced "Walking on Eggshells" around the Vampire constantly during the relationship. This is the feeling of uncertainty about what the Vampire will do next, and the feeling of fear that is induced by that uncertainty. What's actually going on is that the Vampire is attempting to create a Drama Triangle and is attempting to force the Target into either the Persecutor or Rescuer positions in order to carry it out. The "Walking on

Eggshells" part is the Target instinctively trying to avoid being placed in either position and takes an enormous amount of vigilance and effort on the part of the Target, which is why it is so exhausting.

Regardless of how the Vampire initiates a Drama Triangle, once they have decided that they want one they will not cease trying to provoke one. The narrative of the Vampire is that they are always the Victim in their own lives and therefore will always seek to play that out at every opportunity. It is a part of the False Self that they are never the initiator of conflict and always the Victim of it, so adopting the Victim position is second-nature to the Vampire. The Vampire is so extraordinarily well versed in playing the Victim that the Target can never hope to keep up, and it is so vital to the narrative of the False Self that the Vampire will always excel at doing it because not to requires them to re-evaluate who they truly are, which is never going to happen.

Being in a Drama Triangle is always, without exception, a no-win situation for the Target, and therefore, the best and only advice is always to leave the situation, and preferably the relationship.

Why the Target can never occupy the Victim position

The Vampire's occupation of the Victim position is deliberate and if they find that the Target has occupied that position, they will attempt to "Out-Victim the Victim". Whatever the Target has said or done from the Victim position will be turned around by the Vampire so that they become the Victim themselves. This deliberately invalidates whatever the

Target was trying to say or do and allows them to eject the Target from the Victim position so that they can occupy it.

This ultimately means that whenever the Target raises legitimate concerns about the Vampires despicable behaviour towards them, or in general, what will follow is the Vampires deliberate (and always successful) attempt to eject the Target from the Victim position and occupy it themselves, nullifying the concern and turning the Target into either a Rescuer, or a Persecutor. This explains why Targets will always end up in one of two states when attempting to discuss the Vampires behaviour: apologising for their own behaviour; or feeling like the bad guy.

When (not if) the Vampire manages to occupy the Victim position, the Target will have nowhere to go except trying to placate them (Rescuer position), which means the issue will go unresolved, or trying to press the point (Persecutor position) in order to try for resolution. This will fail because the Vampire will not move from the Victim position, making the whole process of resolving the issue impossible. Once again, this is a typical example of how the Vampire places the Target in no-win situations and engages in crazy-making behaviour. Any attempt to continue will only harm the Target, meaning they will eventually leave the Drama Triangle without resolving the issue, which is exactly what the Vampire wants. They will also leave the Drama Triangle feeling either exhausted, guilty, or both.

The Drama Triangle and Splitting

For the Vampire, the Drama Triangle is an on-going

way of dealing with the world and individuals within it. As far as the Vampire is concerned, people do not exist as people, they exist as sources of Narcissistic supply. If a given individual is providing positive Narcissistic supply, the Vampire will consider them to be in the position of Rescuer in an on-going Drama Triangle.

This explains the prevalence of Flying Monkeys in the social circle of the Vampire. It also explains how the Vampire grooms other sources of Narcissistic supply as potential replacements for the Target. In their interactions with these individuals, they will play the role of the Victim in a relationship they claim is abusive (it is an abusive relationship of course, but the Vampire is actually the Persecutor, not the Victim).

If the individual in question appears to be able to serve the needs of the Vampire for positive Narcissistic supply on an on-going basis more than the Target (who by this time almost certainly cannot due to emotional exhaustion), the Vampire will seek to Discard the Target and replace them with this individual who they perceive will serve their needs for positive Narcissistic supply better. They won't, of course. No one can, but that won't deter the Vampire.

If an individual is not supplying positive Narcissistic supply, the Vampire will consider them to be a Persecutor in an on-going Drama Triangle. This explains why they will attempt to isolate the Target from them; because they perceive them to be a Threat. In all cases, the Vampire will consider themselves to occupy the most powerful position in all of their social interactions: the Victim. Any and all providers of positive Narcissistic supply are Rescuers and any and all providers of negative Narcissistic supply are Persecutors, their position as the Victim is secure and they will do anything and everything in their power to ensure that this continues.

The Drama Triangle and Triangulation

Individuals outside the relationship will always be dragged into the relationship by the Vampire in order to facilitate their Drama Triangles. Those perceived as Rescuers will be Idealised, and those perceived as Persecutors will be Devalued. In all cases, however, there will never be a time in which the relationship is occupied by only the Vampire and Target; it will always be occupied by the Vampire, the Target and whoever else the Vampire chooses to complete the Drama triangle. Flying Monkeys serve the purpose of Rescuer, and Threats serve the purpose of Persecutor.

Potential replacements for the Target serve the purpose of Rescuer, and previous Targets serve the purpose of Persecutor or Rescuer. The Vampire may even invent other people who the Target does not know (because they don't exist) that they refer to positively to serve as Rescuers or negatively to serve as Persecutors if real people are not available.

The Vampire will conduct emotional and sexual affairs with their Rescuers openly or covertly depending on which would serve their needs for Narcissistic supply best. They will suggest that the relationship becomes "open" so that they may do this and if that fails, they will do it anyway, and the Vampire will Triangulate with as many others as they feel necessary to maintain their Drama Triangles.

It is not unusual, therefore, for Vampires to maintain a coterie, or harem of past, present and potential other Targets to be used in Drama Triangles. Some of these may be known to the Target, others may not but they are always there. As has been pointed out previously, monogamy has no meaning for the Vampire because it involves too high a risk to place all Narcissistic supply in the hands of one individual and this explains the constant Triangulation because it facilitates multiple sources that can be elevated or diminished at any time in terms of their importance to the Vampire.

In essence, then, any Target will be surrounded by others that they may or may not know about that the Vampire is actively Triangulating at any given time. It is entirely probable, in fact, that the Target was part of the Vampires Triangulations when they met them. Many Targets report that the Vampire they were involved with was in an unhappy relationship when they met them. All that this means is that the Target was being Triangulated at the time as a Rescuer and the Vampires current Target was being Triangulated as a Persecutor. It is impossible for a Vampire not to Triangulate because they need to do so in order to manage their sources of Narcissistic supply.

Therefore, the best and only advice for any Target is to remove themselves from the Triangulation and leave the relationship permanently.

The Drama Triangle and the Target over time

After leaving a relationship with a Vampire, the overwhelming majority of Survivors report that they were subjected to a "Dr. Jeckyll / Mr. Hyde" type character. The experience is one of not knowing what to expect next. Will they be kind or cruel? Will they be vulnerable or malicious?

The truth is that the Target will never know what is coming next because it depends on the needs for Narcissistic supply of the Vampire in question at any given time, and therefore which position they will try to force the Target to occupy in order to provide for those needs.

The overwhelming majority of Survivors report feeling "beaten down" by constant demands that they could not keep up with and feelings of never being good enough, which is a result of repeatedly being forced to occupy the Rescuer position and the feelings of guilt and Shame reported by the overwhelming majority of survivors is a result of repeatedly being forced into the Persecutor position.

Over time, the emotional work of trying to avoid being forced into the Persecutor position, and only having the Rescuer position available to them accounts for why Survivors overwhelmingly report emotional "burnout" by the time the relationship with the Vampire ends. Targets never, ever get to occupy the position that is actually the one that they deserve to occupy: the Victim and so their existence with the Vampire is one of constant invalidation, guilt and emotional exhaustion.

This is because the Vampire will always use the Drama Triangle to their advantage, and will always deny the Target access to their deserved Victim position. They will always seek to occupy the position if the Victim themselves, from which they can claim that nothing the Target-as-Rescuer does is ever good enough, and the Target-as-Persecutor is an ever-present possibility should they fail to function adequately as the Rescuer. In this way, the Vampire is a small child with the "Big Book of Rules for Making Grown Ups Do What You Want", absolutely no limits on how, when or why they dictate those rules and absolutely no remorse for using them.

Over time, once they believe the Target to be fully controlled by their use of the Drama Triangle, the Vampire will begin to overtly occupy the Persecutor position. They will begin to be explicit in their demands of the Target and will remorselessly attack the Target, believing that they will not use the Victim position to defend themselves by calling out the Vampire as the Persecutor. For as long as that is the case, the abuse of the Vampire will escalate, and this is therefore the most dangerous part of the relationship the Target has with the Vampire. Should the Target seek to express their Victim position, the Vampire will immediately adopt that position as their own, forcing the Target to occupy one of the other two.

This use of the Drama Triangle is disgusting, despicable and highly abusive, and it was the intention of the Vampire all along. DARVO is often employed at this point to reverse the Victim-Persecutor positions of the Target and Vampire. This highly abusive employment of the Drama Triangle on an on-going basis explains why the overwhelming majority of Survivors suffer from Stockholm Syndrome (see

Chapter 9), because no matter how abusive the Vampire was, they occupied the Victim position as soon as possible after their abuses, and the Target was forced into the Rescuer position so often that they came to accept it as their identity in the relationship.

Undoing the damage this despicable practice causes is central to recovery (see the Chapters 11 & 12). Overall, since the Vampire will never cease creating Drama, and they will never cease creating Drama Triangles and Triangulating, the best and only advice for anyone involved is to leave the Triangulation and the relationship. The relationship was never a relationship anyway, the Target was simply one point in any number of Triangles that featured the Vampire at the centre, immovably occupying the position of the Victim.

OK, so let's leave the Vampire to their Triangulations for now, shall we? It's time for an Interlude.

Interlude 6

"Difficulty is inevitable. Drama is a choice" – Anita Renfroe

Hello again, dear Survivor!

Drama: We've all been there, huh? Trying to have a reasonable conversation with the Vampire = Drama. Ignoring them because you're fed up with trying to have a reasonable conversation = Drama.

There is a really good reason why Targets always feel that they're in no win situations with the Vampire. It's because the Vampire constantly creates win-win positions for themselves by playing the Victim and doesn't want them to win. Target not providing positive supply? Provoke them to become a Persecutor. Target not being a Persecutor? Play the Victim some more and see if you can get them to be a Rescuer. In all cases, Triangulate so that whatever the Target does doesn't really matter. Been called out on something? DARVO, then storm out and Triangulate.

Targets don't spend all day every day trying to get Narcissistic supply and figuring out how to do that to maximum effect without looking like an asshole. Vampires do that. All day, every day, which is why the Target is always behind the curve in the relationship and the Vampire is always ahead of it.

As Targets, we have all walked straight into their Drama traps over and over again because what we want and what they want are completely at odds. We want a loving relationship. They want Narcissistic supply. And that creates a total war-zone where the Vampire is always attacking and the Target is always on the defensive. Of course it's crazy. Crazy is what the Vampire does.

The relationship with the Vampire is a war, people. The moment you got involved with one, they declared war on you. I shit you not. They saw Narcissistic supply in you and then launched a Blitzkrieg on you to get it, all of it. That transition from Idealisation to Devaluation? That's just a different tactic with the same goal: Attack, attack, attack.

Once you get your head around how utterly single-minded they are, it becomes much easier to handle. It's why Grey Rock is so effective. Grey Rock is described in detail in Chapter 12, but for now it's basically just plain not responding to anything the Vampire says or does. All the Target has to do is let the Vampire do all the work for a change and watch them Drama themselves into oblivion. I thought I'd go through a couple of examples just for fun:

Scenario A: The Drama Palaver

Step 1. Vampire: "Drama, Drama, Drama"

Step 2. Target: "Grey Rock"

Step 3. Vampire: "NO! Drama, Drama, Drama!"

Step 4. Target: "Grey Rock"

Step 5. Vampire: "NO! NO! NO! DRAMA! DRAMA! DRAMA!"

Step 6. Target: "Grey Rock"

    The Vampire explodes and leaves the situation, fully intent on picking on some other poor bastard to get their Narcissistic supply. Either that or the Vampire becomes so deranged that the Target leaves the situation. Assuming that the Vampire has left, the Target takes the opportunity to slip away for the rest of their life and never looks back. When the Vampire gets back (and they will) they come back to a home that is now permanently sans- Target. If the Target leaves, they just don't come back ever and they get on with the rest of their life. In either case, situation resolved permanently.

Scenario B: The Silent Movie

Step 1. Vampire: "Silent Treatment"

Step 2. Target: "Grey Rock"

Step 3. Vampire: "Silent Treatment"

Step 4. Target: "Grey Rock"

Step 5. Vampire: "Silent treatment"

Step 6. Target: Grey Rock"

The Vampire has nowhere to go with this. They either have to continue the Silent Treatment, which won't work, or they have to leave (in which case it's abandon ship and get on with your life time), or they have to start Scenario A, and we already know how that plays out, right?

What it all adds up to is that the best way to get rid of the Vampire is to act like they don't exist. They hate that. The one thing the Vampire hates most is to be ignored, so that's exactly what should happen. Works every time.

You may be wondering if Grey Rock is the equivalent of the Silent Treatment. It isn't. The Silent Treatment is a form of attack. Grey Rock is a form of defence. There is a cast-iron guaranteed way of telling the difference, and it's the use of "The Reasonable Conversation". A Target using Grey Rock will stop doing it to have a Reasonable Conversation. A Vampire using a Silent Treatment won't.

To normal people, a Reasonable Conversation is a thing that people do. To the Vampire, it's a myth that they use to scare their children. "Beware the Reasonable Conversation, little ones..." they say, "...for it is a trap that Targets use to steal your soul." "But what should I do if a Target tries to have a

Reasonable Conversation with me?" say the little ones. They don't get an answer, of course, because the Vampire has already left the conversation because it's not about them anymore. Further enquiry will probably result in a Silent Treatment.

Anyway, that's enough about Grey Rock for now. There's plenty more later on in Chapter 12, and you can discover for yourself the peace and harmony you can restore to your life when you learn to use it. For now, t's time for the last of the burning questions.

How much of this is my fault, and what could I have done differently?

Technically, this is two questions in one. A twofer, if you will. That's OK though because they basically add up to the same thing. The bottom line is that we all have to take a long look at what got us into a relationship that involved abuse. I have a saying about these things. It goes like this:

No-one is 100% responsible for a relationship, but we are 100% responsible for our 50%

If we do look after our 50%, then we can walk away happy that we did our part. The Vampire never will, of course, and the real mind-fuck for Survivors is that not only did the Vampire not look after their 50%, they tried to blame the Target for not looking after the 100%. That is all the different colours and flavours of wrong.

Not only do they spend all their time attacking the Target to get Narcissistic supply, they don't take any responsibility for any of their actions and, when the Discard occurs or the Target leaves, they try to pin the blame for their despicable behaviours on the very person who tried to do everything to help them. There's a word for individuals like that, but I use Vampire instead.

I find myself in a very odd position as I write this because I'm about to use a sports analogy. It's not something I do very often, but it seems an appropriate way of explaining so here goes. There's only one sport I actually like and it's American Football. I've never been sure why, maybe it's because it makes a good relationship analogy. Anyway, the game is pretty simple, despite all the complex rules that people bang on about. You have two teams. At the start, one is the Offense, and the other is the Defence. The Offense has to get the ball to the end of the Defence's half of the pitch. The Defence has to stop them. That's it. Yes, Football fans, I know it's not that simple. It's an analogy. Shush, please.

It just so happens that the pitch is 100 yards long. See where I'm going? It's not, but never mind, it is now. The pitch represents the relationship. Each half represents the personal sovereignty of each person within it, their rights, feelings, emotions, body, hopes, dreams, and aspirations. Everything that makes them who they are and everything they have a right to enjoy and develop as they see fit. The Offense and Defence start in the middle, at the 50 yard line. In a healthy relationship, that's where the game ends. The players greet each other and then clear off and do something they all love to do, like have a healthy relationship. Because a healthy relationship is not a fucking game! But the relationship with a Vampire is. Oh, dear me yes.

The relationship with a Vampire is always a game. In that game, play starts and the Offense tries to get the ball into the Defence's half of the pitch. They usually don't do it all in one go. They do it bit by bit, yard by yard. It's a gradual erosion of the Defence's territory. In other words, the Vampire invades the sovereign territory of the Target a piece at a time.

Vampires are really, really good at being the Offense. Terrible in Defence, of course, but they never play that side. If they were required to, they'd just run off the pitch and call the Offense names to anyone who will listen. Bad sports, Vampires. On Offense though? Incredible. The Target, as the Defence, is constantly trying to defend their sovereign territory from the Vampire. How fucked up is that?

The vast majority of Survivors never even knew they were in a game in the first place, which is why the whole experience is so painful and confusing. The worst case scenario is that their sovereign territory has been invaded over and over again, the Vampire has taken over the whole relationship, they actually feel beaten, even though they never wanted to play the game in the first place and, what's more, once the Vampire thinks they have scored enough points and the Defence can't stop them any more, they fuck off to the lockers, set fire to the stadium, claim they lost by the same margin they actually won by and then start another game with another Target that don't know they're playing either.

So, how much of the relationship was the Survivor responsible for? 50%. Given a fighting chance, they would have looked after that 50% and the game would have ended as soon as it started. But they were in a game. When they were the Target, they were under relentless attack from the Vampire, who had the express intention of taking over the whole relationship while simultaneously not taking responsibility for any of it. Since Targets don't know they're in a game, they are completely forgiven for giving ground.

A good Defence is built of one thing: Self Respect. With that in place, the game would not have even started. Without that at the start, in the game with the Vampire, at some point, one of two things will happen. Either the Target will put up a good Defence somewhere in their half of the pitch, in which case the Vampire will run off the pitch, blame the Target, smear the Target, steal their clothes and wallets from the locker room on the way out, claim they never wanted to play in the first place and then eat the ball, or the Target will be subject to the worst case scenario above. In either case, this is good news because the Vampire has finally buggered off.

But here's the thing. If the Survivor doesn't sort out their Defence, they will be drawn into another game again. In healthy relationships, the Defence isn't necessary but it is there just in case people find they've been drawn into a game. Love is not a game, dear Survivor. There is no Offense and Defence in Love. While Vampires and Targets are busy playing the game, Love is in the parking lot making out, or at the movies, or at home cuddling on the sofa. You know where it isn't? It's not at the fucking game and it sure as shit isn't on the pitch.

So, how much of the Survivor's relationship was their "fault"? Well, insofar as all Survivors need to sort out their Defence, 50%. Once the game is over, there are two things that the Survivor needs to consider. First, how can they learn from the game so that they never, ever get drawn into another one and second, how can they build such an amazing Defence that if they do get drawn into another game, they leave as soon as they hear the kick-off whistle? What the Survivor is not responsible for is that they ended up playing against a Vampire. They were not responsible for the invasion of their half of the pitch, they were not responsible for the defeat, they were not responsible for the loss of clothes, wallets, stadium or ball, but they are now 100% responsible for their 50% of the pitch.

And could the Survivor have done anything differently? Well, given that they didn't know they were in a game in the first place, the answer has to be No. It was always going to end that way. What happens next, however, is entirely up to the Survivor. As I've said before, the greatest gift the Vampire can give is their absence and a savvy Survivor won't be returning to the sport.

There we go: The sports analogy, which seems to work. Anyway, we're off to Chapter 7 now. See you on the other side.

Chapter 7

How the Vampire trains their Target

To explain how this works, I'd like to use an analogy from my own experience. To give you a heads-up, you may not like it but then this isn't exactly a comfortable read, is it? That's why the Interludes exist...

Shortly after I gained my Psychology degree, I trained as a Behaviourist and worked with dogs. I love dogs. They're amazing. Basically, I was on referral from Veterinary surgeries and clients would call me if their dog was doing stuff they didn't want it to do like being aggressive, tearing the place up, running off and not coming back, all that stuff. It was great work and I enjoyed it immensely.

What I noticed, though, was that it was never the fault of the dog. The dog was just being a dog. The problem was always the owner. You'd be amazed how many people have no idea what a dog is. Oh, there are plenty of people who think they know what a dog is, and a lot of them are right, but I never went to their houses. I went to the houses of people who thought that their dog was something else.

What most of these people thought was that their dog was an extension of themselves. They would go to great lengths to tell me about the dog's personality, how much they loved the dog, how upset they were about the dog's behaviour etc. All the big sob-story. All the time, I'd sit there thinking "Dude, it's a dog. How do you not know what a dog is?" The truth of the matter was that the humans in the situation were trying to get the dog to be what they wanted it to be, not what it actually is.

Quite rightly, the dog was pushing back in their own doggy way, going "Hello? I'm a dog! What do you want from me?" In my successful cases, I managed to get the owner to understand that they were dealing with a dog, not whatever they thought it was, to change their behaviour so that the problem stopped (because they were the problem in the first place), and to understand that what was living in their house was an actual dog! It's amazing what you can achieve with a little authority and persuasion. I only had a few unsuccessful cases, and all of them had one thing in common: The owner rejected the dog because it wouldn't be what they wanted it to be.

Let's put that into perspective, shall we? What I used to get called to were abusive relationships in which one side was trying to force their reality on the other side, and I never got a call from a dog. By the time I arrived, the Smear Campaign against the dog was in full swing, and I was supposed to be a Flying Monkey. Nope. Never worked. I would go to great lengths to explain everything from the dog's perspective (even in one case when the bastard had just bitten me), elicit some Empathy from the owners and find a resolution that meant that everyone could get on with life. In most cases it worked, but I am absolutely convinced that my unsuccessful cases involved Vampires.

Once these individuals realised that they were the problem and that they would have to change something about themselves to make things better, it was Game Over for the dog. Thankfully, I only lost one of those dogs to euthanasia, and that was without my knowledge at the time. The rest were successfully re-homed. I was pretty good at what I did. Ask me sometime. I've got lots of stories.

So here's the thing. I'm going to give you a free lesson in how to train a dog. Bear with me please, I promise I'm doing it for a really good reason.

In training, there is a set of simple principles that really works. It works with any mammal and it works consistently. It's called Operant Conditioning and it's based on Punishment and Reinforcement. Punishment is anything the recipient finds bad. In the case of a dog, that might be withholding something it likes, like a bit of bacon. If you're a shitty trainer, then punishments might be direct, like physical attacks. Reinforcement is anything the recipient finds good. In the case of a dog, that might be giving it a bit of bacon. Behaviours that are punished will die out. Behaviours that are reinforced will continue.

The key to training a dog is to figure out what they will work for. Some love bacon, others cheese. Some love toys, others affection. Whatever it is, you have to find it. And then you have to create scarcity. If your dog works for bacon and there's bacon all over the place, your dog will not work for you. What you're trying to do there is to establish yourself as the source of the thing the dog wants most. Wherever possible, you want to make sure that you are the only source of what the dog wants most. That way, the dog will look at you as the "Master of All Bacon", or whatever fancy title you want to give yourself. Once you get there, you have control over what and when your dog learns, because you've "got it by the brain".

The way to train a dog is to reinforce the behaviours you do want and punish the behaviours you don't want. If the dog does something you want, you reinforce that behaviour by giving it a little "bacon". If the dog does something you don't want, you punish that behaviour by withholding "bacon". All you need to know is when to give and when to withhold.

Then you can start training, and here's how that goes. Pick a behaviour and ask for it. When the dog does it, reinforce it. Don't reinforce any behaviour you didn't ask for. Ask for it again. When they do it, reinforce again and don't reinforce anything you didn't ask for. Continue until the dog knows what to do when you ask, and does it every time. Easy. What you're doing is using your power as the "Master of All Bacon" or whatever to give out small amounts of the good stuff when the dog does what you want, and you're withholding the good stuff when they don't.

From time to time, your dog is going to do things you don't want. To stop it doing those things, you want to be able to punish those behaviours, right? So what you do is you establish a signal that means that you're going to withhold "bacon". It's really easy. All you do is go through a few sessions where you offer the dog some "bacon" in your hand, and when it tries to take it, you close your hand and say "No". Do that often enough and the dog learns that "No" means "no bacon for you". It doesn't matter what the word you say is, what matters is that to the dog it means "no bacon for you". In future, whenever you say that word, the dog thinks "oops, no bacon for me". What that lets you do is say whatever word you chose whenever the dog does something you don't want and it knows that it won't get bacon. You're punishing the behaviours it does that you don't want, so it will stop doing them.

Now, that's the humane way of punishing, but it's not the only way. Really shitty trainers will use active and direct punishment on their dogs. They will apply things they know the dog doesn't like, such as scolding, shouting, the God-awful-shock-collar (don't ask), or physical beatings. All trainers that have appropriately qualified never do that stuff because they learn the Cardinal Rule: Whatever you do, remember that a living thing is on the other side. Sadly, not every trainer qualifies and some that do still resort to active and direct punishment because it gets results. What they forget is that the only reason it works is because dogs are loyal creatures. But then so are humans, as it turns out...

With reinforcement, you can't go around reinforcing the dog all the time, right? That's gonna give you one fat dog.

So you use the most powerful tool there is in training: The Intermittent Reinforcement Schedule. What that means is that you reinforce the behaviour at random. The dog never knows when it's going to get that "bacon", so it just keeps trying in the hope that it will. When it does, great! When it doesn't, maybe next time. An advanced technique that goes along with that is "Jackpotting". That's when you reinforce the behaviour big time every so often. That way, the dog never knows whether it will get "bacon", will have to wait, or whether it will get loads of "bacon". A dog on an Intermittent Reinforcement Schedule with Jackpotting in place will keep doing the trained behaviour indefinitely.

Now let's take a quick look at the Extinction Burst. It works once a behaviour has been learned, and it's a great way to make it bigger. Ever seen an impatient person calling an elevator? They push that button and wait. The elevator doesn't arrive, so they push that button again. It still doesn't arrive. So they push that button like "bam, bam, bam", right? If the elevator still doesn't arrive, they give up and walk away. You've just witnessed an Extinction Burst. All mammals do it. They increase the learned behaviour hugely before they give up. Well, a good trainer knows this. You deliberately withhold reinforcement from the dog until the dog ramps up the behaviour you want and, just before the dog gives up you reinforce it. It's called "Surfing the Burst" and it's a great way of getting a bigger and bigger response from the dog to the same request.

So, here's how it works in the Trainer-Dog relationship:

1) Figure out what your dog will work for

2) Create scarcity and establish yourself as the "Master of All Bacon"

3) Reinforce what you want and Punish what you don't want

4) Place the behaviours you want on an Intermittent Reinforcement Schedule

5) "Jackpot" occasionally

6) "Surf the Burst" to bigger versions of the same behaviour

What you end up with is a dog that will work harder and harder for less and less reinforcement. You know what that sounds like? An addict, because that's exactly what it is. When you're training a dog you are creating an addict. You want the dog to be entirely dependent on you for its supply of "bacon", to work harder and harder for less and less "bacon", and you want to be able to dictate when and how much "bacon" the dog gets.

I wish I was kidding here, but I'm not. All trainers create an addiction in their dogs. They do it on purpose and they know exactly what they are doing. Now, good trainers know all this stuff and they train their dogs with the welfare of the dog in mind. Bad trainers also know this stuff and they only care about what they can get the dog to do. Guess which type of trainer the Vampire is...

So there we are. That's your free lesson in dog training and, as promised, here's why I gave it to you:

The Vampire trains their Target in exactly the same way a dog trainer trains their dog. Now, before we all get upset about being called dogs, I'd like to point out I have been there too. When the penny dropped that I'd been trained the way I used to train, I was just as fucked off about it as you probably are reading this. Please bear with me while I draw the parallels as far as the Vampire and Target are concerned. If you still want to argue with me after that, please send me an e.mail.

I'll be coming back to this next point at the end, but I wanted to flag it up out now so that the reasons for the Vampire doing all this are clear. The Vampire is obsessed with Power and Control. Because their Self Respect is so impossibly low, and their Shame so impossibly high, they believe that allowing the Target the freedom to be who they want to be and do what they want to do will lead to them leaving the relationship and the Vampire will lose them as Narcissistic supply.

The Vampire would never admit it, but they are terrified of that. That would mean that they would have to be alone with themselves, and that would be a living hell for them. So, when they do all the things I'm about to describe, they are doing them to exert Power and Control over the Target to make sure they don't leave the relationship. That's their only reason for doing them, they will never stop doing them, and the only way to deal with it is to get the hell away and stay the hell away from them.

OK, so let's take the stages of training in turn and apply them to the Vampire-Target relationship.

Figure out what your dog will work for

During the Idealisation Stage of the Attack Cycle, the Vampire figured out exactly what the Target would work for. 9 times out of 10, that was love and affection but there would have been a whole raft of other things in there too. Maybe it was sex, maybe it was compliments, maybe it was fine living. Basically, fill in the blank. But that's not all. At the same time, the Vampire was learning exactly how to punish the Target. They learned what the Target's weaknesses were like their insecurities, their fears, what they were ashamed of. Again, fill in the blank.

The Vampire was looking for the vulnerabilities in the Target where they could make the Target feel the Shame they refuse to look at in themselves. Whatever the Target feels ashamed of, or insecure about will be used later to control them. The Vampire fully intends to project their Shame onto the Target by using this information, and fully intends to exploit the Target's insecurities using Gaslighting. In other words, the Vampire will use whatever they have learned about the Target in the Idealisation Stage to figure out the reinforcements and punishments they will use to control them later on.

Create scarcity and establish yourself as the "Master of All Bacon"

This is exactly what Isolation and Gaslighting are for. The Vampire wants the Target to be cut off from all other sources of what is important to them, and they want the Target to believe the Vampire's version of reality. If the Target has access to other sources of what they want and need, the Vampire cannot create scarcity and the Target won't work for them. Not only that, if the Target has access to objective reality, there is a danger that they will become immune to the Gaslighting and Shame the Vampire will use to control them. Therefore, the Vampire will pull out all the stops to make sure that they become the "Master of All Bacon" as far as the Target is concerned.

Reinforce what you want and Punish what you don't want

The Vampire will systematically train the Target to provide them with Narcissistic supply through reinforcement and punishment. If the Target does what they want, they will get a little "bacon" in the form of whatever is important to them. If they don't provide Narcissistic supply, they will be punished by withholding or direct punishment. During this phase, the Vampire will establish signals that indicate that they are currently punishing the Target, or are about to. The Silent Treatment is a classic. So are the "sigh", and the "eye roll". Every Target's experience will be unique, but I challenge any Target or Survivor not to be able to name at least one sure-fire signal that they were about to be punished.

And now the nasty part: The Vampire is a really shitty trainer and has absolutely no problem with using all of the Target's weaknesses against them here as active and direct punishment. Remember how they were gathering all that information at the start? This is where they use it. Does the Target fear abandonment? That's a potential punishment used by threatening to leave the relationship. Is the Target insecure? That's a potential punishment used by criticising them. Does the Target fear being unattractive? That's a potential punishment used by flirting with others. Basically, fill in the blank.

Whatever the Vampire can use against the Target as a punishment, they will use as a punishment. Of course, the Vampire would much rather not leave a mark on the Target so where better to do it than in the Target's mind and without physical trace. That's what Gaslighting is for. In this phase of the training, and until the end of the relationship, the Vampire will be a very shitty trainer and directly punish whatever they want to, whenever they want to if they think it will serve them in controlling the Target. Remember all the stuff I talked about in the first half about how the Vampire attacks? This is why. They're training the Target to take their shit over and over and over again.

Place the behaviours you want on an Intermittent Reinforcement Schedule

Once the Vampire has the Target trained to provide Narcissistic supply, they will start to cut down on the "bacon" and expect bigger and bigger amounts of Narcissistic supply from the Target. It's all a matter of economy now. The Vampire is figuring out how to get the maximum amount of Narcissistic supply for the least amount of "bacon". At this point, the Devaluation Stage of the Attack Cycle is well underway, and the Target will be trying harder and harder to please the Vampire while receiving less and less of what they need. This is exactly how you create an addict, and the Target is now addicted to the Vampire's behaviours. When the Vampire reinforces, the Target feels elated. When the Vampire punishes, the Target feels terrible. The Intermittent Reinforcement Schedule is doing all the work to keep the Target hooked, and the Vampire is still the "Master of All Bacon". The Vampire can reinforce and punish at will. Calculated? You bet your ass it is...

"Jackpot" occasionally

Every Target or Survivor remembers the good times, don't they? The romantic dinners? The great sex at the beginning? The occasional kind gestures? Those moments that felt like an oasis in a desert of pain? That's Jackpotting, and it works like a charm. You know when a Vampire is most likely to Jackpot? When they think they're about to lose the Target, that's when. They are enormously sensitive to changes in the Target's behaviours, and if they sense that the Target is slipping away from their control, they will use Jackpotting to draw the Target back into the Attack Cycle again and, of course, it's only a matter of time before the punishments begin again.

"Surf the Burst" to get more of the same behaviour

Show me a Target or Survivor that didn't decide to give up on the relationship at some point. You can count them on the fingers of one leg. Every single Target and Survivor will at some point have made that "one last ditch attempt" to fix the relationship, right? You know what the Vampire did with that? They waited until the Target had almost given up and then they reinforced. They may even have Jackpotted. The Vampire "Surfed the Burst" and that meant that the Target's attempts to save the relationship just kept getting bigger, and bigger, and bigger...

So there it is. That's how the Vampire trains their Target. As a Target or Survivor reading this, you're almost certainly reflecting on what a disgusting process it is to train another human the way a human trains a dog. You may even be reflecting on how unpleasant the process may be for dogs. In any case, that's because you have Empathy. Remember, though, that the Vampire doesn't, and therefore has absolutely no problem doing any of this.

For the Vampire, the Target is simply a source of Narcissistic supply, and therefore has the same status in their lives as a dog. I have seen first-hand how Vampires treat their dogs, and I have lived first-hand how a Vampire treats their Target and I can tell you that there is no difference whatsoever.

Now, I believe that this is calculated on the part of the Vampire, but as I said earlier, it's important to realise that even if it wasn't the Vampire would do it anyway because they are compelled to do it. Once the relationship is underway, the Vampire is terrified of losing Control of the Target and potentially losing their source of Narcissistic supply.

All their behaviours are therefore geared towards training the Target to do what they want. The Vampire is a creature of instinct, they don't know how to be anything else, they will never admit that they are wrong because they cannot look at themselves for fear of experiencing Shame and they will never believe that the Target is anything other than a source of Narcissistic supply. All the Gaslighting, creation of FOG, Lies, Projection and everything else from the Vampires Tactics are used over and over again to make sure the Target does not leave. In other words, the Target has no choice in whether they are trained or not, unless they leave the relationship. If they don't submit to training, the Vampire will leave. If they do submit to training, the Vampire will train them compulsively, and they will never stop. Even if they wanted to stop, they couldn't because they fundamentally believe that if they let the Target out of their Control, they will leave. Anyone who stays with a Vampire will be trained.

What you are dealing with is an individual that is addicted to Power and Control in the same way they are addicted to Narcissistic supply. They really do believe that the Target will leave if they are not controlled, and they cannot let go their power for the same reason. It doesn't matter how hard you work to convince them otherwise, or how much you try to reason with them about it, they will never be able to convince themselves that the Target will stay with them if they don't control them. Essentially, what you have here is a relationship in which one individual that is addicted to Narcissistic supply trains the other individual to become addicted to their behaviour, so that they do not leave and continue to provide them with that Narcissistic supply.

By the time the relationship is in the Devaluation Stage, there are two individuals whose lives are being run by the Vampire's addictions to Narcissistic supply, Power and Control.

I'm so sorry, dear Survivor. I know that's not great news. I've been there. If I thought there was a better way of telling you, I would have done it. The truth of the matter is though, that the Vampire got you hooked on their addictions. But actually, I believe that's pretty empowering. Think about it for a moment. The addict in the relationship was the Vampire, not you. In order to get their "fix", they had to make you an addict too. So who was the problem here? I'll give you a clue, it wasn't you.

The Vampire will never overcome their addictions to Narcissistic supply, Power and Control because they are broken, for all the reasons I've already told you. You got drawn in, but are you addicted to Narcissistic supply? Well, the very fact that you're reading this book tells me the answer to that is "No". So you are not the problem, are you? The Vampire was, still is and always will be the problem. What's more, there are two pieces of really great news here.

1) *It is not your fault.*
2) *You can choose to stop.*

It's not your fault you got involved with an addict. How could you possibly have known? Addictions are usually really obvious, right? Alcohol, drugs, whatever. Most people would see the signs and they could say to themselves "I think this person might be an addict". But who ever heard of an addiction to Narcissistic supply? Almost no-one. It's not in the news, it's not on TV, it's not on Social Media. Even terms like "Narcissist" don't really cover it because they refer to the behaviours, not the addiction. There was no way on Earth that you could have seen this one coming because to the majority of the population it's not even a thing.

Also, please remember that this can happen to anyone. Because no-one really gets this stuff, the vast majority of people just don't see it coming. Before they know it, they're involved with a Vampire and the Vampire's addictions to Narcissistic supply, Power and Control have taken over the whole relationship. By the time the Devaluation Stage kicks in, the Vampire is already the "Master of All Bacon", so the Target is basically stuffed from the start and it doesn't matter who they are.

The very strongest, smartest, most talented and successful people get drawn into this stuff. In fact, it's usually them anyway because that's what the Vampire is attracted to. So don't beat yourself up. No, seriously, don't do that. None of this was ever your fault. In the next chapter, I'm going to explain what happened to your brain that meant that your biology was running the show. The brain of an addict is different than a "normal" brain. Yours was made that way by the Vampire and you can change that. Theirs is going to stay that way forever. So again, it's not your fault, OK?

Second, you can choose to stop. You were involved with an addict, who got you hooked and kept you hooked. They had to, because that's what their entire existence is about. Without their addictions, they cease to exist. The Vampire will never change, but you can. What you can do now is make the conscious decision to get clean. Now that you know what the Vampire was doing and why they were doing it, you can choose to stop and choose to do something else.

Basically, what you've currently got is a brain that was re-wired by the Vampire to serve their need for Narcissistic supply. They re-wired you because they have to. If they didn't re-wire you, you would pose a threat to their reality, which they cannot stand because it would involve looking at themselves, and we both know they will never do that. But you can un-wire what they did.

It will take time, but it can be done. I know because I've done it, and so have loads of other people. You can undo the re-wiring that was done to you. The first step is to get the hell away and stay the hell away from the Vampire, because every single thing they do will be an attempt to re-wire you again. So choose to stay away please. OK?

OK. That's enough from Chapter 7. Let's have another Interlude, shall we? See you on the other side.

Interlude 7

"Outside of a dog, a book is man's best friend. Inside of a dog it's too dark to read" – Groucho Marx

Hello again, dear Survivor!

Dogs: Amazing creatures. Not, as many people believe, pack animals. That's wolves. Dogs don't work in packs and they don't seek "dominance" over humans or any other bullshit you might have heard Cesar Milan say. Dogs aren't wolves, they don't think like wolves and they don't behave like wolves. They think and behave like dogs.

Life's a funny thing, isn't it? Who'd have thought that knowing the difference between how wolves and dogs think and behave would key me in to the difference between how Vampires and Healthy people think and behave? It did, though. I'm gonna take a moment of your time to explain the difference and I'm hoping it will make things a bit clearer when it comes to understanding the difference between Healthy people and Vampires.

Dogs and wolves want different things, just like Healthy people and Vampires want different things. Dogs are looking for contact with humans. Wolves don't give a shit. To a dog, humans are a source of affection, and security. To a wolf, humans are either a hazard, or they are prey. Sound familiar? If you hurt a dog when it's trying to get affection and security, it will try a different tack. Try that with a wolf and it will either attack you or it will leave because it wasn't looking for affection or security in the first place. Dogs want to coexist with you. Wolves don't. Healthy people want to coexist with you. Vampires don't.

This all goes back to the origin of the dog as a species. For the longest time, we used to believe (and some people still do) that the dog is a sub-species of wolf. Nope, they are a totally different species. Ask a Biologist. Specifically, ask the Biologist Ray Coppinger, who wrote the seminal work on the subject. His explanation goes something like this:

Thousands of years ago there were humans, and wolves. Humans were really; really good at creating garbage (we're still good at that). For wolves, human garbage represented a food source. Those wolves that were genetically predisposed to fear humans stayed away from human garbage. Those wolves that weren't ate it, which required them to get closer to humans.

Add time, and lots of mating.

The "stay away" wolves interbred, passing on the "stay away" gene, and making more "stay away" wolves. The "get closer" wolves interbred, passing on the "get closer" gene, and making more "get closer" wolves. One strain led to the Wolf, an animal genetically predisposed to "stay away" from humans. The other strain led to the Dog, an animal genetically predisposed to "get closer" to humans.

Add more time, and lots more mating.

The "get closer" wolves are now more Dog-like than Wolf-like, and they get closer and closer to humans. After all, it's an evolutionary advantage to fill a niche like garbage-hunting, right?

Add more time, and a bit more mating, obviously.

Dogs learn that being around humans leads to security and affection. And show me a healthy dog that doesn't love that stuff. Wolves never learned that because they got on a different evolutionary train. What you end up with is one species that lacks fear of humans on a genetic level and actively enjoys the affection and security afforded by peaceful coexistence with humans and another that avoids the affection and security afforded by that coexistence and sees humans as potential prey. If we could talk directly to their brains, it would go something like this:

Dog: "Hello! I'm a dog! I reckon those human type things are pretty cool. I like them 'cos I'm pretty affectionate and when I get close to them, they're affectionate too! I have no idea what reciprocity is because I'm a dog, but I do know that we get along really well and I really want to be close to humans". Wolf: "Fuck you, man! I'm a wolf. Humans are dodgy at best, so I don't want anything to do with them. Sometimes they're OK if I can get something from them but I'll stick to my own kind, thanks".

So what's that got to do with Healthy people and Vampires? I'm glad you asked. In exactly the same way that wolves are not dogs and vice versa, Vampires are not Healthy people. Vampires have taken a different train to the one Healthy people are on. Healthy people are on the "affection and security" train. Vampires are on the "Narcissistic supply" train. And the reason for the behaviour of both is all in the motivation. Healthy people are motivated to make contact with other humans for affection and security. Vampires are motivated to make contact with other humans for Narcissistic supply.

But instead of it being about evolution, it's about upbringing. Over here, you've got your Healthy person: Self-respecting, grounded and capable of love (decent upbringing). Over there you've got your Vampire: Little to no Self Respect, deluded and incapable of love (shitty upbringing). And they want different things. If we could talk directly to their brains, it would go something like this:

Healthy person: "Hi! I like me and I'm prepared to like you, too. I treat myself well, so I can treat you well too. The voice in my head says nice things about me because that's what I heard growing up. I can understand things from your perspective, so we can have a meaningful relationship where we understand each other. If we get along well enough, we might get into an intimate relationship. If that happens, we'll both look after ourselves and each other and we'll have a two-way relationship based on trust."

Vampire: "Hi! I pretty much hate me, and I pretty much hate you too. I don't treat myself well, so I'm not capable of treating you well. The voice in my head says horrible things about me because that's what I heard growing up. I haven't got a clue how to understand things from your perspective because I don't care. I'd like to have an intimate relationship with you because attention makes me feel good. If that happens, I'll look after me and so will you. I'll expect you to look after you, too. Our relationship will be a one-way street based on what you can do for me."

Interesting analogy, don't you think? I reckon the most common mistake people make when it comes to Vampires is similar to the most common mistake people make when it comes to dogs: They think they're looking at something else. I keep reading stuff online and watching Youtube videos where people talk about Vampires as "dark entities", or "evil", or "demons" or some-such. Fair enough, if that helps you but I do think those conclusions are drawn from trying to understand the Vampire by comparing them with Healthy people.

It's a bit like trying to explain a crocodile by comparing it to a gecko. If your standard is gecko and you expect the crocodile to be like that, you're going to be very confused, right? They're both reptiles, but they're totally different. Imagine calling one of your friends and asking how their reptile is, only to be given the answer "the fucking thing just tore my arm off!" If we keep expecting Vampires to behave like Healthy people, we're going to keep having our figurative arms torn off, aren't we? Bottom line? Wolves are not Dogs, Crocodiles are not Geckos and Vampires are not Healthy people. Treat them like they are, and you could lose a proverbial arm, which they'll blame you for, by the way.

Right, then. That's enough about animals. On with the next chapter.

Chapter 8

The Biological effects of the Attack Cycle on the Survivor

In this chapter, I want to address the very real damage that the Modern Vampire does to their Target's body and brain. These issues are significant and, if you've survived a Vampire, enormous damage will have been done by them that now needs to be repaired. The Vampire attacks their Target remorselessly, deliberately and with only one goal: to obtain Narcissistic supply. They do not care what damage they do to the Target in obtaining that supply, so it is the Survivors job to care about themselves.

The damage incurred by the Survivor occurs at the biological level, not just the emotional and psychological level. In fact, it is the biological damage that creates the experience of psychological and emotional damage. Everything that will be explained in Chapter 9 about the psychological effects and in Chapter 10 about the emotional effects experienced by the

Survivor is a result of the damage done by the Vampire at the biological level. Therefore, for repair to be effected, it needs to occur beyond the emotional and psychological. But there is hope. Enormous numbers of Survivors can and do recover from the damage I will describe here. In later chapters I will be addressing some ways that recovery can begin and I will highlight again the role that a good therapeutic professional plays in facilitating that repair.

Because the damage that has been done occurs in a variety of ways, I will be breaking this chapter down into several sections:

1) The effects of chronic stress
2) The symptoms of PTSD and C-PTSD
3) The addicted brain

The effects of chronic stress.

As humans, we are hard-wired to respond to perceived threats in our environment. It is part of a healthy survival mechanism that the brain responds to such threats by preparing the body to run from, fight or otherwise evade things that could harm us. The process by which the brain affects the body in this way is called the stress response. Most people refer to it as the "fight-or-flight" response.

Stress can take several forms: Acute stress refers to the body's response to a sudden occurrence, such as an attacking dog, or an unexpected loud noise. The brain perceives the threat, and triggers the fight-or-flight response; Traumatic stress is more severe. It refers to the body's response to a traumatic event, such as personal injury, physical attack, or sudden loss of a loved one. The brain perceives a threat to the body's existence, and hence the stress response is more elevated and severe. This can lead to mental health issues such as Post Traumatic Stress Disorder (PTSD); Chronic stress refers to a state in which the perceived threat is on-going. The activation of the fight-or-flight response is constant, and the net effect is that the body is on high alert all the time. This can also lead to PTSD, as well as Complex Post Traumatic Stress Disorder (C-PTSD)

In normal life, many things are a source of chronic stress. Whenever the brain perceives a threat and triggers the stress response on an on-going basis, whatever caused that can be considered to be a source of chronic stress. For many people, that may include certain elements of their job. Life events such as financial insecurity may be a source. On-going noise pollution or chemical pollution may be sources. I maintain that life with a Vampire is a source of chronic stress.

The reason for this is simple. The Vampire is a disordered individual. They do not think or function as normal individuals do. They cannot live without drama, create constant conflict, attack their Target constantly and remorselessly, Gaslight permanently, require an endless supply of attention and will provoke that wherever necessary, are constantly in crisis, are never happy, have no capacity to give, only to take and create around them at all times an atmosphere of fear, obligation and guilt.

The overwhelming majority of Survivors report living their lives with the Vampire as "walking on eggshells", with which I broadly agree, but I would suggest that it is actually more like walking on landmines. The potential for the entire world of the relationship to explode at a moment's notice with no apparent reason and no apparent provocation is what characterises life with the Vampire. As discussed in chapter 6, if the Vampire does not create Drama, they cease to exist. As discussed in Chapter 5, if the Vampire does not Gaslight, they lose control. In both cases they are compelled to do these things as part of their very existence and since this is so, and because of their other behaviours, the brain of any "normal" person living with one is experiencing a perceived threat 24 hours a day, 7 days a week, 365 days a year.

Before we examine how that affects the Survivor, we need to take a look at how the stress response normally works in response to a threat. Here's how that goes:

The HPA axis

Once the brain perceives a threat, a small part of it called the Hypothalamus sends a chemical signal to the Pituitary gland. In turn, the Pituitary gland sends a chemical signal to the Adrenal Cortex. This triggers the Adrenal gland to release the hormones Cortisol and Adrenaline. This system is known as the HPA axis (Hypothalamus - Pituitary - Adrenal).

Cortisol is released into the bloodstream. So is Adrenaline. These cause several changes in the body

a) Increased heart rate and blood pressure
b) Decreased digestion

c) Dilation of blood vessels in the muscles, so blood is diverted from other body areas
d) Release of Glucose (blood sugar) into the bloodstream
e) Suppression of the immune system
f) Increased muscle tension

When the blood concentration of Cortisol reaches a certain level, the Hypothalamus realises this and turns off the response.

Under normal circumstances, this process would prepare the body to take on the perceived threat by providing for the physical needs of a body that was either running away from or fighting a perceived threat in the short-term only, which is why the process is turned off once the chemical balance reaches equilibrium.

The problem is that the important word here is: perceived. If the brain perceives that a threat is present, it will continue to trigger the HPA axis for as long as it perceives the threat. In the case of the Vampire, that threat is 24 hours a day, 7 days a week, 365 days a year, which leads to the HPA axis being triggered constantly and not turning off. As discussed before, the name for the constant triggering of the stress response is chronic stress. Therefore, the Vampire is a walking, talking source of chronic stress in the life of anyone in a relationship with one.

Clearly, a constant state of high alert is no way to live. Humans are not designed to live that way, and neither is any other animal. The issue here is that the impact of chronic stress can have effects on the individual that are very, very serious and in some cases fatal. Let's start with the list from earlier and take each in turn:

a) Increased heart rate and blood pressure can lead to Hypertension (high blood pressure), coronary disease, heart attack, stroke and potentially death.

b) Decreased digestion can lead to long-term digestive problems, intestinal pain, bowel problems and lack of appropriate nutrition

c) Dilation of blood vessels in the muscles, so blood is diverted from other body areas, which can lead to internal organ damage, sexual dysfunction and heart and lung problems

d) Release of Glucose (blood sugar) into the bloodstream can lead to diabetes, high cholesterol levels, heart disease and potentially death

e) Suppression of the immune system can lead to increased risk of infection, susceptibility to colds/flu, decreased ability to fight disease and potentially death

f) Increased muscle tension can lead to skeletal muscle problems, back and neck pain, headaches and/or migraine However, there are additional effects of chronic stress that go beyond this. Cortisol in the bloodstream is supposed to ensure that the body prepares for short-term action. We have already seen what happens to the body when it stays in the bloodstream over extended periods. What follows is a list of effects on the brain caused directly by high levels of Cortisol over extended periods of time.

1) Cortisol creates high levels of a chemical called Glutamate, which in turn creates molecules called "free radicals". These attack the walls of brain cells, killing them.

2) Cortisol causes the part of the brain that handles the emotion of fear (the Amygdala) to over-respond. Over time, the Amygdala becomes overactive, and actually gets larger, which makes the individual fearful on an on-going basis.

3) Cortisol stops the brain making a chemical called BDNF, which is used to make new brain cells, so fewer brain cells are made to replace the ones being destroyed

4) Cortisol stops the brain making Serotonin and Dopamine. These are the "happy chemicals" that allow us to feel pleasure. Lack of them is associated with depression

5) Cortisol stops a part of the brain called the Hippocampus from adding connections that allow memory and learning. The result is lack of short-term memory and an inability to learn

6) Cortisol stops a part of the brain called the Pre-Frontal Cortex from adding connections that allow for decision making. The result is indecision, confusion and impulsivity.

In short, the chronic stress of life with a Vampire causes extensive damage to the brain and the body. Targets end up physically ill, depressed, confused, fearful, indecisive, unable to remember or learn and with a brain in cellular free-fall. Life with a Modern Vampire is a threat to the body and the brain of the Target. The result could easily be both mental and physical illness and even death. This is not hyperbole, it is a fact.

The symptoms of PTSD and C-PTSD

People who experience chronic stress and traumatic stress are at very high risk of developing PTSD and C-PTSD. Both are the result of the continued stress response over long periods of time as we have already seen and/or exposure to traumatic experiences. If you're still in doubt about whether exposure to the Vampire is traumatic, please re-read Chapters 4, 5, 6 and 7. PTSD refers to Post Traumatic Stress Disorder. The symptoms of PTSD are many, and they account for everything the Survivor experiences emotionally during the Devaluation and Discard Stages of the Attack Cycle. Here's the list:

Flashbacks (feeling like the trauma is happening right now)

Intrusive thoughts and images (thoughts and memories

forcing themselves into everyday life)

Nightmares

Intense distress at real or symbolic reminders of the trauma

Pain, sweating, nausea or trembling

Panic when reminded of the trauma

Being easily upset or angry

Hypervigilance (extreme alertness)

Sleep disturbance or insomnia

Irritability

Lack of concentration

Being "on edge"

Recklessness or self-destructive behaviour

Wanting to keep busy

Avoiding reminders of the trauma

Amnesia (memory loss) of the trauma

Emotional numbness (not being able to feel normal emotions)

Feelings of detachment from the body

Being unable to be affectionate

Drug or alcohol abuse

Feelings of mistrust

Feelings of lack of safety

Believing that no-one understands

Self-Blame

Overwhelming feelings of Anger, Sadness, Guilt and Shame

Any Survivor will be able to relate to this list of symptoms, and the reason is simple: Survivors of the Attack Cycle usually suffer from PTSD to some degree. This is what the Vampire does to their Target. They assault their mind and leave them damaged on a biological level. This is the direct result of living with a disordered individual. The Vampire is devoting their entire time to tearing the Target apart for Narcissistic supply, dominating them, controlling them and manipulating them and the result is the physical devastation of the Target. The good news, however, is that the damage can be treated with work and guidance and I will be discussing that in Chapters 11 and 12.

C-PTSD refers to Complex PTSD. The "Complex" part of the title refers to trauma on an on-going basis. Therefore, many Survivors suffer from C-PTSD as a result of exposure to the Vampire. The symptoms of C-PTSD are the same as for PTSD but with the following additions:

Difficulty controlling emotions

Hostility or mistrust

Feelings of emptiness or hopelessness

Feeling worthless or damaged

Feeling different from others

Avoiding friendships or relationships

Experiencing "dissociative" symptoms, such as feeling unreal or not being present

Suicidal thoughts

Again, many Survivors will be able to relate to this experience and again, it accounts for their experience during the Attack Cycle. C-PTSD may have existed in the Target before they became involved with the Vampire, only to be made worse by their exposure to them, or it may have come about as a result of that exposure. In either case, the news is good. C-PTSD, like PTSD can be treated with professional help and Chapters 11 and 12 should help point Survivors in the right direction.

The addicted brain

As if all this wasn't enough, the Survivor or Target has also had an addiction induced by the Vampire, as described in Chapter 7. Addiction is nasty, not least because it takes quite a long time to recover from. The reason is simple: The brain has changed. It has been re-wired by the Vampire by the way they behave. Here's an outline of what happens in the brain of a person who is addicted to the behaviour of a Vampire.

During the Idealisation Stage, the Vampire bombarded the Target with attention, flattery, praise and all the stuff I've already talked about. At the same time, they Mirrored the Target to get them to believe they were a perfect match. What that achieved was getting the Target hooked on the Vampire's behaviours. What happens next is that the Target spends the whole relationship trying to get back to that initial "Honeymoon Period", which will never return because the Vampire lied. The whole thing was a fake.

During training, the Vampire reinforced the Target when the Target gave them Narcissistic supply. They also punished the Target when they didn't. What that did was work the pathways in the brain to do with two chemicals called Dopamine and Serotonin, and a part of the brain called the "Reward Centre". It runs on Dopamine with the help of Serotonin and it kicks off like crazy when it thinks it's going to get something good. Basically, it floods with Dopamine every time something good happens like nice food, fun stuff, sex, attention, you name it. Whatever the individual thinks is good will kick off the Reward Centre. That "rush" you get when you get something you like? That's your reward centre kicking off. The reward centre will also kick off just in anticipation of getting good stuff. That excitement you feel when you know you're going to get something good? Same thing.

But here's the thing. If you control the source of pleasure, you can manage when that reward centre kicks off. In an ideal world, we would all control our own sources of pleasure and could trigger our reward centres at will. The problem for Targets is that they have been convinced by the Vampire in the Idealisation stage to give up that control to the Vampire. They trusted that what was shown to them was real and would continue. The Target effectively surrenders their own ability to control the activity of their reward centre to the Vampire because they believe that the Vampire will continue to trigger it on an on-going basis the way they did in the beginning.

But what does the Vampire do with that? They exert control over all the good stuff, and start to starve the Target. They deny the Target any good stuff that would kick off the reward centre and dictate when and how much good stuff they get. The really messed up part of this is that the Vampires addictions to Narcissistic supply, Power and Control cause them to behave in ways that dictate how and when the Target receives the stuff that triggers their reward centre.

Controlling by withholding love and affection and using Silent Treatments are prime ways in which the Vampire gets their "hit", while at the same time denying the Target theirs. Essentially, the Vampire feeds their addictions by abusing the Target, and the Target sinks into withdrawal until the Vampire decides to throw them the proverbial bone. In other words, when the Vampire feeds their own addiction to the good stuff of Power and Control, they deny the Target the ability to feed their own addiction to the good stuff of whatever the Vampire has them hooked on.

What that creates is a Target that goes longer and longer in withdrawal while the Vampire stays longer and longer in gratifying their addictions. Plus, the Vampire can feed their addiction to Narcissistic supply by creating Drama whenever they feel like it. And, the Vampire also has the option of finding Narcissistic supply outside of the relationship while the Target does not, because they've been isolated.

The net effect is that the Vampire feeds their addiction at will, and the Target gets to feed their addiction when the Vampire says so. Not only that, but the Target has to work harder and harder to get even the smallest scrap of the good stuff from the Vampire and, over time, loses the physical and mental resources to do so. And what does the Vampire do with that? They attack the Target even more because the Target is not giving them Narcissistic supply. Tell me that deliberately getting someone hooked on supply that you deny them just because you want to while you get your fix whenever you want to isn't just plain evil. Go on, tell me. I dare you.

And then there's the mother of all hormones: Oxytocin. This one will keep Targets hooked into relationships for years, or possibly for life. Oxytocin is the hormone secreted by mammals in relation to bonding. It is sometimes known as the "Love Hormone" because it gets released during physical contact, sex, is heavily involved in maternal bonding and lactation and the feeling associated with its release is that feeling of "mmmmmmm" that we get when we have human contact. Oxytocin makes us want to touch people, to hug people, to kiss and caress, to make love.

In the right hands, Oxytocin will make you happy beyond your wildest dreams. In the hands of a Vampire, Oxytocin will make your life a living nightmare. Because and it's a big because, Oxytocin is also released during times of stress. It's the body's way of saying "for fuck's sake, get some human contact NOW". We all need people when we're stressed, right? That's Oxytocin at work. When a Vampire gets involved with all this stuff? It's Game Over for the Target.

In healthy relationships, Oxytocin just flows all over the place. It keeps couples together, gets them to make babies, gets them to raise those babies into healthy adults and makes the whole process pleasurable. Stress releases Oxytocin, and so does closeness, so they bond in times of hardship, which brings them closer, which releases more Oxytocin, which keeps them together and then they do the stuff that makes more babies. That's the magic of a healthy relationship, people. It's really cool and its basic biology.

At the same time that they are controlling the supply of Dopamine, the Vampire is also dictating the flow of Oxytocin in the Target. When humans are stressed, they release Oxytocin, and that makes them want to bond with others. What do we all want when we're stressed? Human contact, and what does the Vampire create more than anything else? Stress. But will they hug you? Why would they? They don't even like you, let alone love you. But that won't stop you wanting to, which is why Targets are constantly trying to re-establish closeness with the Vampire, while the Vampire has no interest in doing so, and will actively withdraw from contact with the Target in order to punish them.

When humans are separated from the people they have already bonded with, their Oxytocin levels go through the roof. You know that feeling of missing someone close to you when they go away for a few days? That's Oxytocin. But what is the Vampire's go-to form of punishment? You guessed it - the Silent Treatment. What does the Target's body do during that? It pumps out Oxytocin like there's no tomorrow.

And that's why Targets chase, and Vampires withhold. The Target wants to bond because they can and Oxytocin tells them to and the Vampire doesn't want to, couldn't even if they did and uses withdrawal of affection to punish the Target because they get off on it. And then there's the Discard. When the Vampire goes there, the Oxytocin levels in the Target don't just go through the roof, they go through the stratosphere. The Target's body is screaming at them: "Bond! Bond! Bond! Do it now! NOW!"

And that's why Targets go back time after time, which is why Hoovers work. The Targets Oxytocin driven impulse to bond overwhelms their good sense, tells them to do it at all costs, and when they do they actually feel better for doing it, even though they know it's wrong. We've all been there, right? It sucks, but it really does come down to basic biology.

That's what the Vampire does to the Target's biology. They mess with it to the point of addiction, mental and physical breakdown and even death. Essentially, the Vampire is an addict, addicted to Narcissistic supply, Power and Control. Being in a relationship with one will turn the Target into an addict, addicted to the behaviours of the Vampire.

Ask any Survivor how it feels to go and maintain "No Contact" (more on that later) and they will tell you it feels like coming off Heroin. The reason for that is simple: It IS like coming off Heroin. The structural and chemical changes in the brain of a Heroin addict and the Survivor are exactly the same.

Add to that the fact that the Survivor almost certainly has a dose of PTSD or C-PTSD and by the time the relationship is over, the Survivor is not only addicted to the behaviour of the Vampire, the experience has made them into someone they barely recognise as their former selves.

But you know what? It can be fixed. Chapters 11 and 12 talk about what can be done to tackle all the brain-scrambling the Vampire has done to the Target. PTSD and C-PTSD can be treated. Addiction can be recovered from. The damage can be repaired and a new and better life after the Vampire is not only possible, with the right treatment it is probable. Everything in this chapter is a description of what happens, not what will always be the case. Recovery from this damage is very, very do-able and it is the right of every Survivor to achieve it.

Well, that was tough going, huh? I reckon we need an Interlude, don't you?

Interlude 8

"What would you do with a brain if you had one?" – Dorothy, "The Wizard of Oz"

Hello again, dear Survivor!

    Well, it seems that I've set myself up quite a treat here, doesn't it? The last chapter was pretty serious, right? So, how to follow that with something funny? Well, I'm nothing if not optimistic, so I figured we could have some fun examining the Vampires brain and behaviours and figuring out what to call them. I thought it'd be a laugh to make up some terms for the various messed up parts of the brain of a Vampire and their equally messed up behaviours in the spirit of the awesome book "The Meaning of Liff" by Douglas Adams and John Lloyd.

If you haven't read it, read it. It's hilarious. The basic premise is to take a word that doesn't appear to have a meaning and then give it one, preferably a funny one. I have a good mind to make this an on-going project, so if you reckon you've got a doozy of a definition, please feel free to e.mail it across. The great thing about having a website devoted to this subject is that I can run a page devoted to fun stuff like this, so let's make this a thing in its own right and keep the laughs going. It's what life is for, after all.

And so, without further ado, here's the beginning of what I hope will be something we make together. I give you:

"The Vampire Encyclopedia"

Amphisbaena: The brain region responsible for categorising the ownership of joint resources into those belonging to the Vampire and those belonging to the Vampire.

Anfractuous: The behaviour of the Vampire at all times of happiness and celebration through which they communicate their general emotional malaise and seek to ruin the occasion. Creating drama, sulking, refusing to participate and demanding to leave are all examples of anfractuous behaviour.

Brabeum: The brain region responsible for identifying the least plausible reason for being annoyed about something and then fixating on it to the extent that that reason seems plausible to the Target, at which point the Vampire abandons the reason and accuses the Target of being petty.

Buccellation: The series of unconnected topics that the Vampire has specifically pre-planned to raise in order to turn the conversation into an argument so that they can return to the one point that can never be resolved without ending the relationship and have the Target either fall apart or promise to work harder.

Canitude: The behaviour of the Vampire by which they show excessively positive behaviours to everyone present at an event except the Target. This is especially evident when the Target has facilitated the entire event, in which case they will be subjected to an additional Silent Treatment.

Commendaces: Twin brain structures entirely devoted to deciding whether the Vampire is either the Victim of a narrative, or the Hero of it. Since their function can alternate, the same narrative may be told from either position, or both on any given occasion.

Diribitory: The kind of compliment routinely given by the Vampire that is actually an insult. For example: "You're pretty for a large girl", or "Most guys would care about their looks, but you're more confident than that".

Dodrantal: The brain region responsible for regulating how long a Silent Treatment should be applied for. Over extended periods, this region expands to the extent that it can erase all memory of why the Silent Treatment was initially applied, leaving the Vampire to imagine new reasons to justify its use.

Ensorcell: The region of the Vampire's brain that measures what is enough to make them happy. Scans have shown that this brain region is entirely unresponsive to any form of stimulus.

Embaphium: A specific behaviour on the part of a Vampire that defies the Vampires own logic. Stating that they would never do something, and then immediately doing that thing is an example of an embaphium.

Futz: The state of overload in the brain of a Vampire that comes about as a result of the successful application of Grey Rock. The derivative "Futzed" refers to the expression on the face of a Vampire that has just been denied all Narcissistic supply and now has no idea what to do.

Fuscous: The language used by a cornered Vampire when presented by hard evidence of their behaviour. Vague, contradictory and entirely lies, the objective when using fuscous language is to confuse the Target and allow the Vampire to escape the situation.

Gabelle: The brain region responsible for convincing the Vampire that nothing you're experiencing could ever come close to the time they experienced something so pathetically dissimilar it's not even in the same league as what you're experiencing.

Haruspex: While not actually connected to any brain region that allows for emotional expression, this brain region allows the Vampire to engage in extraordinarily bad simulations of emotion. When the Haruspex is fully engaged, the Vampire could win Anti-Oscars.

Incunabula: The enlarged brain region that allows the Vampire to perceive and adopt the Victim position in any interaction featuring more than two people. The Incunabula is highly active in Vampires and toddlers.

Jentacular: Any public behaviour on the part of the Vampire that would be perceived as harmless by others yet is specifically designed to inflict hurt on the Target with the express intent of causing them to become emotional in front of other people, and thus be labelled as "crazy" by the Vampire.

Krioboly: The embittered behavioural process whereby the Vampire ridicules and belittles the Targets achievements while simultaneously taking credit for them.

Labarum: The brain region responsible for perceiving the wants and needs of others and reacting in direct opposition to them via passive obstruction.

Loblolly: The region of the brain responsible for forgetting everything the Target has ever said to the Vampire and replacing it with what they want the Target to have said.

Minacious: Usually part of a Hoover, the behaviour of a Vampire in desperate Victim mode. Prolonged eye contact, puppy-dog expressions, crocodile tears, promises of change and above all, really bad acting are all examples of minacious behaviour.

Mumpsimus: The bizarre repetitive behaviour of one hand finger-to-thumb touching, nail clicking, or finger drumming that precedes an attack from the Vampire either out of boredom or premeditation.

Nepheliad: The brain region that handles all information about the Vampires appearance and attributes and categorises the people saying it in a hierarchy regardless of whether or not they are the Vampires partner or family. A fully engaged nepheliad accounts for why the Vampire has affairs, which they will attempt to explain to those they have cheated on.

Oncethmus: The brain region responsible for time management, in particular for ensuring that whatever disgusting behaviour the Vampire has done exists solely in the past and therefore should be "got over".

Ossifragant: The behaviour of a Vampire who has decided to abandon all hope of manipulating the Target and is simply projecting emotional bile directly at them instead. Spiteful, childish and hilariously obvious, ossifragant behaviour often precedes a discard.

Pinguid: The behavioural state of the Vampire in which they are not currently engaging in an attack on the Target, usually associated with a recent successful Hoover. Pinguid states are usually brief unless the Vampire is actually dead.

Pedicular: The brain region responsible for convincing the Vampire that they are right about something, even in the face of overwhelming, tangible, hard evidence. Scans indicate that this region may be composed of granite.

Quaeritate: The brain region that is responsible for converting everyday questioning about the Vampire's behaviours into all-out attacks on the Vampire's very existence. Research indicates that removal of the quaeritate renders the Vampire inert, because the procedure is fatal.

Quibbleism: The excessive and unreasonable questioning of the Target's behaviour regardless of logic, evidence or reason that arises simply as a result of the Vampire projecting their own behaviour onto the Target.

Rogalian: The behavioural state the Vampire adopts whenever they feel even remotely insecure. Rogalian behaviour involves attacking the Target endlessly until the Vampire is satisfied that the Target is more miserable than they are. This is a normal behavioural state for the Vampire.

Redamancy: The Vampires behavioural process of ensuring that all discussions end in circular arguments in which the Target has the choice to either concede, die of starvation and exhaustion, or both.

Sedecuple: The brain region responsible for disconnecting from reality. Research shows that the seducuple travels around the Vampire's brain limited only by the confines of the skull and can be employed to support the Vampires version of reality at will.

Speustic: The peculiar behaviour of the Vampire in which they leap to such a bizarrely disconnected subject during an argument they themselves started with such force that the Target is temporarily stunned.

Thysiastery: The odd behaviour of an ill-informed Vampire attempting to convince the Target that they are a Vampire. Relying on pseudo-psychology, projection and Gaslighting, thysiastery is the process of getting the argument catastrophically wrong and hoping the Target won't notice.

Urette: The brain region that allows the Vampire to claim all of the Targets positive qualities as their own while simultaneously projecting their own negative qualities onto the Target. Sometimes known as the "what the fuck cortex".

Veprecose: Comments made by the Vampire about what other people have said about the Target. Such comments are designed to induce doubt and fear in the Target and are always a part of the Vampire's narrative (i.e. lies).

Woundikins: The excessively hurt behaviour that is exhibited by the Vampire after the Target finally asks to be left alone following a nagging or attacking session that has gone on all day specifically for the purpose of getting the Target to ask to be left alone so that the Vampire can behave in an excessively hurt way.

Xenization: The behavioural process of finding out what's wrong with the Target's friends and family in the Vampires opinion and bringing it up whenever the Vampire feels attacked.

Yelve: The brain region that deals with self-examination. To date, no evidence has been found for the existence of the Yelve.

Zygostatical: The Vampires peculiar behaviour regarding their children in which they claim all glory for their achievements and all but disown them when they are anything less than perfect.

So there we are, folks. The beginnings of what I hope will become something fun as we go forward together. I'm serious about your contributions. As I see it, the Vampire is an attempted blight on our lives, and we don't deserve that. At the heart of it is a joke, and that joke is the Vampire themselves. They want us to take them seriously and the moment we do that they start to destroy us. The antidote is humour. Let's laugh at the very thing that can't stand to be laughed at. And let's do it for us. Deal?

And now, let's delve into Chapter 9. See you on the other side.

Chapter 9

The Psychological effects of the Attack Cycle on the Survivor

So, all that biology from the previous chapter must mean something, right? Well, yes. Everything that happens to humans in terms of their behaviour and experience has a biological basis. That's why these chapters follow the order they do, because once we understand the biological, the psychological makes more sense. And once we have our heads around that, the emotional experience makes sense too. With that in mind, I'd like to look at a couple of psychological phenomena here to explain what's going on "under the hood" of the Survivors experience.

The Trauma Bond

Trauma bonding is the psychological phenomenon that

keeps Targets trapped in relationships with Vampires and the Vampire sets up the trauma bond deliberately with the express purpose of keeping the Target trapped. Effectively, they hijack a normal human process and use it for their own ends, because trauma bonding is actually a normal process. Humans are designed to form trauma bonds with others as a means of survival. The experience of a threat to the survival of a group of individuals will lead to them working together, trusting each other, fighting together, fleeing together and so on.

We've all been there, right? At least on a small scale. That moment when an emergency has occurred among a group of strangers and suddenly all the normal boundaries and barriers we put up come down and now we're a group? That's healthy trauma bonding. Ever wondered why people are so happy in the company of someone they went on a rollercoaster with? They trauma bonded with each other. That shared experience of surviving the trauma brought them together. So in many ways, trauma bonding is actually a good thing because it helps humans co-operate in threatening situations for mutual benefit.

But trauma bonding can be extraordinarily dangerous. A commonly used example of trauma bonding is Stockholm syndrome, so called because it first came to light following a hostage situation during a bank robbery in Stockholm, Sweden in 1973. The hostages were under an immediate threat to their survival because their captors had the power to kill them, but they also had the power to save them from that fate. Over the course of 6 days, the captors exerted their power over the hostages and the resulting trauma caused the hostages to go to a psychologically "safe" place by befriending their captors.

Again, this is the hijacking of a normal human response. The hostages knew that if they fought their captors, they could die, but if they befriended them, they stood a better chance of survival. In other words, the hostages were working with their captors, and so the trauma bond was formed.

Other examples come from prisoner of war camps, particularly during the Korean War. Prisoners were routinely exposed to techniques used by their captors in which they were tortured (the trauma), then befriended (the survival), then tortured again (trauma), then befriended again (survival). The North Koreans used this technique to break the will of the prisoners and brainwash them, and it was highly effective. Once an individual has trauma bonded to their captor, they become extremely malleable and will accept the captor's version of reality simply as a means of survival.

The really scary part of all this is that Vampires use this exact technique to trap their Target in the relationship. Vampires by their very nature create trauma, and it is the creation of and alleviation from the trauma they create that sets up the cycle of Trauma-Survival dynamic that lies at the heart of the trauma bond.

The Attack Cycle is expressly designed to create a constant reoccurrence of trauma and survival in which the Target bonds with the very individual that is creating the threat to their psychological survival. Everything I described in the previous two chapters about training and the addicted brain comes into play here. The cycle of devaluation, punishment, intermittent reinforcement, Jackpotting, Surfing and so on creates a constant reoccurrence of Threat-Survival-Threat-Survival-Threat-Survival and the individual in charge of dictating that cycle is none other than the Vampire themselves.

Over time, the Target becomes addicted to that cycle and forms a trauma bond with the very individual that is creating the trauma. On a biological level, the chemical and structural changes that occur in the Target simply facilitate the trauma bond and serve to maintain it.

Once an individual is trauma bonded, they will go to great lengths to actually defend their abuser. They make excuses, deny the Vampires bad behaviour, justify it to others, claim responsibility, side with the Vampire against others, self-isolate, attack family and friends who criticise the Vampire, and unquestioningly accept the Vampires version of reality. The reason they do this is simple: It's safer to do all that than face their abuser. Remember, trauma bonding is about survival. Once the Target is trauma bonded, they will focus solely on ensuring that the Vampire does not attack them by doing everything in their power to appease them.

This is entirely why the questions "Why don't they just leave?" and "Why can't they just get over it?" are so fucking annoying and totally redundant. A person who has trauma bonded can't do either of these things because their biology won't let them, and neither will their training. Once a trauma bond has formed, it is incredibly resistant to being broken because it is a primal response in humans that goes all the way back to the dawn of civilization. We've been doing it for thousands of years, so a quick conversation over coffee with a concerned but ignorant other isn't going to break that trauma bond, now is it?

While I'm at it, the other statement that concerned but ignorant others have a tendency to say is something along the lines of "They must be addicted to the abuse, because they won't leave". That's not just ignorant, that's dangerous.

Targets are not addicted to abuse; they are trauma bonded. Suggesting that they are addicted to abuse is a form of victim-blaming, and it validates the Vampires behaviour. It's never acceptable and if you ever find yourself having someone say that to you, get the hell away from that person. They are not helping you, they are blaming you. In all probability, the person saying that is a Flying Monkey. As we'll see later, the only way to break a trauma bond is to get the hell away and stay the hell away from the Vampire that caused it and anyone who supports them.

Now, before I move on, a quick word of caution. In the vast majority of cases, Survivors who have been trauma bonded have an overwhelming fear of being alone. That is a direct result of the trauma bond, not a sign of weakness. The danger for trauma bonded Survivors is that they will be tempted to bond again quickly once their abuser has left. That is a really bad idea.

There is a name for individuals that can innately sense a trauma bonded individual: Vampire. They know exactly what they are doing, can recognise the handiwork of other

Vampires in the Survivor and will gladly step in to the role of the abuser if the Survivor tries to bond with them. Let's not forget that Vampires always appear to be "safe" in the Idealisation Stage, right? They're doing that on purpose. They want trauma bonded Survivors to believe that they will take care of them. In reality, nothing could be further from the truth. What they're actually doing is setting the stage for another trauma bond, and what would ensue would be a duplicate of the same abusive pattern.

Please, please, please don't do that. I will be talking about the "Big Year" later on, which is about how to break the trauma bond before entering another relationship, but for now please accept that trauma bonded Survivors are extremely vulnerable to attack from other Vampires and it is critical to not repeating the same pattern that the trauma bond is broken first.

Cognitive Dissonance

Cognitive Dissonance refers to the existence in the mind of two differing explanations of a situation or occurrence at the same time. The effect of that is to create anxiety, because humans are hard-wired to have a single explanation for things so that they can make sense of their world. Whenever we encounter conflicting narratives in life, we automatically seek to resolve the conflict so that we can feel safe. It's perfectly normal and natural and, just like with trauma bonding, we've been doing it since the dawn of time. Humans have a basic drive to render the world predictable and understandable. If we didn't do that, everything would appear to be random and chaotic, which translates into most people as "unsafe".

Resolving Cognitive Dissonance is therefore something we do so that the stories we tell ourselves about the world, ourselves and others make some sort of unified sense to us and we can get on with life with a sense of safety.

To illustrate that, I'll use an example. Let's say that you're out with some friends and you meet a stranger. You and your friends are chatting with this person and you go off to the bar. By the time you get back, one of your friends and this new person are in the middle of a heated argument about something. Naturally, you want to find out what's going on, so you ask. The new person tells you that your friend insulted you while you were away, and that they were defending you. Your friend tells you that the new person insulted you while you were away, and they were defending you.

Now you've got two versions of reality to contend with that are at odds with each other. You've got Cognitive Dissonance. In order to create a narrative you are comfortable with, you will have to decide who to believe, because you can't believe both people. In all probability, you will believe your friend, politely ask the new person to leave and get on with your evening. By doing so, you resolve the Dissonance and you can continue with your narrative that your friend loves you and will defend you, which makes you feel safe in the world.

The very real danger with Cognitive Dissonance is that the Vampire deliberately creates a version of reality that is at odds with actual reality, and then insists that you believe it.

The reason they do this goes back to the False Self. Vampires are liars. They lie to themselves about who they really are, and they lie to everyone else about who they really are in order to protect themselves from feelings of Shame.

The False Self they create is a protection against the world, and it is a complete fabrication. If they didn't create and maintain the False Self, they would be forced to look at what they really are and they will never, ever do that. Narcissistic supply serves to prop up the illusion they have created and without it, their False Self would come crashing down and the True Self would be revealed to the world. In other words, their narrative about the world and their place in it is completely distorted. The reality they live in and actual objective reality are two completely different things. If they were forced to accept actual, objective reality, even for a moment, they would quite simply lose their minds.

The Vampire has no way of admitting that the False Self they have created is a lie, because even attempting to do that would mean that all their feelings of Shame are real. Not only that, they would have to accept that that is all they are. This is never, ever going to happen. Instead, the Vampire seeks out constant sources of Narcissistic supply to feed the False Self, to reinforce the distorted reality they are projecting out into the world. The more that false reality is reinforced, the more they believe it and the more they believe it, the more they seek Narcissistic supply to reinforce it.

This is why they will never change. They would have to dismantle their very existence to do so. What you end up with is an individual that must insist for their very survival that what they are telling you about who they are and how the world is are true, despite the fact that it is all the direct opposite of actual, objective reality and demonstrably false. In other words, everything a Vampire says about themselves and the world creates Cognitive Dissonance.

This process of pushing the false narrative starts When the Target first meets the Vampire. In the Idealisation Stage, the Vampire creates the illusion that they are a good person because that is what they need to believe about themselves. They project their false version of reality about themselves and they do it extraordinarily well because it is crucial to their existence that they believe it, and even more importantly that the Target believes it. But this amount of effort can't be sustained for long, which is why that initial period tends to be brief.

However, what does occur is that the "Uber-False Self" the Vampire created during that phase is what the Target will be trying to get back for the rest of the relationship. That's never going to happen, of course, but at least now we know why. It's because none of it was ever true, and once the Vampire realised that they had the Target hooked, they could start dropping the act and working on the addiction in the Target instead. The big question here is "Does the Vampire know they are doing this?" Yes. Yes, they do know. The Vampire knows that their False Self is false, they just choose to ignore that and convince themselves that it is true anyway, and the more Narcissistic supply they receive, the easier it is for them to delude themselves.

So, given the Vampires compulsion to feed and project

the False Self, how does that play out in creating and maintaining Cognitive Dissonance? Well, it happens all day every day. Objective reality and the Vampires reality are two completely different things. If the Vampire accepted objective reality, they would have to endure the agony of realising what they truly are and dealing with all their Shame, so they just don't. Instead, they systematically go about convincing the Target that their reality is true, the Targets reality is false, and anyone who disagrees with the Vampire about their reality about themselves is a threat to the relationship.

This should be sounding familiar by now. It's Gaslighting, and the whole reason the Vampire does it is to control reality. In any objective reality the Vampire would be exposed for what they truly are, so the imposition of their false reality is of paramount importance to them. They will not tolerate any contradiction of their false reality and will do whatever it takes to make sure that never happens.

During the Devaluation Stage, the Vampire works on the Targets sense of reality. They Gaslight them so that they would believe that they were at fault, meaning the Vampire can maintain the False Self. They criticise them to run down their Self Respect, so that the Vampire can maintain the superiority of the False Self. They never accept responsibility for their behaviours, because in their minds the False Self doesn't do such things.

They project all their negativity onto the Target, because in their minds the False Self has no negativity. They create Fear, Obligation and Guilt in the Target to ruin their Self Respect, so that the Vampire can maintain the False Self's illusory status as worthy of love and admiration. If you take a look back at Chapters 4 and 5 on Weapons and Tactics and consider each in turn, it is very easy to see how they are all used to maintain the False Self as the only version of reality in the relationship.

Normal, healthy people don't need to insist on reality because reality is just reality. But Vampires do, because they know that their reality is false. They spend all day every day trying to impose a twisted, distorted reality onto those around them in order to exist without collapsing in on themselves and using Narcissistic supply to fuel the process. The combined effect of being with a Vampire is that two versions of reality exist in the mind of the Target: the real, objective version and the Vampire's false version. The Target ends up never being able to reconcile the two, or if they do, they are forced to accept the Vampires version, because it is being insisted upon all day every day. Sooner or later, the Target just buckles under the pressure.

Once the relationship is over, however, the Survivor is left to piece back together the nature of reality. By the time they have escaped or been discarded the Survivor often simply does not know the nature of reality. What is to be believed? The Vampires version in which they are perfect and the Survivor is the bad guy? The Vampires version in which the Survivor was the abuser? The Vampires version in which the Survivor believes that the Vampire will be happy with the new supply?

Or actual, objective reality?

This is often one of the hardest parts to deal with, because Cognitive Dissonance as a result of emotional abuse is very little understood by the general public. It is generally only other Survivors and therapeutic professionals that really get it because let's face it, what the Vampire told the Target makes no fucking sense whatsoever, does it?

Therefore, how can people who don't get it expect the Survivor to make any fucking sense? This is why it was so easy for the Vampire to claim that the Target was the "crazy one", because people who are trying to make sense of basic reality sound crazy! The Vampire sounds fine, because their version of reality makes sense, at least to them. But the Target has two versions going on and that is the definition of "Crazy-Making". And after the relationship ends, the dissonance usually continues until it is healed.

But here' the great news: It can be healed. Time, self-love and compassion and a good therapeutic professional can help the Survivor remove all the Cognitive Dissonance from their mind and return to objective reality once more. Just like with PTSD and C-PTSD and overcoming the addiction the Vampire created, Survivors can and do recover from this.

And, just like with the Trauma Bond, it is vital to get away and stay away from the Vampire and their Flying Monkeys, who will seek to push the Vampires version of reality.

Moreover, it is essential to avoid new relationships until the Cognitive Dissonance is gone. Vampires admire each other's work and it would take no time at all for one to realise that the Survivor has been subject to Cognitive Dissonance. They find that out in the Idealisation Stage. Once they have that, all they need to do is put their name on the false reality instead and the whole cycle repeats again.

Please, please, please do not allow them to do that. Again, I will be explaining the "Big Year" later on in Chapter 12 but for now, if you are a Survivor suffering with Cognitive Dissonance, please stay away from relationships. The risk of attack by another Vampire is way too high.

OK, so that's a look at the psychological effects. All that stuff is pretty scary, right? I think we need an interlude, don't you?

Interlude 9

"Comedy is acting out optimism" – Robin Williams

Hello again, dear Survivor!

So, we've just been through quite a journey into the psychology of surviving a Vampire and I thought it would be fun to spend some time exploring my favourite psychological phenomenon: Comedy. Specifically, I'd like to have a light-hearted look at how humour can be used as an antidote to the Vampire's ridiculously serious behaviour. Before we get started, though, a word of caution. Do not, under any circumstances, share what you're about to read here with a Vampire. They don't get it, they don't think it's funny, and it's guaranteed to upset them and you don't want that. Safety first, OK?

OK, so ever noticed how the Vampire hates to be laughed at? How even the slightest light-hearted mockery will send them into a rage? There's a reason for that: They don't understand comedy, and they think you're attacking them because that's what they think comedy is. Poke fun at a secure adult and they'll laugh along with you. But you try poking fun at a Vampire and they go all the flavours and colours of crazy. But why is that the case? Bear with me, I'm getting there.

It seems to me that there are 3 components to good comedy. The first is that it involves people failing at things. Success isn't funny; failure is. If it's human to fail, and comedy is human, then failure is comedy, right? The second is that when people fail, they fail because of themselves. Ever gone looking for a remote control you're actually holding? Ever looked for the glasses or sunglasses that are on your head? You did that to yourself, that's funny. The third is optimism. When we see people trying, and failing, and trying again, we feel their optimism and we feel for them. We share their optimism that they will succeed and we celebrate when they do, however short-lived that may be.

In other words, we engage in empathy. To my mind, if you have those 3 things going on, you've got comedy. I also believe that we're really not laughing at characters that do those things, we're laughing with them because they could easily be us. We're actually laughing at ourselves. We share their human failings and we share their optimism and that's what makes the world go round.

There's a 5 minute video on Youtube of the character Nials from the show "Frasier" which starts with him wanting to iron out the tiniest crease in his trousers and trying to do so involves him destroying the trousers, the sofa, his dinner, and ends with him passing out. At no point did any accidents occur; he caused the whole thing himself. He failed, he failed because of himself, and throughout the whole thing he believed he could fix it. Hilarious. But we're not laughing at him, we're laughing because that could be us. We've all made things worse while trying to fix them and that's why it's funny.

And then there's what I call "Mean Comedy". That's the one where people really are laughing at other people. The German word "Schadenfreude" refers to "pleasure derived by someone from another person's misfortune." The waitress is tripped by a customer, drops a tray of glasses and you laugh at that? That's Schadenfreude. That's not comedy, my friends, because it lacks 2 of the 3 required components to be comedy. It's just plain mean. She failed at something, and only a Vampire would find that funny on its own.

See, Vampires are mean, they love Schadenfreude, and they don't have the capacity to identify with others which means they never sense the optimism that is inherent in comedy. They laugh at, not with, and will settle for a person's failure as a source of amusement because they can't see the second component and are incapable of the third component. If someone fails at something, they don't discriminate between whether the cause of that failure was external or the person themselves, they just laugh.

And they are natural pessimists, as any Target or Survivor will tell you. They suck all the fun out of things because they're always finding fault, or causing an issue, right? The Vampire is incapable of seeing the optimism inherent in comedy because they aren't capable of it themselves. In other words, Vampires are very basic and they have a crappy sense of humour.

And what's worse, they assume that everyone else is doing the same because they lack empathy. They assume that, because when they laugh at someone it's coming from their world view, when you laugh at them, that's coming from the same place. Because Vampires just don't get comedy. Not in the slightest. It's part of the reason why they're so bloody exhausting.

Oh, they love a good laugh but it's always at someone else's expense, and they never, ever laugh at themselves. And God forbid you should laugh at them, because as far as they're concerned, that laughter is coming from the same place it does when they do it. As they see it, you aren't laughing with them, even if they've just been utterly ridiculous, you're laughing at them.

Now, I issued words of caution about this whole thing earlier and I'm going to do it again. Please don't laugh at a Vampire. They don't get it, and they don't think it's funny. In fact, they think you're attacking them because that's what they're doing when they do it. I speak from experience here because I tried it once. The Vampire pushed me down a flight of stairs. I know they don't get it, and I know you know they don't get it either.

We both know that it's just plain tiring having to explain to a Vampire that you're not laughing at them when they did something ridiculous, right? They would like us all to think that what they think is funny really is, but they're just plain wrong. What they think is funny isn't funny. It's mean.

Comedy isn't mean. It's wonderful. It's human, it's optimistic, it's sharing and it cares. It's silly, and it's frivolous and no-one gets hurt. Comedy is another way that humans can show that they understand each other. For as long as there are humans, comedy will always be with us and I think that's great. I also happen to believe that it's the antidote to the Vampires ridiculously serious behaviours. Just because they take themselves seriously doesn't mean we have to. Just because they laugh at people doesn't mean we're laughing at them. Just because they don't get it doesn't mean we have to explain it, or sink to their level. We are truly blessed to be able to engage in great comedy, and I see no reason to throw that away just because the Vampires among us can't.

This whole book is designed to be funny to some extent, but that doesn't mean I'm laughing at the Vampire, I'm laughing at their behaviour, because they behave in comedy ways just like all humans do. That they don't get it is not my fault and not my problem any more than it is yours. If they want to have their form of comedy and take themselves seriously, and be mean, let them. We don't have to do that. We can just go right on laughing with each other about the silliness of the world and let them get on with it. Just don't tell them you know the secret, OK?

Right, then. Off we go into Chapter 10. See you on the other side.

Chapter 10

The Emotional effects of the Attack Cycle on the Survivor

Now that we've looked at the biological and psychological effects on the Survivor, we can now take a look at the emotional effects. As I stated before, I believe that the emotional stems from the psychological, and the psychological stems from the biological.

However, it is the emotional effects that are the most powerful in our experience of being with a Vampire. They are how we feel during and after a relationship with one that dominate our lives, and that's completely normal. Emotions are there to tell us something. That's what they do. When we feel afraid, there's a threat. When we feel happy, there's something good going on. When we feel angry, we're defending ourselves. In normal, healthy interactions and relationships, our emotions are there to guide us in how best to navigate that experience. Having those emotions validated tells us that what we feel is real and that we are experiencing is actually happening in reality. Normal, healthy partners listen to each other's emotional experiences. They validate them, and therefore our reality. They understand how we feel and they honour and respect that.

The Vampire does not do any of that. It's so important to remember that the Vampire has no capacity for empathy. They don't understand the Targets feelings and what's more, they don't care. They will not listen to the Targets expressions of their emotions unless those expressions are serving to give them Narcissistic supply. Even then they don't care because they can't care. All they know is that the Target is providing them with attention. Whether the Target is angry at them, fearful of them, happy around them, sad at what they've done doesn't matter. None of it matters. They simply don't care.

What's more, the Vampire will never validate any emotion in the Target that does not align with their False Self. If the Target is expressing an emotional response about something the Vampire has done that goes against their version of reality, they will invalidate that response. Basically, they will tell the Target directly that they are wrong for feeling that emotion and that there is something wrong with them because of it. To the Vampire, their emotional reality is the only one that matters. They will never accept any other version of reality, and that most certainly includes that of the Target. The Vampire will never respect or honour the Targets emotions if they run contrary to their false narrative.

What the Vampire will do, however, is provoke emotional responses in the Target in order to validate their own existence. If the Target is not responding emotionally to what the Vampire does, they are effectively invalidating the Vampires entire existence. There's a phrase that sums this up nicely: "Love me or Hate me, just don't ignore me". That's what goes on in the head of a Vampire all day every day, and they are compelled to provoke emotional responses in the Target to make sure that attention keeps flowing towards them.

The real mind-fuck for the Target is that once the emotional response has been provoked, whether it is validated or not depends on the extent to which it chimes with the Vampires False Self. Therefore, some emotional responses are "allowed" in the Vampires reality and others aren't. Adoration, Excitement, Love and all the positive emotions are "allowed". Sadness, Anger, Frustration and all the negative emotions are not "allowed". They don't make the Vampire feel good and therefore don't support the False Self. Those emotions will be invalidated, ignored and turned back on the Target because the Vampire doesn't "allow" them in their false reality. What's occurring is that the Vampire is having their emotional needs met whenever they want, and in doing so they are ensuring that the emotional needs of the Target are met as close to never as possible.

It's not just that they don't care about the Target's emotional needs. That's bad enough. What's worse is that they get off on denying the Target their emotional needs because it makes them feel superior. Their False Self dictates that they must be superior to the Target, and denying them their emotional needs achieves exactly that.

And that's where the emotional damage starts to set in. Because the Vampire only wants an emotional response to validate their existence, they will provoke those responses at will. If the response is positive, the Vampire wins because they get to prop up the False Self and feel superior to the Target because they provoked that emotional response. But if those responses are negative, the Vampire wins again. They will use them to invalidate the Target, undermine their Self Respect, paint them as having "anger issues" or being "crazy", claim the victim position and then sit there calmly enjoying all the attention they are getting while simultaneously hurting the Target and enjoying that too. Make no mistake about this.

It is deliberate, malicious torture and to the Vampire, it's a fucking game. It serves to prop up the False Self and make the Vampire feel superior to the Target. It's basically Win-Win for the Vampire and Lose-Lose for the Target. As a wise man once said:

"The only way to win is not to play."

Before I go any further, I want to make one thing abundantly clear. The emotional damage caused by the Vampire can be repaired. In the same way as the biological and psychological damage can be fixed, so can the emotional. There is always hope, dear Survivor. Always.

OK, so let's take a look at some basic human emotional needs and then ask how many of them are met in a relationship with a Vampire.

accepted	free	private
acknowledged	fulfilled	productive
admired	heard	reassured
appreciated	helped	recognised
approved of	helpful	respected
believed in	important	safe / secure
capable	in control	supported
cared about	included	treated fairly
challenged	listened to	trusted
clear (not confused)	loved	understanding
competent	needed	understood
confident	noticed	valued
forgiven & forgiving	powerful	worthy

I would argue that in the Idealisation Stage, as many of those needs the Target has will be met by the Vampire, probably to excess. However, once the Devaluation Stage begins, the Vampire will systematically cease to meet them until they have stopped even trying to meet them at all. By the time the Target is in full Devaluation, not only is the Vampire not making any effort to meet those needs, they are actively making the Target feel wrong for even having them. Any and all emotional needs the Target has will be invalidated by the Vampire if they don't chime with the False Self.

But more significantly, if the Vampire believes that fulfilling those emotional needs will threaten their superiority over the Target (which is part of the False Self), those needs will not only go unmet, they will be used against the Target to paint them as "weak", "needy", "clingy", "crazy" and the personal favourite of the Vampire: "Abusive".

That's right, folks. The Vampire actually believes that having emotional needs that mean that the Vampire has to do something they don't want to do, like caring for the Target is abuse. That's how they always manage to come off to Flying Monkeys and the world in general as the Victim. They truly believe in the False Self, and that the Target is the abuser because they demand something from them that essentially criticises that False Self. Asking a Vampire to do something they are incapable of doing (like caring for another person) makes them feel threatened because in their mind, the False Self is already doing that.

The False Self is loving and caring, right? The False Self is wonderful, right? Therefore, anything the Target needs must be unreasonable, right? And the more they ask for those basic things that normal, healthy humans have a right to ask for in a relationship, the more demanding and abusive they are right?

Wrong. Totally wrong. All the different colours and flavours of wrong. Wrong all day, week, month and year and wrong six ways to Sunday. But can you tell a Vampire that? Not a chance in hell. You might as well be talking astrophysics to a chimp.

Now take another look at that list. How many of the Vampire's emotional needs on it are being met by the Target? I would say all of them, wouldn't you? Now, call me old-fashioned, but I happen to think that's unbalanced. The Vampire wins at every turn in the emotional needs stakes, and the Target loses at every turn. And the real bastard of it all is that is exactly what the Vampire wants. They want the Target to have none of their needs met, while they get all of their needs met and they want to hurt the Target as much as possible in the process to prove their superiority over them.

That, Ladies and Gentlemen, is what you're dealing with. On an emotional level, the Vampire wants all of their needs met while giving nothing back, using every single opportunity to punish the Target for even existing in the process and claiming they are the Victim of the whole thing. Tell me that isn't the definition of insane. Go on. I dare you. To illustrate how this all plays out, let's take a look at the Attack Cycle and how the Target feels at each Stage of the Attack Cycle.

The Idealisation stage.

Ask any Survivor what this stage felt like at the time and they will tell you that it felt amazing. Ask them what it feels like looking back after the Discard stage and they will tell you that it feels fake. That's because it was fake. Survivors are often encouraged to carry out a thought experiment in recovery. I was taught this by my Therapist. It goes like this:

"Imagine the Vampire walking toward you the first time you met them. They are wearing a T-shirt with one word on it that describes your first impression of them. What is that word?"
"Now imagine the Vampire walking away from you after the Discard. On the back of that T-shirt is one word that describes them now. What is that word?"

The truth of the matter is that the word on the back is what the Vampire really is. What they presented in the first

Stage of the Attack Cycle was a lie. During that stage, the Vampire was engaging in an attack, of course, but the attack was different to the other stages. In this stage, the attack took the form of attempting to overwhelm the Target and rush them into a relationship.

The Vampire knows full well that they need to lock down the Target and secure them as a source of Narcissistic supply. This is when they are doing two things, both related to the Targets emotional needs. First, they are figuring out what the Targets emotional needs are and overwhelming them with whatever they happen to be. Everyone is different in terms of emotional priorities and the Vampire needs to tailor their approach based on the information they gain here. Second, they are mining the Targets past to find out what their weaknesses will be. They will want to know everything about the Target in order to know where their weak spots are.

Does the Target fear being alone? Does the Target feel shameful about something in their past? How did other Vampires successfully hurt the Target? The Vampire will come off initially as entirely attentive to the Targets emotional needs, not because they want to be, but because they are figuring out what works. Yes, it really is that calculated.
All that attention to the Targets emotional needs will ensure that they drop their guard and let the Vampire in, so to speak.

On an emotional level, this creates an emotional experience that looks like this:

During the Idealisation Stage, the Target feels:

Special to the Vampire
Important to the Vampire
Powerful as an individual
Desired by the Vampire
Similar to the Vampire
Perfectly matched
Fulfilled emotionally
Deeply in love

All of this is deliberate on the part of the Vampire and none of it is true. Occasionally, the Vampire will return to the behaviours they showed here if they think they are about to be discovered, but once this Stage has been effectively carried out and the Target is locked into the relationship, the Vampire will move to the Devaluation Stage. This will be a gradual process, because otherwise the Target would notice, but it is happening and it will get worse.

The Devaluation Stage

This is the Stage where the emotional damage will be done. The Vampire will start to drop the mask of the False Self and reveal their true intentions for the Target: To Dominate, Control, Manipulate and Destroy them.

Have another look at the Weapons and Tactics chapters while you consider this Stage. They will all be employed with the goals set out above. In terms of emotional needs, the Targets needs will gradually be ignored, undermined and used against them while the Vampires needs will be elevated to the position of prime importance in the relationship. This was the goal all along. The Vampire aimed to get the Target into a position whereby they would serve the Vampires emotional needs without any regard for their own, and no regard for their needs from the Vampire either.

Make no mistake, the Vampire feels fully entitled to do this. This is what the Vampire calls love. As far as they are concerned, they are superior to the Target, and therefore ignoring their emotional needs is completely normal. Because they feel superior, they feel entitled to everything the Target has to offer and as far as they are concerned, the Target has no needs. In a bizarre twisteroo of thinking, the Vampire views the Targets emotional needs as a sign of weakness, completely ignoring the objective fact that the truly weak one in the relationship is themselves. It's all about the False Self. They've managed to convince themselves that their needs are minimal, or normal, because they have completely cut off from their true, needy selves.

Essentially, they are a bottomless pit of emotional needs that they completely deny exists. They will never see the objective truth of the situation, and any attempt to show them will result in them attacking the Target. The upshot of all this is, of course, that the Target never has their emotional needs met, are attacked for expressing them, are accused of being "weak", "needy", "clingy", "crazy" and "abusive" while all the time the Vampire is insisting that the Target meets their emotional needs. It's exhausting and crazy-making. Rather like raising a toddler because, emotionally, that's exactly what they are. The Vampire is a permanent emotional child.

During the Devaluation Stage, the Target feels:

Powerless to resist the Vampire
Entirely responsible for the relationship
Fearful of losing the relationship
Fearful of the judgement of the Vampire
Fearful of the judgement of others
Guilty for their actions, or lack of them
Obliged to stay in the relationship
That they don't matter
That they are unlovable
That they cannot survive alone
That their future depends on the Vampire.

When compared, these two lists of phrases look very, very different. Here they are, side by side:

Idealisation Stage	**Devaluation Stage**
Special to the Vampire	Powerless to resist the Vampire
Important to the Vampire	Entirely responsible for the relationship
Powerful as an individual	Fearful of losing the relationship
Desired by the Vampire	Fearful of the judgement of the Vampire

Similar to the Vampire	Fearful of the judgement of others
Perfectly matched	Obliged to stay in the relationship
Fulfilled emotionally	That they don't matter
Deeply in love	That they are unlovable
	That they cannot survive alone
	That their future depends on the Vampire

The Discard Stage

And then comes the inevitable Discard. Before I go there, I'd just like to point out how incredibly powerful Survivors are. Look back at that list of emotional needs. How many of them did the Target get met by the Vampire? None of them. How many of them did they meet for the Vampire? All of them. And how long did that go on for? Months? Years? Decades?

Survivors are incredible. They can meet the emotional needs of another individual while receiving only abuse in return. And they can do it for years, and years, and years. That's staggering. When the Discard finally arrives, it will be for one of two broad reasons. Either the Target is just plain exhausted and can't meet the excessive demands of the

Vampire any more, or they got wise to what was going on and either changed so that they started looking after their own needs and they stopped looking after the Vampires needs. In any event, the Discard occurs because the Vampire knows that they cannot rely on the Target to fill their endless void of emotional needs.

So why is the Discard so brutal? Why does it make no sense at all? Why is there never any closure? Because the Vampire is crazy, that's why. As far as the Vampire is concerned, the Target has failed to do their job, and they resent that. Remember, the Vampire feels superior to the Target and entitled to everything they have to offer, so how dare they stop functioning as a means of fulfilling the Vampires emotional needs? Their lack of Empathy, sense of entitlement, sense of superiority derived from the False Self and total disregard for the Target as anything other than a source of Narcissistic supply puts the Vampire in a position in which they feel entirely justified in throwing the Target away as they would a broken appliance.

In many cases, the Vampire is actually outraged that the Target is no longer "doing their job". They take it personally. And because they take it personally, they want to hurt the person who they see as hurting them as much as they possibly can. I know I say this a lot, but tell me that's not the definition of crazy. Go on. I dare you.

On an emotional level, the Discard Stage is without doubt the most painful Stage. At this point, the Vampire has absolutely no inclination to wear the mask of the False Self at all. They are done with the Target now, and want them to know exactly how they have "failed" them.

This is the point at which the Target finally gets to meet the Vampire face-to-face, because what they show here is precisely who they really are. In part, that's why it hurts so much, because the Target gets to see just how much of an illusion they were dealing with all along. Make no mistake here, the Vampire has been building up that resentment for some time because they are grudge-holders. They will have filed away every single "failure" of the Target to meet their emotional needs and now is the time they unleash it all. It's also the time that the Vampire will unleash all the Shame, Rage, Fear and Envy that they could not keep at bay because the Target wasn't providing the necessary Narcissistic supply to do so.

In short, the Discard gives the opportunity to the Vampire to finally reveal themselves for what they are, take out all that resentment on the Target, use them as an emotional toilet for all their Shame, Rage, Fear and Envy and then walk away.
So how does that leave the Survivor feeling? Like this:

During the Discard Stage, the Target feels:
Guilty and Shameful
Emotionally devastated
Uncertain and Fearful about the future
Paralysed
Self-Loathing

All of this was deliberate on the part of the Vampire and all of it was done to maximise the probability that the Target would remain in place, be unable to move on with their life, continue to abuse themselves in the absence of the Vampire and remain vulnerable to future attacks.

Again, the experience of the Survivor in Stage 3 of the Attack Cycle is enormously different to that of Stage 1. Here they are side by side:

Idealisation Stage	**Discard Stage**
Special to the Vampire	Guilty and Shameful
Important to the Vampire	Emotionally devastated
Powerful as an individual	Uncertain and fearful about the future
Desired by the Vampire	Paralysed
Similar to the Vampire	Self-Loathing
Perfectly matched	
Fulfilled emotionally	
Deeply in love	

The Hoover Stage

It is an experience common to all Survivors following the Discard Stage that they do not recognise themselves. The disparity between how they felt at the start and end of the relationship is vast. It is for this reason that it is imperative that the Survivor realises that the Discard represents an opportunity to escape the Attack Cycle. At this point, they are enormously vulnerable to attack from the Vampire during the Hoover Stage of the Attack Cycle.

On an emotional level, what has occurred is that the Vampire has finally revealed their True Self, unleashed their full fury at the Target for "failing" to serve their needs, blasted them with all the Shame, Rage, Fear and Envy they can no longer contain and then departed. What the Discard Stage afforded the Vampire was an opportunity to "get clean". Once they spewed all their disgusting negativity into the Target, they really thought they could start over again with a new Target and that everything would be different.

That's how delusional they are. Because of their denial of the True Self, they simply don't get that all those negative emotions will keep coming back over and over again. And, because they don't get it, they expect that the new Target will save them from all those feelings. And yes, they really are that delusional. If they weren't so vile, it would be funny.
But of course that won't work. The source of the Vampires negative feelings is themselves.

After a while, once the Idealisation Stage with the new source of Narcissistic supply has ended and the Devaluation

Stage is underway, the Vampire will completely fail to understand the basic truth of objective reality: That they are the cause of all of their problems. Their False Self just won't let this happen. After all, they're never to blame, right? And that may create a problem for the unwary Survivor, because the Vampire might come back. In the Hoover Stage, Survivors who are not actively working on their recovery are vulnerable to the attacks of the Vampire due to the simple fact that they are still where the Vampire left them at the Discard Stage. If the Survivor hasn't moved on, the Vampire can find a way back in. We've all been there.

If the Vampire does come back, they will attempt to Idealise the Target the same way they did in the First Stage. All too often, this is successful. It's tragic, but like I said, we've all been there. I'm not going to go into great detail here because the emotional experience of being Hoovered is uncannily similar to Idealisation, and we all know how that goes. Suffice to say that all too often, Hoovers work and the Survivor winds up feeling the exact same way they did in the beginning, so when we put the experiences side by side, they look like this:

Idealisation Stage	**Hoover Stage**
Special to the Vampire	Special to the Vampire
Important to the Vampire	Important to the Vampire
Powerful as an individual	Powerful as an individual
Desired by the Vampire	Desired by the Vampire

Similar to the Vampire	Similar to the Vampire
Perfectly matched	Perfectly matched
Fulfilled emotionally	Fulfilled emotionally
Deeply in love	Deeply in love

It really doesn't take a genius to work out that the emotional experience in the Hoover Stage is exactly the same as in the Idealisation Stage. But, like I said at the start, we can only understand the emotional effects once we understand the psychological and biological effects. Everything that occurs at the emotional level is driven by the psychological and biological. Therefore, despite the very natural tendency to blame ourselves for our feelings, we can rest assured that none of it is our fault. I'm going to say that again, dear Survivor.

None of your emotional experience is your fault.

As a Survivor, you were subjected to a sustained, deliberate and malicious attack on your very being. Your emotional experience is a result of the psychological and biological trauma you experienced at the hands of a disordered individual. You did not invite this and neither did you deserve it. The Vampire knew exactly what they were doing every step of the way.

The only thing that matters now is that you accept the statement above and take action based on it. Just as with the psychological and biological effects, the emotional effects can be repaired. People recover from them every day, and so can you. In the next chapters, I'll be talking about how to move forward and recover from this and I promise you can.

For now, please, please, please remember that the emotional experience is not the be-all-and-end-all. It is a symptom of the psychological and biological damage that the Vampire has inflicted. All of these levels of damage can be healed.

OK. That was heavy. Interlude, anyone?

Interlude 10

"I put a dollar in a change machine. Nothing changed." - George Carlin.

Hello again, dear Survivor!

So I was reading this article recently on why giving advice to people won't change their behaviour and thought it might be fun to see how it applies to the Vampire. It was fascinating stuff, and all of it completely true. There's a bunch of research out there on "reactance theory" that backs up the idea that people just don't listen to advice. Not only that, they actively push back against it, even if they've asked for it. Odd behaviour, but distinctly human. Like losing your keys, or forgetting why you opened the fridge.

Just like you, I've been in situations where I've offered advice to people who've asked and had them ignore it, do the opposite or do nothing at all. Fair enough, of course. It's their life and they can do what they want with it, but I was always left feeling a bit weird because I wondered why they asked in the first place. It's one of those things I've learned and I hope you have too, or do learn if you haven't. If people directly ask me for advice now, I either don't give it, ask them what they think instead and let them walk towards their own answers, or give it and walk away from any hope that they will take it. It's just not worth it to expect anyone to take advice because that's not what humans do.

What humans do, apparently, is they have a kind of reflex when given advice. It's a kind of "up yours" reflex. No-one likes to be told what to do, right?

What does work, though is modeling. Not strutting about a catwalk, that would be silly. What modeling means in this context is being the example of the behaviour you want to see in others. If you really want someone to do something, do it first and have them observe you doing it. Whatever reward you're getting from doing it will be observed and DING! Light bulb Moment! The other person will start to adopt that behaviour to get the same reward! There you go, a bit of free information on how to get people to do stuff. Don't advise; Model.

So, how does that apply to the Vampire? Well, I'm going to go out on a limb here and say that it doesn't. I reckon that modeling only works when people can see the benefit of what you're doing, change their motivation to do that thing and then do it. It's what I call the "why should I? hypothesis". Why should I change my behaviour? Well for most people that's easy: because it gets you rewards if you do. They see the motivation to change and off they go. Change the motivation, change the behaviour. But Vampires don't think like normal people, do they? The Vampire only has one motivation: Dominate and Control to obtain Narcissistic supply.

Let's take an example. We all know how infuriating it is to try to explain why being a decent person is a good idea to a Vampire, right? It makes you want to blow your brains out, doesn't it? It's like talking to a wall, or your cat. Actually, your cat is more likely to listen. So let's say the behaviour we're looking for is the Vampire to stop giving Silent Treatments. Fat chance, yes? Bear with me though, it's just an example.

OK, so we know that people in general don't listen to advice, and we know that Vampires don't listen to requests either. So let's try modeling instead. Let's have tons of conversations in front of the Vampire with people we'd much rather not talk to. Let's develop our communication skills to world-class levels, and let's have the Vampire watch us reap the rewards of those skills over and over again. Let's have the Vampire observe us building our popularity and being enormously well liked. You know, like you are.

You know what the Vampire will do with that? They'll get jealous. And probably give you a Silent Treatment for being more popular and well liked than them. Not a scrap of any of that modeling will have any effect at all because they have zero motivation to stop doing Silent Treatments. All the rewards in the world are not going to get them to stop, because it works for them and the power and control it gives them is a far greater reward than popularity or being liked.

Oh, they like the Narcissistic supply they get from the popularity, but what do they use it for? You guessed it, power and control. Before you know it they've boarded the Triangulation Express to Smear Town and are using those interactions to tear relationships and friendships apart for Narcissistic supply.

So if advice won't change their behaviour, and having them walk them to their own answers doesn't work, and modelling doesn't work, what does? In a word: nothing. I can't say this clearly enough. Nothing the Target ever does will have any effect on a Vampire's behaviour. Their motivation for power and control to obtain Narcissistic supply is the only motivation they have, and that will take precedence over any other motivation ever.

It's a bit like takeaway food. Bear with me here. See, I love Indian food, specifically chicken Madras. If I'm with friends and the subject drifts to takeaway, I do the whole Meerkat thing. My friends don't even bother asking any more, and some of them just say the word "Takeaway" occasionally just to watch me become a Madras-Meerkat. That's not to say I won't go for, for example, a nice Chow Mein because I absolutely will. But you better believe that if someone walked into the room with a chicken Madras while I was eating it, I would go full Meerkat and it's anyone's guess what happens next.

You simply can't stop me being a Madras-Motivated-Meerkat, and you simply can't stop Vampire being a Narcissistic supply-Motivated-Vampire. Given that, why try to change their behaviour? Well, the simple answer is: Don't.

Nothing you do will change the Vampires behaviour. I think it's worth bearing in mind that The Vampire will actually ask you for help. It's also worth bearing in mind that they're not actually looking for help; they're looking for Narcissistic supply. So when they ask for advice, it's probably worth considering doing what you'd do with a normal person, which is ask them what they think and have them walk to their own answers.

Regular folks will do that because they actually want to resolve the issue. Vampires won't because they only want Narcissistic supply, so when you do that, they just get fed up and walk away. They'll blame you for not helping them, of course, but so what? They'd end up blaming you anyway, this is just quicker and less costly for you.

OK, so that's the main bit. I'm conscious that it's not fall-about funny, so I thought I'd throw in a few things that are more likely to occur in order to illustrate how enormously unlikely it is that a Vampire will ever change their behaviour based on anything their Target tries to do. I reckon all of this lot are more likely to occur:

Getting the Pope involved in a game of Twister.

Receiving a kiss from a Velociraptor while wearing a meat helmet.

Correctly guessing someone's phone number while being struck by lightning. And a meteor.

Witnessing a pianist playing Beethoven's Moonlight Sonata perfectly. With their face.

Scoring a hole in one in a game of golf. In space.

Getting Julius Caesars autograph. And selling it on eBay. To Adolf Hitler. In the year 1066.

Knitting a sweater made of helium.

Licking the back of your own head.

Finding the city of Atlantis. On the moon.

Successfully hiding from the other person you're in the bath with.

That'll do for now. I think we get the idea. Do feel free to e.mail me any you've thought of. It's always a good idea to share the laughter. Right then, onward to Chapter 11. See you on the other side.

Chapter 11

How Targets are made, and how they can become Survivors

In this chapter, I'd like to take a look at what it is about the Target that made them attractive to the Vampire. In addition, I'm going to make some recommendations about what to do about it so that you can start to tackle the underlying issues and begin a happy, healthy, Vampire-free life.

Just as there are characteristics that are common to all Vampires, as described in the first part of this Field Manual, there are characteristics that are common to all Targets. However, unlike the Vampire whose core characteristics are negative: Envy, Fear, Rage & Shame, the core characteristics of the Target are positive: Empathy, Compassion, Love and Reciprocity. In other words, the Target possesses the very things that the Vampire lacks, and cannot generate for themselves.

At the heart of what attracted the Vampire to the Target is that exact dynamic. The Target has what the Vampire lacks. The Target can generate Narcissistic supply, whereas the Vampire cannot. The Empathy, Compassion, Love, and Reciprocity inherent in the Target draws the Vampire to them like a moth to a flame and, once they get their hooks into the Target, they simply will not let go until all of those things have been "sucked" out of the Target to the point that they cannot give any more. The great news for the Target is that their inherent ability to generate these things means that they can recover once the Vampire is gone. The really terrible news for the Vampire is that they will never be able to generate these things, and they can never recover.

Just as with the Vampire, the Nature-Nurture debate is still raging concerning the Target. However, whether they are born or made doesn't really matter. What matters is that those of us who are Survivors come to realise that our characteristics are truly amazing, and that we deserve to live a life that is Vampire-free so that we can enjoy the enormous joy and satisfaction that possessing those characteristics brings.

But it doesn't end there. Vampires are not attracted to "ordinary" people. Think about it. The Vampire is addicted to Narcissistic supply, right? So what provides the best Narcissistic supply? The best people. The attention from great people is the richest, most delicious source of Narcissistic supply to the Vampire, so there are several things that all

Targets have that the Vampire is attracted to outside of the core characteristics.

Vampires are attracted to intelligent people. They are attracted to good-looking people. They are attracted to successful people. They are attracted to passionate people. They are attracted to funny people. They are attracted to positive people. They are attracted to confident people. They are attracted to popular people.

As a Survivor reading this, you may find it hard to take this in, but I promise you it is true. The reason that you're having a hard time taking it in is actually because the ultimate Target for the Vampire is people who possess all these qualities, all the core characteristics and one important other thing: Low Self Respect. Targets all have one thing in common, and that is that they don't realise just how attractive they are. If they did, they wouldn't have put up with the Vampire's bullshit in the Devaluation Stage, and they wouldn't have fallen for the Idealisation in the first place.

Now, here's the bit that might be a bit of a struggle. Targets don't just wake up one day with Low Self Respect. They have usually carried that with them for many years, and possibly all their lives. At some point in their history, all Targets have developed Low Self Respect as the result of the actions, or inactions of others and have come to believe that they are somehow unworthy. I'm sorry to have to tell you this, dear Survivor, but that includes you, just as it used to include me. The reason you were vulnerable to the Vampire was that when you met them you had Low Self Respect, and you didn't do that to yourself. Someone else did it to you.

The thing is that without that Low Self Respect "chink" in your armour, the Vampire's attacks would have bounced off, but if there's one thing the Vampire excels at, it's finding the Target's weaknesses, particularly their Low Self Respect. Sometimes, Low Self Respect is temporary, and comes about because of a recent loss (a relationship, say, or bereavement or other life loss, like a job, or a home).

Mostly though, Low Self Respect had been going on in the Target for some time before they met the Vampire. There could be loads of reasons for this, like being bullied at school, maybe a bad prior marriage with another abuser that the Target hasn't recovered from, overcritical parents, mistaken beliefs about the Target's appearance, you name it. The list is effectively endless. One thing that I will stand by, however, is that in the vast majority of cases, the Target became a Target because someone, somewhere, at some point in their past, groomed them to accept abuse.

That's right, folks, I said it. Targets of the Modern Vampire were groomed to accept abuse.

Before we all throw our toys out of the pram, I'd like to define what grooming really is. Some commentators on the subject of abuse have gone so far as to say that abusers groom their Targets like paedophiles groom children. As it happens, I agree with those commentators, so I'm going to emphasise my point by using a definition of grooming] from "Psychology Today".

"Grooming involves desensitising a Victim to inappropriate social or sexual advances through

progressive boundary probing, while at the same time developing a foundation of trust."

The similarities are striking, no? The key word is "trust". The Vampire pushes the Targets boundaries one at a time to see how much of their shit they will take while simultaneously appearing loving, kind and attentive in order to gain the Target's trust. There's a phrase for that: Love Bombing. It is disgusting, deliberate and morally bankrupt and all Vampires do it for the purposes of figuring out how best to manipulate the Target to get what they want from them. Once the Vampire has all that figured out, they have everything they need to progress to the Devaluation Stage, which they will.

The short version of explaining the dynamic between the Vampire and the Target is the idea of conditional love. Real love doesn't come with conditions. It isn't given when the person giving it feels the other person deserves it, it is given freely and without question and it is never withheld. When we truly love another person, we never stop loving that person regardless of what is going on between us. That is not how the Vampire thinks, and all too often it is not what the Target has experienced in life.

The Vampire thinks in terms of Black and White (see Splitting), never shades of Grey. It's how they view themselves, and it's how they view others. How they view the Target depends on what they are doing for them at any given time. If the Target is providing Narcissistic supply, they are White. If they are not, they are Black. All good or all bad; never somewhere in between. The way the Vampire abuses their Target is to withdraw positivity towards them and actively punish them if they aren't doing what the Vampire wants, and only to offer smaller and smaller amounts of positivity towards them when they are.

In other words, what the Target receives from them is conditional based on how the Vampire feels about them. That is all the different colours and flavours of wrong. Love is unconditional. What the Vampire calls love is abuse. If the Target has been conditioned to accept that as somehow normal, the Vampire gets away with their abuse because the alarms are not going off in the Target to tell them that what is going on is not normal. That's not the Target's fault, by the way. It's how they have been programmed earlier in life. Their Self Respect is determined by outside sources and they are all too familiar with the idea that love and affection can be withdrawn by others at will.

Whenever people with Low Self Respect meet abusers, the abuser will begin grooming them. It's automatic, and the Vampire is no exception. The Vampire is full of self-loathing, and their way of thinking about themselves is utterly deranged. If left alone, they attack themselves emotionally because they hate themselves. Finding someone with Low Self Respect provides them with the opportunity to turn all that negativity outwards onto that person instead of themselves. In other words, attacking the Target gives them reprieve from attacking themselves, and since the Target has been groomed and programmed to accept that, the Vampire gets away with it.

What keeps them away are boundaries. Vampires hate boundaries, because they stop them from attacking in order to secure Narcissistic supply, so they will test the Targets boundaries to see how secure they are. This could easily be smaller things to begin with, like seeing if the Target is alert to their lies, seeing whether the Target will chase them if they draw away, or throwing an emotional fit to see if the Target will offer comfort. It may be bigger things like sulking or silent treatment to see how the Target responds, starting a fight to see if the Target tries to appease them, or suggesting the relationship should end to see whether the Target works to preserve it. All the time, the Vampire will be building trust with the Target by engaging in Love Bombing or Seduction.

What all that tells the Vampire is the amount of prior grooming the Target has received, and therefore what they will be able to get away with in order to lure them into a relationship. Once the Vampire has discovered that the Target can be attacked, they will attack them because it means they can stop attacking themselves. It's utterly deranged, but it's true.

But the Target wouldn't accept Love Bombing if someone else at some other point hadn't already groomed them in exactly the same way. They wouldn't accept Devaluation if they hadn't been programmed to accept the idea of conditional love either. What every Survivor has to ask themselves is this:

"Who groomed and programmed me to accept abuse in the first place?"

That question is absolutely key. Without an answer to that, and appropriate action on the part of the Survivor, they absolutely will become the Target of another Vampire at some point. See, anyone with Low Self Respect is vulnerable to a Vampire because their number one skill is finding people like that. Not only that, but the more attractive that person is, the more likely they are to attract a Vampire, and we already know that all Survivors are extremely attractive. So, if the Survivor doesn't figure this shit out pronto, they will be very unlikely to enjoy being the gorgeous person they are for very long before being trounced by another Vampire that sees exactly how gorgeous they are and wants to utterly destroy them for it.

The chances are extremely high that if you are a Survivor of a Vampire, someone somewhere at some point in time groomed you, destroyed your Self Respect (or made a bloody good go of it), programmed you to believe that love is conditional, and left you vulnerable to being groomed for abuse again, which the Vampire you encountered did with delight. What you have to ask yourself is: Who?

Now that's a huge question, and only you will come to know the answer, but there is a special type of person out there who will be able to help you answer it: Therapists. They come in all shapes and sizes, but they all have the same goal which is to heal people, and Survivors are all in immediate need of healing before they even consider entering another relationship.

Having said that, I am well aware that many Survivors are left with little to no resources once the Vampire has left, so please don't think that all is lost if you cannot afford to engage one right now. There are many other resources out there that can help you, and I will be pointing them out in a bit. However, I would urge any Survivor to consider this: Vampires will destroy your life, so how much are you prepared to give up to make sure that never happens again? The price of engaging a therapist is nothing compared to what it will give you in terms of making yourself immune to Vampires. If you ever find that you can afford one, get one.

However, in the immediate term, as a Survivor myself, I can offer you the resources that have helped me. There are many more, of course, but this is a start.

Online

Thank whatever higher power you prefer for the Internet! Many Survivors start their journey to recovery by searching online and eventually coming across the various websites and YouTube channels that are specifically geared towards helping Targets of abuse to recover. It often takes Survivors a while to compile their lists of the ones that really help them, but they often end up in a similar place and that community is growing, and growing, and growing. It truly is a beautiful thing to behold. The resources below helped me in my recovery, and all of these people are outstanding at what they do.

For each of these online resources, put the whole thing into a YouTube search or a standard web search and you'll find them:

Kris Godinez We need to talk

Melanie Tonya Evans Thriver TV

Richard Grannon Spartan Life Coach

Kim Saeed Let me Reach

Quinn Holliday ASSC Direct

Angie Atkinson Queenbeeing
Tara Palmatier A Shrink for Men

David DeMars CNXG

Shahida Arabi Self Care Haven

Books

There are so many books out there on this subject that can help you. These are the ones that helped me in the immediate term during my recovery, and should at least give you a start point.

Psychopath Free by Jackson McKenzie

Complex PTSD: From Surviving to Thriving: a guide and map for recovering from childhood trauma by Pete Walker

Becoming the Narcissist's Nightmare: How to Devalue and Discard the Narcissist While Supplying Yourself by Shahida Arabi

The Inner Child Workbook by Cathryn Taylor

The Human Magnet Syndrome by Ross Rosenberg

The Self-Esteem Workbook, 2nd Edition by Glen Schiraldi

The Object of My Affection Is in My Reflection: Coping with Narcissists by Rokelle Lerner

The Wizard of Oz and Other Narcissists: Coping with the One-Way Relationship in Work, Love, and Family by Eleanor Payson

Running On Empty by Jonice Webb

Codependent No More by Melody Beatty

Therapists

Earlier on, I talked about the emotional, psychological and biological damage that the Vampire does to their Target. All of that really matters. Survivors who find themselves in recovery will almost certainly be dealing with PTSD or C-PTSD, be suffering from Stockholm syndrome as a result of Trauma Bonding, have had chemical and structural changes to their brain as a result of chronic stress, and experience Cognitive Dissonance as a result of Gaslighting.

And there is great news. A good Therapist can help with all of that. The process of healing is gradual but is usually steady and it is designed to rebuild the Survivors Self Respect and help them love themselves first, and stop seeking love and esteem from outside sources. Once Survivors are doing that, they are well on their way to becoming Vampire-free, because that is what being a Survivor is all about. Being a Survivor is not an all-or-nothing state. Rather, it is an ongoing process of self-improvement and building self-love and self-esteem. In other words, Survivors can start referring to themselves as Survivors the moment they make the conscious decision to become one. There is no exam, there are no medals and the status of Survivor is not awarded by any outside agency. It comes from within, and there is really only one thing that Survivors need to do:

To say to themselves, and thereby to the world that they are finished accepting abuse.

That is the first step. Saying that we are finished accepting abuse is enormously powerful. It is a statement of intent to the world and the self that we will no longer accept abuse of any kind from anyone for any reason. It is saying that we are done with conditional love, and will from now on only accept unconditional love. And it is the polar opposite of what we said before because, through our actions as Targets, we were saying that we do accept abuse.

As soon as Survivors make the conscious choice to stop accepting abuse, we are changing our entire mind-set, and the thoughts and behaviours that go along with that can now change too. Just like stopping using any drug or behaviour that is harmful to us, the decision must be made to put it down, never pick it up again and walk a different path that does not involve doing that thing.

Therapists exist for this very reason, to help Survivors make that decision, understand why they made the choices they made when they were Targets, change the things they need to change, heal their wounds and move on with a life that is abuse-free. They exist to help Survivors re-program their beliefs about love as conditional, and allow them to come to love themselves unconditionally. That is the goal of healing from abuse - to learn to love ourselves unconditionally because once that's in place we will only ever accept unconditional love from others, never conditional love because that is abuse.

Finding a good Therapist is actually pretty easy. Depending on where you live, just Google "Therapy" and the town or city you live in. You may find that sponsored links come up, but it's often better to look for a directory of therapists because that way you can shop around a little. Some important points to bear in mind will be to look for therapists, counsellors or life coaches who have a good understanding of what Survivors have been through.

Good Therapists understand about trauma, PTSD, C-PTSD, domestic violence, emotional abuse, personality disorders and childhood abuse. It's a good plan to check out whether your prospective Therapist knows about these things before you commit to therapy because they will "get" you straight off the bat. And, if you find that a particular therapist doesn't work for you, if you don't feel safe with them, or that you can't see yourself trusting them, move on and pick someone else. A good Therapist isn't offended by that because they know that those things are at the heart of the healing

process, so don't be afraid to make a different choice if you feel you need to.
So there we have it.

Becoming a Survivor is no mystery. It is a conscious choice, and it starts with a statement of intent. A good Therapist will aid immeasurably in making that choice and changing any faulty programming that led to accepting abuse. If you find that you cannot get access to a Therapist, please access as many resources elsewhere as possible. The ones I have given here are excellent, but I encourage you to keep searching because education about your experience is incredibly useful in recovery.

What's more, all of these resources are aimed at the most important thing of all: Learning to love yourself unconditionally. Whatever works for you in achieving that can only be a good thing. As a Survivor, you are now part of an ever growing community that exists to help you achieve that. Everyone in that community wants to help you love yourself, which is a beautiful thing. Please accept it into your life, because you truly deserve it.

OK: Interlude time.

Interlude 11

"Oh the places you'll go! There is fun to be done!" – Dr Seuss

Hello again, dear Survivor!

Well, having had a look at how we can get mixed up with Vampires and their games, I'd like to riff on the subject of games for a bit. Games are brilliant, aren't they? I love a good game, me. I'm very lucky to have wonderful friends who also enjoy a good game, and we've spent endless happy hours playing together for the sheer fun of playing. It never really matters what we're playing, what matters is the great company, the laughter, the play and most importantly, the sharing.

Anyway, I thought it worth mentioning before we proceed that Vampires really suck at playing games. I've honestly never met one that enjoys a game in which they are not the centre of attention. I think it's because they don't get to dictate the rules. Oh, and have you ever seen one lose? Yikes, that's not pretty is it? They just suck all the fun out of it all. Funnily enough, there is a game out there called "Sorry". Vampires don't play that one.

Anyway, with all that in mind, let's have a look at what might happen if we launched same games specifically for Vampires. We could take classic games and rework them so that the Vampire would be happy for a change. How would that look, I wonder? Well, how about...

Vampire Cluedo (or Vampire Clue, if you prefer)

A detective board game in which the players are required to solve a murder. Players identify the location, weapon and suspect by using information gained from other players to eliminate possibilities. The winner is the first player to correctly identify all 3. The Vampire is only required to identify the location and weapon and may accuse suspects at will, including other players. If their deduction turns out to be wrong, the Vampire is free to deny that they ever made it and/or accuse other players of making it instead. The Vampire is also free to claim that they are in fact the murder victim and therefore are entitled to as many free turns as they wish. The Vampire is under no obligation to give other players any information they have, and may also choose to give whatever information occurs to them on the spot.

Vampire Scrabble

As in the standard version, in Vampire Scrabble, players take it in turns to use their letter tiles to spell out words on the board and score points accordingly. In addition, the Vampire may engage in the practice of Word Salad whereby they may spell out and claim points for words for as long as they wish, regardless of whose turn it is, none of which have to make sense or even be real words. When another player spells a word, the Vampire may claim that word has hurt their feelings and immediately take their turn again. Play proceeds until the Vampire has used up all the letter tiles.

Vampire Monopoly

Similar to standard Monopoly, this is a board game in which players move around the game board, buying and trading properties, and developing them with houses and hotels. Players collect rent from their opponents, with the goal being to drive them into bankruptcy. Money can also be gained or lost through Chance and Community Chest cards, and tax squares. The winner is the last player standing when all others have been bankrupted. The Vampire may refuse to pay rent at will and manipulate other players into paying it for them. When another player buys a property, the Vampire may immediately place a house on it and claim that it belongs to them. Loans made by other players to the Vampire are not required to be repaid and whenever another player lands on any property owned by the Vampire, the Vampire may accuse them of trying to steal it and immediately steal one of theirs instead. At any point in the game, the Vampire may accuse any other player of stealing from them and demand that a third player give them the sum of money they claim the first player has stolen. If the Vampire is required to pay tax, they may ignore this and pass the bill onto another player, claiming that they have no money. When the Vampire passes Go, they may claim that £200 is not enough, that the other players clearly don't love them and then refuse to move their playing piece again until the other players have given them an amount they are not required to disclose.

Vampire "I-spy"

Similar to standard "I spy", players try to guess the object the other player has selected given only the first letter of the objects name. The purpose of the game for the player is to identify the object. The purpose of the game for the Vampire is to keep the other player guessing for as long as possible. The Vampire may change the selected object at will, change the letter its name begins with or not select an object at all. Play proceeds until the other player gives up, at which point the Vampire may accuse them of being stupid for not guessing the object regardless of any of the above.

Vampire Chess

Similar to standard Chess in terms of rules, Vampire Chess is a game for 3 or more players, but the Vampires opponents do not know of each other's existence. Each of them believes that they are playing against the Vampire when in fact they are playing against each other, and themselves. In addition, any move made by an opponent that the Vampire does not approve of may be classified as cheating. Claiming their opponent is cheating allows the Vampire to move between games at will, and each time they do so, take a turn in the game they are leaving and the game they are joining. This usually leads to it always being the Vampires turn. Some games may be abandoned by the Vampire for weeks, months or even years but when the Vampire returns to a game, they may take their turn. If the Vampire returns to a game and is told that it is not their turn, they may remove themselves to another game, claim that their last opponent cheated and then immediately take both their turn and their opponents turn. If opponents become aware of each other, the Vampire may tell both that the other is a cheat and immediately take two turns in either or both games. Play continues until all opponents leave their respective games.

Vampire Hide-And-Seek

The only thing that separates this from the usual game is that when it is the Vampires turn to hide, they have the option to "hide" by leaving the game and pursuing whatever other activities they see fit for as long as they wish. The Vampire is under no obligation to explain this to the other player. When they choose to return to the game, they may accuse the other player of not trying hard enough to find them and then immediately take their turn again.

Vampire Battleship

Similar only to the original game in that they have the word Battleship in the title, this game involves taking turns to guess the location of the other players ships on a board divided into a grid by calling out grid locations. Players inform each other that they have either scored a "Hit" or a "Miss" according to whether their ships occupy the stated grid location or not. The Vampire is not required to place any ships in their grid at the start of the game. The game ends only when either the other player has either called out all the grid locations, or gives up.

And there we have it: End of Interlude 11. I think this one might have legs, dear Survivor, so please feel free to drop me an e.mail if you have any other suggestions. For now, let's get into Chapter 12. See you on the other side.

Chapter 12

The key skills of the Survivor

I'm going to open this Chapter with a story. It is relevant; I'm not just rambling. Back in the day, I'd just bought house, with a Vampire as it happens, but that's another story. On the day we moved in, there was a police car outside and two uniformed officers approached me as I was unlocking the front door. "Excuse me, Sir", one of them said, "Were you here last night?" "No, I'm just moving in. Why?" said I. "Oh, it's just that there have been a spate of burglaries in this street. One of them happened last night and we wondered if you'd seen anything", was the reply.

I'm now thinking: "Great! I've moved into Gotham City!" and after assuring the police that I was not, in fact, a burglar using a house purchase to cover my tracks, I completed the move-in. All day, though, I was wondering what to do about living in a crime-zone and finally decided to spend actual money on a security system. But here's the thing:

I didn't get a security system to make my home safe, I got a security system to make my home a harder target than the guy next door, who didn't have a security system. See, the thing about burglars is that they will always go for the easy target. All you have to do is make yourself a harder target than your neighbours and you're done.

Thanks for bearing with me on that, because the point of the story is that the Vampire will always go for easy Targets. They are actually very easily deterred once you know what you're doing and the skills I'm going to talk about here are based on one very simple principle: Make yourself a harder Target than the Vampire is willing to deal with and wait for them to go attack someone else. The skills in this Chapter are all based on the simple understanding of what the Vampire is, how they think and behave and their motives and once the Survivor has that clear in their mind, they become much easier to use.

In essence, the entire Field Manual has been building up to this Chapter, because once that understanding is secure, these skills make complete sense. The bottom line when engaging with a Vampire is the phrase "The only way to win is not to play". Once you master that, no Vampire on the planet has any power over you.

Now, I've made that sound easy, and it can be, but it will take clarity of mind. Before any Survivor implements these skills, it is essential that they get clear in their mind that they are NOT dealing with a "normal" person. There may well be a struggle there because of societal conditioning, Gaslighting, Cognitive Dissonance, Flying Monkeys,

Stockholm syndrome and, of course, the Vampires continuing and relentless attacks. However, this really is a case of making a decision either to give ground and question whether the Vampire is really a Vampire or to accept whole-heartedly that the Vampire is a Vampire and stick with that conclusion forever.

I cannot overstate the importance of a good Therapist in making this happen, and if that's not possible, Survivors are well advised to surround themselves with as many resources mentioned in Chapter 11 and beyond as humanly possible. The Vampire will seek to undermine the Survivors attempts to use these skills at every turn, and without complete conviction on the part of the Survivor, that might work.

I'm going to invite you, dear Survivor, to answer a question for me. That question is this:

"Are you finished with being abused?"

If the answer to that is "Yes", please go ahead and read the rest of this Chapter. If the answer is either "Maybe", or "No", please go back and read whatever Chapters and Interludes are necessary, and pursue as many resources from Chapter 11 and elsewhere are necessary, engage a good Therapist and then revisit that question. By all means, read on anyway but please, please, please be finished with being abused. Until you are, the Vampire will be more than happy to continue abusing you.

Now, the really great news about these skills is that they actually take very little effort to put into practice. All that's really required is a thorough understanding of what the Vampire is and how they operate, and then to apply the principle that "The only way to win is not to play". Remember Chapter 6 on the Drama triangle? Here's where that knowledge pays off. The Vampire will try every trick in the book to draw you into a Drama Triangle, and the way to deal with that is to remember plainly and clearly that they want you to provoke you to be either a Rescuer or a Persecutor. Here's the key to dealing with that:

Be nothing in their life and everything in yours

Any engagement with the Drama the Vampire will try to create plays directly into their hands. Any emotional response you give to the Vampire is Narcissistic supply, full stop. They see you as a source of Narcissistic supply just as they do all people, so the only way to get them to leave you alone is to close yourself down as a source.

Be so preoccupied with your own life that you have nothing to give them; give everything to yourself and nothing to them; give them nothing and you will, step by step, deter them from bothering you because the effort required to extract Narcissistic supply from you will far exceed the Narcissistic supply gained, and the Vampire will simply move on to other, easier Targets. Just like the burglar who looked at my home and then decided to rob the guy next door, the Vampire will look at you, decide that you are no longer a viable source of Narcissistic supply and move on to another Target.

The thing the Vampire absolutely does not want you to know is that their entire strategy is one of Strike

and Retreat. For all their diverse weapons and tactics, they are all designed with only one purpose: to provoke you into responding. Master the Art of not responding and you defeat the Vampire.

And all that is required to do so is nothing at all. Allow me to explain please. The Vampire strikes out with provocations, and attempts to draw you into Drama. If they succeed, they withdraw to the Victim position and remain there while they extract Narcissistic supply from you as you function as either Rescuer or Persecutor, both of which are active positions. The moment you give no response, you are neither Rescuer nor Persecutor, and therefore there is no Victim position. Get it?

Without a Victim position, there can be no Drama. The Vampire cannot exist without Drama. Therefore, without Drama, there is no Vampire.

And that's exactly how you defeat them: By doing nothing at all. The fundamental truth is that the Vampire wants to start a fight, but doesn't want to fight it. Vampires are basically very, very lazy. They want to provoke an emotional response in others using the minimum amount of effort possible and then let them do all the work providing Narcissistic supply. They "Provoke and Retreat", but they don't fight. Instead they take the Victim position as soon as whatever they kicked off starts. What they really, really don't want to have to do is put effort in, so the way to defeat them is to put in less effort than they do. If they have to do the work, their lazy attitude dictates that they just won't. What they'll do instead is go find someone else who's more easily provoked.

Once we step away from the fight, we automatically win because the goal of our opponent has been defeated by our own inaction. So, what I'm going to do in this Chapter is lay out the key skills used in protecting against the attacks of the Vampire. It's not a set of instructions to follow word for word; rather it is a description of what actually works. Once you get your head around the logic of why they work, it should be easier to use them.

Resisting the urge to attack or defend

In almost every case, Survivors are angry, and with good reason. They have been betrayed, lied to, cheated on and attacked. During the process, the Vampire constantly placed themselves in positions that meant that the Target could not fight back without causing further problems for themselves. The experience often feels like having your voice stolen and fighting fog. No attack lands, nothing that is said is validated, many people don't understand and some of them don't believe the Target, the Vampire has smeared the Target so that their reputation is damaged and the Target ends up being attacked and damaged over and over again with no meaningful way of fighting back.

What that leads to is what I call "Futile Rage". The experience is one of being full of boiling anger and rage with nowhere for it to go. The over-riding feeling is one of total injustice. Survivors want to lash out at the Vampire, to damage them in some way, to warn the new Target, to convince the world of the truth. That is all completely normal and entirely justified.

But here's the thing. All of that is exactly what the Vampire wants. When the Vampire discards the Target, they want them to be crippled and broken, full of emotions both positive and negative and to stay exactly where the Vampire left them both figuratively and literally. That would make it much easier for the Vampire to swing back at some point to Hoover.

What lies at the heart of resisting the urge to attack or defend is an understanding that attacking or defending is exactly what the Vampire wants. They want the fight to continue. For as long as there is conflict, the Vampire feels powerful. If they believe that they can affect another person and draw them into conflict, it makes them feel that they have potency, and the more they can do it, the more superior they feel.

What's important to remember here is the phrase "The only way to win is not to play". That's often a struggle for many Survivors because it appears to lack the power of either an attack or defense. Basically, it sounds too Zen, New Age and annoyingly ineffective. But it's not. It really isn't. In fact, it is one of the most powerful weapons against the Vampire, and I'll explain why.

Vampires need Narcissistic supply. Without it, they cease to exist. Cutting off that supply as a form of attack or defense feels like nothing to the Survivor, but that's because they don't think like Vampires do. For the Vampire, losing

Narcissistic supply is death to the soul. It really is that important to them.

Remember, you are dealing with an individual that has absolutely no sense of self and must therefore get that from outside sources. If they can't get a response from people, they take that as an injury because it invalidates them. The world wounds them with its indifference to them every single day and when people ignore them, they feel that as an attack, a slight against them.

The Vampire does not want you to know that they fear your ability to hurt them with your indifference, which is why they spend their entire lives creating Drama and conflict. The Vampire doesn't want you to become indifferent because that would crush them utterly. I'm not kidding here. If a Vampire knows you have the power to be indifferent to them, they will avoid you like the plague. Not just because they won't get any Narcissistic supply from you, but because you and your indifference are an active threat to them.

Please bear in mind that the Vampire lacks empathy. They know that the most hurtful thing that could happen to them is the indifference of others, and therefore cannot consider any other form of attack. That's why they attack with withdrawal, silent treatments and feigned indifference. They know it hurts them, so they assume it hurts you. They know they hate it and it causes them incredible pain, so they do it to you. But they've given away their weakness there, haven't they? Their lack of empathy has betrayed them, because they have shown us how we can hurt them most: Indifference.

Imagine for a moment that you are a boxer. You are fighting in a World Championship and this fight means more to you than anything else in the world. You know that you have to beat your opponent by putting them on the floor or knocking them out. But they don't fight back. They just stand there. No matter how hard you hit them, they don't move or react. They don't feel any of your punches and appear to be made of granite. Every time you hit them, nothing happens. You are fighting an immovable statue and you know full well that, if things continue this way, your opponent will win because your technique looks weak. The judges will favour your opponent because you look like an amateur, and you will not be able to put them down or knock them out.

As the fight goes on, you become more and more frustrated. Losing this fight could end your career but you have absolutely no way to win. Now, every punch you throw makes you feel weaker. You're starting to be humiliated by the ineffectiveness of your attacks. In front of thousands of people, you are showing yourself to be completely impotent. Nothing you do makes a difference and the harder you fight the more powerless you become. Eventually, the final bell rings and sure enough your opponent takes the championship and you have been defeated and humiliated.

Sound familiar? It's how most Survivors feel at the end of a relationship with a Vampire. Impotent, humiliated and that they have lost.

But that's the key thing, isn't it? We all have an intimate knowledge of the pain the Vampire inflicts with their mind games and manipulations. We all know exactly what it felt like to be robbed of our power. So now is the time to turn all that pain away from us and onto the Vampire and the beautiful thing is that in order to do it we have to do absolutely nothing.

Not engaging in either attack or defense is actually the most highly effective form of both. It is an expression of power because it attacks the Vampire where it hurts the most: their need to feel powerful. When we become that statue, we turn all the pain away from us and onto them and they feel that pain way more than we ever did.

By not engaging, we are attacking because the most effective way to hurt a Vampire is to show them that they mean nothing. By actively being indifferent, by actively focussing on turning our attention from the Vampire, by actively focussing on ourselves and not them, we are landing blow after blow on them and every single one of them counts. And the more we do it, the more we hurt them.

Is it easy? No. But does it work? More than you could possibly imagine. But this comes with a caveat. All that "Futile Rage" needs to be expressed. It can't be used directly against the Vampire because that would defeat the purpose but it does need to come out or it will damage you. The good news is that there are loads of ways to release it. Here's a few:

1. Exercise
2. Talking about your experience with trusted friends
3. Working through it with a Therapist
4. Did I say exercise? Exercise

And here's the best part. Every single time you get some of that Rage out and don't turn it inwards, you are attacking the Vampire. By taking care of yourself, you are hurting them. Your actions show the world that they mean nothing, which is more damaging to them than you could possibly imagine; the more that you become that statue boxer and the more they slide towards humiliation and defeat. By resisting the urge to attack or defend, you are doing both more effectively than you can possibly know. Your indifference is killing them.

No Contact

This is by far and away the most powerful technique in the Survivors arsenal. Its function is very simple: It removes ALL access to the Survivor from the Vampire. Once No Contact has been implemented and maintained, the Vampire has absolutely no way to affect the Survivor at all, and therefore they lose all power to attack.

There are many misconceptions about No Contact, so I'm going to go through how to use it effectively. The first of these to address straight away, however, is that No Contact is not designed to harm the Vampire. It is not a technique to make the Vampire miss you, or to punish them. These things are outside of your control.

The one and only reason to use No Contact is to allow you to heal. The time and space that No Contact affords is essential in allowing you to repair the damage the Vampire has done. If you are considering using No Contact as a weapon, please think again. Survivors never attack the Vampire, they escape them.

If you are in any doubt about this, please re-read the chapters on the Biological, Psychological and Emotional effects of the Attack Cycle and reflect on just how much damage they have done. Is anyone that damaged in any fit state to fight? Thought not.

In understanding No Contact, it is so, so important to remember that all Survivors are addicts. No Contact is the equivalent of going "Cold Turkey", so don't expect it to be easy, and don't beat yourself up if you take a while to master it. If you fail, start again. No Contact can be mastered. I promise.

No Contact works on several levels:
1. The Practical
2. The Biological and Psychological
3. The Emotional

I tend to look at these as a series of steps in building the "No Contact House". You have to build the foundations at step 1 before you can put the walls up at step 2, and you have to complete the walls at step 2 before you can put the roof on at step 3. Master each one in turn and you can definitely say that you've Mastered No Contact and your "No Contact House" will now keep you safe from the Vampire. OK, so let's take a look at each of those in turn.

The Practical level

On a practical level, going No Contact means removing any means by which the Vampire can contact you, but it also means removing any means by which you can contact the Vampire. It is basically burning every bridge between you and the Vampire <u>permanently</u>. Given the complexity of our world, there are loads of ways that people can contact each other, so you will need to make a full inventory of all the ways the Vampire may be able to contact you. The most common are:

a) Your address. In an ideal world, move. That may not be realistic, so if that's not possible, or you really don't want to, be prepared to call on local law enforcement if the Vampire comes to your home. Trespass and Harassment are crimes. In informed societies, so is Stalking. If the Vampire is coming near your property, call the cops. They take this stuff seriously. If the Vampire sends you mail or notes, destroy them without reading them. A good idea is a "No Contact Buddy" - a trusted friend that will take away any notes or mail and destroy them for you.

b) Your phone numbers. If at all possible, change them. If it is not possible to do that or you really don't want to, block the Vampire's numbers and delete them from your phones. Every telecoms operator and phone manufacturer offers the blocking facility and it will mean that the Vampire cannot get to you, or leave you voicemails. If your telecoms operator sends blocked calls to voicemail, delete the voicemails as soon as they come in. Actually, if your telecoms operator is that ill-informed, change them too.

c) Your e.mail. If at all possible, change your e.mail addresses. If it is not possible to do that, or you really don't want to, set up an automatic response that (in order of preference) blocks the Vampires e.mail addresses, deletes any e.mail from the Vampire or sends them to the junk folder. If you find any that have been sent to junk, or are awaiting deletion, delete them. Also, delete the Vampire's e.mail addresses from your contacts.

d) Social Media. This one's important. Vampires know exactly how to stalk you on Social Media. If at all possible, close ALL your Social Media accounts. If that's not possible, or you really don't want to, block the Vampire on ALL Social Media platforms. Do not simply de-friend them, BLOCK them. Then, do an inventory of all potential Flying Monkeys and block them too. Never underestimate the power of Flying Monkeys to work as agents of the Vampire.

Do not accept contact requests from people you do not recognise. The Vampire has mastered the "fake account", and will use them to stalk you. Go through all of your contacts on each Social Media platform at a time. Use the same inventory as before for Flying Monkeys and cleanse accordingly.

In addition, DO NOT LOOK at their Social Media. The Vampire wants you to look at them. It's all about Narcissistic supply. They will post all sorts of crap about how happy they are, how much in love with their new Target they are, how perfect their life is and all sorts of bullshit that has no more credibility than they do. Please listen carefully:

Every Single Thing The Vampire Posts On Social Media Is A Lie.

I'm not kidding. They lie all the time. They lied when they were with you, and they're lying now. They are not happy. They never will be happy. Everything they do on Social Media is designed to get Narcissistic supply, and none of it is true. If at all possible, they will use their Social Media posts to hurt you, so don't look. Block them and have done please.

e) Your place of Work. Many people overlook this one. Report to your HR department that you have left an abusive relationship and that you have gone No Contact with your ex. Request that all calls and e.mail from the Vampire (you'll need to give them a list of addresses and numbers) are blocked from getting to you. In addition, any decent HR team will inform any Security team (or Reception team) that any visitors should report to HR and/or Security before they report to you, and that goes for deliveries too, so don't be afraid to ask.

HR departments only exist to make sure the company doesn't end up in lawsuits. If you have requested that this happens, they will take notice because harassment can get real ugly real quickly. Any failure on their part to protect you could result in a nasty lawsuit, and even if you haven't realised that, they will have and they will comply accordingly.

f) Your friends and family. Tell your support group that you have gone No Contact, and warn them that the Vampire may try to get to you through them. Request that if that happens, they ignore all contact from the Vampire. If you find a family member or friend is trying to reinstate contact between you and the Vampire, consider them a Flying Monkey and act accordingly.

The Biological and Psychological level

This is the tough part, because it's not about stopping the Vampire from contacting you, it's about stopping you from contacting the Vampire. As I said in Chapters 7, 8 and 9, Survivors are addicts. They have become addicted to the Vampire's behaviours and their brain and thought processes have been fundamentally altered by the Vampire. All of that "reprogramming" that the Vampire did compels them to close the distance and re-bond with the Vampire. But stopping that drive to re-bond is what lies at the heart of No Contact at this level.

At the level of the Biological and Psychological, going No Contact from the Vampire is the equivalent of going "Cold Turkey" from any other drug. It's hard and it hurts. It hurts because the physical and psychological "wiring" that the Vampire induced now wants to function without the Vampire but can't. Those neural pathways and the thought processes that stem from them are trying to run without the input that the Vampire provided. But the Vampire is gone, and the brain doesn't really get that. The pain is psychological because the Survivors' thought processes are now in free-fall and it's physically painful because the Survivors nervous system has been massively disrupted, which results in the sensation of pain. It is serious stuff, and all Survivors have to go through it, but it can be overcome. No Contact is a skill, and it can be mastered. What are required are discipline and a good understanding of what's really going on.

What's really going on is that the brain and body are going into withdrawal, and that's very serious indeed. Withdrawal is a major deal because the brain has suddenly been deprived of all the chemical ups-and-downs that it has become conditioned to. That leads to a physical and psychological experience that is no different from coming off any other drug.

The Survivors body and brain will be screaming out for the intermittent positive rewards the Vampire was providing; the brain wants its "fix". The Survivors' training dictates that they must chase those rewards. Their brain chemistry is all over the place because Oxytocin levels have gone into the Stratosphere, there is a massive drop in Dopamine and Serotonin and the Reward Centre is receiving no stimulation whatsoever, so the first thing it wants is some form of reward: The "fix". In other words, the Survivors brain is now officially a cluster-fuck. It will do everything in its power to make the Survivor reach out to the source of rewards: the Vampire.

But here's the thing. The Vampire has been the source of all rewards and punishments that made the Survivor an addict in the first place. The Biological and Psychological effects of the Attack Cycle are all due to the Vampire. Therefore, the one and only thing that must be avoided at all costs is the Vampire. Once you know that, you can tell yourself what is going on and endure it. If you are in any doubt about this, please re-read Chapters 7, 8 and 9. Read them over as many times as you need to. What is going on during No Contact at the Biological and Psychological level is withdrawal, and it can be endured. The skill here is in mastering the urges that withdrawal induces.

The only thing that needs to be done is to make a solemn vow that you will not contact the Vampire under any circumstances and then stick to it no matter what. Your brain is going through withdrawal, and your thought processes will be leading you to break No Contact so that the brain can restore its conditioned chemical balance. In short, your brain is going to betray you, and you MUST stick to one simple truth:

Any contact with the Vampire will hurt you more than it hurts now.

In the early stages, the drive to contact the Vampire will be overwhelming. It will occupy your mind all day every day. It will be the only thing you think about. Your brain will want that "fix", and it will drive you crazy over and over again trying to get it. Only one thing matters:

Any contact with the Vampire will hurt you more than it hurts now.

Read that again, and again, and again. Make it your mantra if you need to. It is God's honest truth, it is never false and it always applies. Remember that the Vampire wants to hurt you. They live for the Narcissistic supply your contact would give them, and they will take the opportunity to demean, belittle, blame and Shame you for getting in contact.

Any contact you give the Vampire will feed them and hurt you. That is a straight-up fact. I don't want to sound heartless, but I don't care how much it hurts. Breaking No Contact will hurt more. I have been there, and I have done it and I know one thing for damn-sure-as-mustard:

Any contact with the Vampire will hurt you more than it hurts now.

The reason for that is basic. Once you break No Contact one of two things is going to happen:

1) The Vampire will offer rewards for you getting in contact and you're back to square one because the brain has just got it's "fix", the psychological effects will follow, and therefore so will the emotional effects.

2) The Vampire will punish you for getting in contact and you're back to square one because the brain has just got it's "fix", the psychological effects will follow, and therefore so will the emotional effects.

In either case, the result is the same. You go straight back to square one. Do not pass "Go", do not collect £200. Reset, Restart, Rinse and Repeat. You just allowed the Vampire to play the "No Win" on you again. Please, please, please don't do that.

At the level of the Biological and Psychological, No Contact is all about allowing your brain to adjust back to normal levels of activity. Remember that the activity your brain has become accustomed to is completely abnormal. The

Vampire has reprogrammed you to respond in the way they want you to. Your brain has been programmed to function in their reality, which is a total fucking joke, nowhere near actual reality and exists only to serve their needs. At this level, No Contact allows you to literally reclaim your brain and thoughts from the Vampire and their False Reality. Any break in No Contact serves only to sacrifice your brain and thoughts to the needs of the Vampire and their False Reality, and that can't possibly be a good thing. So, at the risk of sounding enormously repetitive,

Any contact with the Vampire will hurt you more than it hurts now.

So, how to master the skill of No Contact at this level? Actually, it's surprisingly simple. You don't contact the Vampire, ever. Every single time you want to, you say to yourself:

Any contact with the Vampire will hurt you more than it hurts now.

And then you just plain don't. That's it. You go do something else. You just keep telling yourself that simple truth over and over again. And over again. And over again. You keep telling yourself that simple truth until it's something you say every day without thinking. Your brain is that of an addict, and it is addicted to lies. It needs to hear the truth all day, every day to replace the lies it has been fed by the Vampire, so you keep telling yourself that simple truth until you believe it 100%, all day, every day.

Will you fail? Maybe. Is that OK? Yes, it is. What matters is that you immediately start again. Remember that you are beating an addiction, and just like beating all addictions it is not about how many times you relapse, it is about how many times you start over. What really matters is that you understand that the Vampire wants you to fail. They want you to relapse. They want you to break No Contact so that they can hurt you some more. They want to enslave your brain and your thoughts. They want to enslave you. They want you to forget the simple truth:

Any contact with the Vampire will hurt you more than it hurts now.

At this level, No Contact is a weapon insofar as it serves to remind you that every time you want to contact the Vampire, they win and every time you stay No Contact, they lose. Count the days. Count the hours. Every single moment of No Contact is a win for you and a loss for the Vampire. Every single moment you resist their reality and insist on objective reality is a win for you and a loss for them.

Every single moment of your independence from them is a victory for you and a defeat for them. Remember that the programming of the Vampire is designed to hurt you and therefore every single piece of "deprogramming" you do hurts them. And it really does hurt them. They hate No Contact because it means that they have lost control of you and control is everything to the Vampire. Every moment of No Contact shows them that they cannot control you. All of these add up to you defeating the Vampire on their own terms: You have control; they don't.

The Emotional level

Once you've got your head around the Biological and Psychological levels, the Emotional level becomes easier to understand and to work through. Survivors have suffered extensive emotional trauma at the hands of the Vampire, and that trauma leads to emotional pain even (and especially) after the Vampire is gone. If the Vampire discards, they will make sure that their final attack on the Target is the worst, most intense emotional savaging they can manage. They will "emotionally nuke" the Target. The reason they do this is as simple as it is sick: They want the Target as close to emotional death as possible without actually killing them.

They know that they will not be around to abuse the Target for a while, so they want to ensure that the Target is as unbalanced, confused, hurt, angry and shamed as possible so that they will continue to struggle in emotional turmoil in the Vampires absence. The way they see it, they don't want the Target toddling off to find support and rescue because that would mean that they have lost control of them.

That's right, folks: the Vampires need for control is so pathological that they even want to do it when they've left the relationship because to them, they haven't. On a physical level, Elvis has left the building, but on an emotional level, he is most certainly still in it, and he's systematically smashing all the furniture.

Survivors who cannot get through the results of the "emotional nuke" tend to stay where the Vampire wants them, both literally because they don't implement No Contact and figuratively because the Vampire is still dictating their emotional reality. This must not be allowed to happen, because if the Vampire still has an emotional presence in the mind of the Survivor, their emotional "furniture" is going to get smashed over and over again.

Going No Contact on the Emotional level is the last thing to happen. The Practical gets implemented and mastered first and then the Biological and Psychological must be endured and mastered. Once those things have been done, the Emotional level can be tackled. Since that's the case, please, please, please don't beat yourself up if you're still experiencing emotions towards the Vampire. That's counterproductive because feelings tell us we're human, right? Feelings are completely normal, and it's not only OK to feel them, it's expected. In mastering No Contact at the Emotional level, there will be several emotions to take into consideration: Shame, Love and Anger.

Survivors feel Shame for several reasons. First, because the Vampire has systematically worked on whatever the Target feel Shame about and made that the focus of all of the problems in the relationship, magnified it to obscene proportions and used it to attack the Targets Self Respect through Gaslighting. Second, because Survivors tend to blame themselves for the failure of the relationship, which sucks and is not true but exactly what the Vampire wants because they blame the Target too. Third, everyone on the planet feels Shame when a relationship fails. It's embarrassing. You failed at something. It's completely normal and natural to feel that way, but in an abusive relationship with a Vampire, that Shame gets magnified to unspeakable levels. Fourth, there is almost certainly some Shame in there left over from the past that needs dealing with. Vampires excel at finding those original wounds in their Targets and they exploit them remorselessly.

So how to deal? Get with a good Therapist and work through all that Shame. It is imperative that the Shame that was instilled in the Survivor be worked through and gotten rid of. Remember, the Vampire is a Shame-based individual, so they will have projected all their Shame onto you, and you need to get rid of it. They don't want to deal with their Shame, and they never will but it does not belong to you, so go get Therapy and get rid of it for good. That goes for the Shame that's probably present from the past. That's got to go too. A good Therapist can help you identify whose Shame is whose, and then put it all back where it belongs.

Also, read and research online. I mentioned some good resources earlier, so maybe start there. They will not only help you understand your experience, they will validate it, and that's so, so important. The very first thing to do in getting rid of Shame is to recognise that it is there in the first place. Vampires never do that, which is why they never change, but Survivors can.

Validating your experience by listening to the experiences of others and interacting with other Survivors will help you realise that what the Vampire did is not your fault. They are sick, twisted individuals whose sole purpose is to destroy the well-being of others for their own survival. They disguised themselves as a normal person in order to trap you, and then systematically set about destroying you because that's what their disorder programs them to do. None of that is your fault, so go get involved with as many resources as possible so that you can come to terms with that and start working on all that Shame that doesn't belong to you.

When it comes to feelings of Love, they're completely normal and understandable too. In fact, if the feelings of love the Survivor has stopped after the relationship ends, that would be extremely worrying. The fact that Survivors still have feelings of love after the relationship means that they are human, and therefore not Vampires.

Survivors often spend many years in relationships with Vampires believing that the False Self the Vampire portrays is really who they are. It's not, but that doesn't mean that those feelings of love are going to go away overnight. Just because the Vampire was false, doesn't mean that the love the Survivor felt was. In fact, what the Survivor felt in the relationship was absolutely genuine; they loved with all their heart. Just because the Vampire didn't does not detract from the real love the Survivor gave, and it's incredibly important to remember that.

So how to deal? First, recognise it. You loved this individual, and that's a beautiful thing. That they are incapable of receiving love is not your issue. That they are incapable of having a functional relationship, and must therefore render any relationship horribly dysfunctional is not your issue either.

You loved. You wanted a functional relationship. You fought for it. You gave. In other words, you demonstrated that you are capable of loving another person, and that is something that is beautiful beyond measure, so recognise that please. As with Shame, get with a good Therapist and work all this through. And, of course, use all the resources at your disposal. All Survivors are having the same conversations about this, and it will help enormously.

Please don't focus on the Vampire. Remember please that they are incapable of love. If you dwell on trying to find reasons why they didn't love you, you won't be able to implement Emotional No Contact. Focus instead on YOU and the way YOU loved. There comes a point in Emotional No Contact when the Survivor has to make a decision: To believe 100% that the Vampire is incapable of love, and therefore destroyed the relationship, or to believe that the Vampire isn't a Vampire.

I would assert that the only way to reconcile those feelings of love that remain after the Vampire is gone is to recognise those feelings, accept them, recognise how amazing that makes you for having the ability to feel them and then "flip the switch" and accept that the Vampire is a Vampire. The problem with love in the relationship was them, not you.

Once you accept that the Vampire is a Vampire, and therefore is incapable of love then the conclusion that they, not you, destroyed the relationship is the only logical one. It doesn't matter what their version of events is. They are disordered, so nothing they say or do makes sense anyway. As soon as you accept that, you can put all the love back where it belongs: on YOU. Self-love is critical to mastering

Emotional No Contact, so use the resources, get a Therapist and find as many ways as possible to love yourself every day.

When it comes to Anger, those feelings are completely normal and understandable. You are going to feel angry. You've been duped, attacked, abused and probably discarded by a disordered individual that has no capacity for love or remorse and has clearly demonstrated that they are not fit to be in a relationship but has blamed you for its failure. That's enough to make the Dalai Lama angry.

Anger is useful, though. It can be used to motivate you, but please beware. Staying in anger is going to hurt you. You are perfectly within your rights to feel it, in fact having your own feelings is something that Vampires don't allow, so now's a great time to feel all that anger good and hard. But channel it please. Find a direction to put it in. Anger that is turned inwards becomes depression and self-loathing, and that cannot be allowed to happen. In Emotional No Contact, allowing your anger to turn inward is doing the Vampires work for them because they can still affect you, and that defeats the purpose.

So how to deal? Get it out. Express that anger in healthy ways. Talk about your experience and feelings with a Therapist. Get stuck in to the resources available and talk with other Survivors. And find a channel. Exercise is a great one; burn it off. Swim, run, walk, play a sport, take self-defence classes (that's a double-win). I used my anger to start this book. Just don't point it at other people or yourself, please. Again, that's what the Vampire wants you to do. Think about it, pointing anger at others is what Vampires do, and you're not a Vampire, right? There you go. Do something healthy instead. The resources available to you will give you loads of great ideas, so take them on board, and go do.

And again, please don't point the anger at the Vampire. Yes, you are angry about what the Vampire did to you, but they never accepted your anger at them while you were in the relationship, and they won't now. Pointing all that anger at the Vampire is what they want you to do. It risks you breaking No Contact so that you can have a go at them, at which point they will hurt you again.

No, that anger needs to go out into something productive for you. Feel it. Definitely feel it, and then channel it so that it benefits you. Maybe even others. That anger is fuel for something, so get active please, and let that anger out in healthy ways. I can't recommend exercise enough. Run, walk, swim, cycle or whatever you choose. Get it all out.

OK, so what happens when you have mastered Emotional No Contact?

This is the great bit. You let go. Mastering Emotional No Contact means getting yourself into a position where the Vampire means nothing to you. There simply is no emotional connection at all. You'll know when you're starting to master No Contact at this level when a few things start to happen:

1) You're dealing with your Shame. You don't feel guilty about the relationship failing, and you know you did everything you could. You know that it was never going to work, and that's the Vampire's fault, not yours.

2) You've started to love yourself. You're doing things for you and you're treating yourself well again. You're enjoying things and getting to know you again.
3) You're channelling your anger. You're doing things that allow you to express your anger in healthy ways, and you feel better afterwards. You're not hurting anyone, and you're not hurting yourself.

Once you start to recognise those signs, you're mastering Emotional No Contact. Keep going with that, and eventually you'll be able to take the final step, which is forgiveness.

If you're a recent Survivor, you've probably just uttered a cuss-word, or a series of them at the mention of the word "forgiveness". That's completely fair. It takes a while, and a fair amount of work to get to a place where you can finally master Emotional No Contact, so no worries. But, it's worth exploring why it's necessary and why it works.

Forgiveness isn't about the Vampire. It's about you. Once you've got a handle on your feelings of Shame, Love and Anger the only thing keeping you connected to the Vampire is the choice to stay connected. If you're still connected, it's because it's serving a purpose. It's allowing you to process your feelings.

But once you've started to master Emotional No Contact, and you've got a really good handle on your emotions again, why stay connected? What purpose does it serve? The question to ask yourself at that point is: Am I better or worse off for staying emotionally connected to the

Vampire? If the answer to that is that you are worse off, then it's time to forgive and move on. If you can do that, you will have mastered Emotional No Contact, the Vampire will have no hold on you at all and you will finally be free. Your "No Contact House" will be secure, and the Vampire has no way in.

The choice to forgive represents you finally letting go of the past. You are consigning the Vampire to their fate and taking control of your own life again. It is a conscious decision to remove them from your mind and focus solely on you and what you want from life. And forgiveness is not the same as forgetting. I would argue that you should never forget what the Vampire did to you because that would be foolish. However, once we forgive, we release all connection to the Vampire and let whatever will happen to them happen to them. If it helps at all, what will happen to them will be very bad indeed. Karma never loses an address.

Grey Rock

In an ideal world, everyone would be able to go No Contact with the Vampire that attacked them and that would be Game Over. But we don't live in an ideal world and many Survivors find themselves having to be in contact with the Vampire, usually because of shared children, which means that another skill needs to be mastered instead: Grey Rock.

This skill gets its name because it refers to giving as much Narcissistic supply to the Vampire as a rock does, in other words, none. It requires the Survivor to engage with the Vampire with the same amount of emotional engagement as a rock. Whatever the Vampire does to provoke an emotional response, the Survivor responds with facts and plain statements, never emotion. Therefore, Grey Rock has a Golden Rule: Give No Emotion.

Grey Rock and No Contact are not mutually exclusive. In other words, it's not one or the other. All Survivors have to master No Contact, even if they are still in contact because No Contact is the process of building towards the complete removal of emotional connection to the Vampire. Given that, even when contact has to be maintained, which requires No Contact at the Practical level to be adjusted, the work at the Biological & Psychological and Emotional levels continues. Grey Rock can therefore be usefully thought of as a way of building a solid foundation for the "No Contact House" with provision for a basement in which the Vampire can be dealt with without risking the rest of the House. The Vampire is never allowed access to any part of the House other than the basement, and the work on that House continues without any input from the Vampire at all.

On a practical level, examine what communication channels are necessary, and reject any that is not. Whatever is the most recordable, and least disputable is the right way to go. The Vampire will try to exploit any communication channel that could allow them to call the communication into question. Vampires are notorious for drawing Survivors into communications in which they can claim that things were said that were not, or that things were not said that were. The content of phone calls will be denied or "forgotten", voicemails will not have been "received", texts will not "arrive", and the same goes for instant messages. Please bear in mind that it won't matter what "received / read" reports exist at your end, the Vampire will deny it arrived at their end in the hopes of drawing you into Drama. Therefore, if at all possible, use e.mail exclusively to communicate with the Vampire.

The only exception to this is when there are children involved, and therefore a phone line is a good idea in case of emergencies. But here's the thing: it's for emergencies. By all means have a phone line open with the Vampire, but make it very clear IN WRITING that phone communications are to be used for emergencies and essential communications concerning the kids ONLY. If the Vampire is going to be late picking up the kids: Fine. Call or text. Same goes the other way round, but if it's not an emergency and it's not essential, it goes via e.mail and that's it.

The Vampire will try to control all communications they way they did in the relationship and that's not going to change. So, have ONE communication channel only. Make it an e.mail channel. Tell the Vampire IN WRITING on the e.mail channel that you will only respond to messages on that channel, and that you will ignore any messages on any other channel. Ignore any other channel. If the Vampire claims an e.mail didn't arrive, do not get drawn into a discussion. Your report will say it's been sent and that's good enough. And here's why:

When communicating in Grey Rock via e.mail, you have to consider how a court would look at the matter, just in case it actually comes to that. However unlikely that may seem, always assume that you will be called on to put your communications in front of a judge at some point. If you have one channel that you have made clear to the Vampire at the start is the only channel that is to be used, then everything that appears on that channel can be printed and put in front of the court. Courts like simple. Not only that, but if you're the one doing the simple and calm presentation, the Vampire can't make you look like the crazy person in the situation. If there are several channels, it could get confusing, and the Vampire wants it to get confusing because then they can control it.

The Vampire will try to confuse the matter, delay court proceedings, run up your legal costs, constantly deny and retract information and generally fuck the whole process up. The Vampire has absolutely no interest in communicating openly and honestly. What they want is to control you by causing chaos for you to respond to and, if you do, they will just keep on doing it. When it comes to presenting information to a court, the Vampire will turn up looking and sounding completely reasonable and claim that you are the disorganised and crazy party because you haven't managed to keep up with all the confusing communication they fucked up in the first place.

Never forget that the Vampire thrives on chaos and drama. Getting drawn into complex, drawn out court proceedings based on their own machinations is exactly what they want, so don't. Stick to one e.mail channel, insist that it is the only one that will be used and ignore everything else. This serves several purposes.

First, it shows the Vampire that you will not be drawn into drama and chaos. Second, it shows the Vampire that there would be no point taking anything to court because the communications are clear and any manipulations they have tried to pull will be obvious. Third, it forces the Vampire to behave themselves in case they say something stupid in writing and finally (and this one's really good), if you ever feel that you are being threatened, you can copy in your lawyer, or a trusted friend to the messages. The Vampire will notice that other people are looking and back down. They want to operate in the shadows, and you will have shown them that you can take those shadows away any time you want. Nothing shuts a Vampire up quicker than an audience they can't control.

Overall, there's an acronym that can help here: BIF. It stands for Brief, Informative and Firm. Originally, BIF had another F in it. It stood for friendly, so I took it out. You don't need to be friendly with a Vampire. They will probably take it as an open invitation to Hoover, so BIF will do. Keep your emails brief, give only the information required and stick to your guns. That's it. If you find that you have to deal with the Vampire face-to-face, for example if there are children involved, then Grey Rock still applies. Here again, an acronym applies: DIP. It stands for Detached, Indifferent and Professional. Let's break that down.

Detached: Keep your emotions to yourself. Do not allow emotion to register on your face or in your voice. The Vampire will try to provoke you, so a bit of practice can be very useful here. Have a friend or a Therapist help you rehearse how to speak and keep your expressions under control. You may not believe it at this point, but that can actually be fun. Always keep in mind what you want to get out of any interaction and keep that at the centre of what you say and do. Don't get drawn into needless pleasantries because they're not pleasantries, they're Hoovers.

Indifferent: Do not respond to anything the Vampire says or does that creates drama. Their objective will be to draw you into some bullshit or other in order to extract Narcissistic supply from you, so just pretend like you don't care. At first that might be tricky, but just like all the skills here, the more you practice the better you get. Rehearsal is a great idea here too. Try developing a few standard responses that clearly indicate indifference. Words and phrases like "Uh-Huh", "Mmm-Hmm" and "Sure" are good for that.

The object of the exercise is to show the Vampire that you really don't care what they say or do. Whenever a Vampire is required to make more effort than other people in a conversation, they just won't. They expect to be able to say very little, provoke a response and then lap up the Narcissistic supply. The less you say, the more they feel invalidated and the harder they have to work. They hate that.

Professional: How great is it when you deal with someone at work who is the consummate professional? They're clear in their communication, no-one gets excited, there's no drama and you just get shit sorted, right? Be that person: polite, clear, calm and straightforward. Professionals stick to the facts and they don't get drawn into emotional crap because they know that's counterproductive and inappropriate. If you're already a professional, engage with the Vampire as though they were a client. If you're not, talk with any friends you have that are, or discuss with your Therapist.

The Big Year (and a day)

And now I'm going to make myself really unpopular. I've included The Big Year in this section because although it is more to do with the passage of time, technically it is a skill because it will probably be unfamiliar and will take some effort to achieve. The "Big Year" means staying single for a year and a day. Yeah, I know. I told you I was going to make myself unpopular. Please bear with me while I explain because there are so many really good reasons why the Big Year is a good idea, and so many really good reasons why not doing it is a really bad idea.

Why not doing the Big Year is a bad idea: The addiction

Survivors are in withdrawal: Fact. Addiction takes time to recover from, and any addict that doesn't stay clear from their drug of choice will relapse. For Survivors, that drug is the behaviours of the Vampire. Not the abuse, but the intermittent positive rewards. Now that the behaviours have stopped because the Vampire is gone, you have to make sure you don't fall back into the same patterns again and that means getting all the poison out of your system.

As I said in previous chapters, the addiction operates at the levels of the Biological, Psychological and Emotional. That's going to take a while to break free from. At least a year, I'd say. The overwhelming majority of survivors that don't do the Big Year end up in another abusive relationship. I'm not making that up, it's the plain truth. If you were recovering from alcoholism and you'd been drinking vodka, what difference would it make if you switched to whiskey? And that's exactly the same as abusive relationships. While you are in withdrawal, you must stay away from relationships, full stop.

Yes, there will come a time when you can go back out there and start dating again, but it's not now. Get your system clear of all the poison, reset, re-start and then go out there. Right now, your brain is a mess. If you're in any doubt about that, re-read chapters 8, 9 and 10. Dating with an addicted brain is about as safe as walking into sawmill while wearing a magnetic vest. You will be drawn to the very thing that will destroy you. Don't do it.

Dolphining

A great term, this. It refers to the way dolphins leap out of the water and dive back in again. Imagine that the water is abusive relationships, the air above the surface is your new found freedom from the Vampire and you are the dolphin. You've just broken the surface and you're in the sunlight and fresh air. There will be an enormous temptation to dive straight back into the relationship world because it brings a source of validation. People will provide you with positive feedback about yourself. It feels comfortable and familiar. But there's a major problem with that. Everything under the surface is a source of validation that comes from outside of you.

Only when you're above the surface can you start to validate yourself and that really matters. The water and everything in it serves to confirm everything you have believed about yourself up to this point, and all that has to change. Once you've broken the surface and you're in the clear, fresh air and all that sunlight you have to stay there.

Diving straight back in is diving back into the past, and we both know what was in your past: The Vampire. And what's in the water? You guessed it: Vampires. Not only Vampires, of course, but I guarantee you they don't live in the sunlight. Diving back into the water is stupid and dangerous, and the Big Year will allow you to make sure that when you do go back in, you will be able to see the Vampire coming from a mile away.

Grief

Grief is something that modern society gets catastrophically wrong in my opinion. When we have lost something or someone important in our lives, our natural and human response is to grieve that loss. Whether that was a person, a job, a home, a pet, you name it, a loss is a loss and it must be grieved. Life without that significant thing will never be the same again, and we have to reconstruct our new reality without whatever it was that we lost.

Grief is a psychological process by which we create new ways of understanding the world that now does not contain someone or something whose existence we relied on to help us make sense of reality. It takes time to readjust and I would argue that the loss of an intimate relationship takes at least a year to grieve because the readjustment that loss requires is profound.

The thing about psychological processes is that even if we deny that they are happening, they are happening anyway. Whether we choose to acknowledge grief is immaterial; we are grieving anyway. Denying it will only cause us damage because we won't have a fucking clue why we're behaving the way we are. In modern society, we seem to have a problem with that. Grief appears to be an inconvenience. Something we should just "get over".

Fuck that. Everyone on the planet who has lost someone or something significant in their lives has the right and responsibility to grieve because grief is the process by which we reinvent ourselves after the loss. And yes, that includes the loss of the Vampire. However disgustingly awful they were to you, they were still a massive part of your life.

In fact, I would argue that the more disgustingly awful they were to you, the more you need to give yourself time to grieve because grief is the psychological process of readjustment. The more unadjusted you were by the Vampire, the more grieving you will have to do. I would say a year and a day would be the minimum requirement here, but a good Therapist can help you manage the grieving process far better. If you can get one, get one.

Why doing the Big Year is a good idea:

The addiction:

As a Survivor, you're addicted to the behaviours of the Vampire and you are in withdrawal. Your hormones, neurochemicals, brain wiring and behaviour patterns are all over the place. For all the reasons I've explained in earlier chapters, you have to let that withdrawal run its course or it will all go catastrophically wrong.

Please remember that you are addicted to the behaviour of the Vampire. And how do all Vampires behave: exactly the same. So what's the first thing you'll attract and be attracted to? That's right folks. You are going to want to get a "hit" of Vampire behaviour, and that will undo all the good work you've been trying to do in recovery. Doing the Big Year will allow you to repair the damage that was done at the Biological, Psychological and Emotional levels and that's absolutely vital if you're going to move on and have healthy relationships in the future.

Think of it like this: Would you want to date an addict? You already did that, right? So why ask anyone else to do the same for you, and why jump into another relationship with another addict? It won't end well, because it's just repeating the same relationship with a different person. You are not a Vampire, so please don't behave like one. Once you've repaired all that damage and you are healthy you will attract and be attracted to healthy people. It's as simple as that.

Fleas

The expression "when you lay down with dogs you get fleas" is especially true of Survivors of relationships with Vampires. It doesn't matter how long the relationship went on for, there is every chance that you will have picked up some of the Vampire's behaviours, thoughts, beliefs and feelings and you're going to have to get rid of them. No-one wants to carry unhealthy stuff into a new relationship, right? Having "fleas" is a very unpleasant way of being.

Take it from someone who's been there. Until you've got yourself clear of all the toxins in your emotional system left there from your relationship with the Vampire, you will in all likelihood try to recreate the drama you were familiar with, even with someone healthy. In other words, you will behave like a Vampire because that's what you're used to. That's what it is to have "fleas".

The most tragic scenario I can image post-Vampire is that you meet a lovely, loving, kind person and fuck the whole thing up because you're still looking for a Vampire. Please don't do that. It will take you a little while to get rid of all those bad habits you picked up from the Vampire and you deserve to enjoy a loving, healthy relationship, so give it time please. A good Therapist can help enormously here, and the Big Year will give you the opportunity to get rid of all those "Fleas" so that you can get into a healthy relationship once your year is up.

The "Firsts"

The "Firsts" are all the significant days in the calendar that you shared with the Vampire: your birthday, their birthday, religious holidays, Valentines, Halloween etc. There's no two ways about this. Getting through the "Firsts" is hard. It will trigger all sorts of emotions in you from nostalgia to anger, and it will threaten your resolve in terms of No Contact. However, they have to be endured and the great news is that you'll only have to do each one once.

The reason getting through them is so important is that it serves to show you that you can survive and thrive on your own. Each "First" you get through demonstrates that your life is about you now, not about the Vampire. Each and every "First" you get through is another step towards a Vampire-free future and each one says loud and clear that you don't need to put anyone before yourself ever again. In practical terms, whenever you find that a "First" is coming up, make plans to do something good for yourself. On the Vampires birthday, go to the movies. On Valentine's Day, buy yourself dinner. The idea here is to get into the habit of putting you first. You matter now, not them. All those days were never about you anyway, right? Well they are now, and you may have to force yourself to do that but it really matters that you do. Reward yourself for getting though every "First" because each one is a marker of your success and freedom.

The New You

Once you're free from the Vampire, you're going to have to figure out who you are. Almost every Survivor reports that they simply don't know who they are because they spend so long defining themselves by their worth to the Vampire that once they're gone, there is a huge hole where their identity used to be.

The Big Year is absolutely vital in recovery because it lets you find out who you really are. Now, that might sound trite, or cliché but I am absolutely serious. If you are coming out of a relationship with a Vampire, your identity will literally have been stolen from you. You have been Gaslighted, lied to, manipulated and treated like you have no worth at all. The Vampire's False Self was all that mattered in the relationship, and if you didn't support that, or you didn't serve the Vampire's never ending need for Narcissistic supply, you will have been made to feel that you are basically a bad person. Nothing could be further from the truth, and you deserve the time and space to piece back together the wonderful person you always were.

The purpose of the Big Year is to allow you to become who you truly are without the toxic input from an individual that was compelled to tell you who you are in order to make themselves feel safe. Your head has been filled with the Vampire's lies that support their False Self, and the objective reality of who you are has been replaced with the Vampires False reality so that they don't have to face the truth. In other words, your very reality has been twisted all out of shape and you're going to have to untwist it and get your identity back.

During the Big Year, you will have an excellent opportunity to rebuild friendships, make new ones, rediscover old hobbies and interests and discover new ones, rebuild your success in your job or business or find new successes elsewhere and most importantly you will have the opportunity to rebuild your Self Respect. The Big Year will give you opportunities every day to prove to yourself that what you were told by the Vampire was a lie. Every single day of the Big Year is a chance to do something that you didn't think you could do, and things that benefit you for a change. Maybe that's picking up an old interest, or listening to music you love, or going to the movies on your own.

Whatever it is, there are 366 days in which you can prove to yourself the very thing the Vampire didn't want you to know: That you can flourish and grow on your own. Remember that the Vampire trapped you and systematically tore down your Self Respect. They had to for their own survival. But they're gone now, so now you can take your own life in your own hands and shape it the way you want.

Now, I've been there so I know how impossible that might sound, but on the other hand, I've been there so I know it can be done, and when you do it it's wonderful. If you don't believe me right now, take a leap of faith, OK? The Big Year is the start of the rest of your life. As time passes, and you do more and more things on your own you will prove to yourself that you are capable not only of surviving, but thriving in a new life that you are in complete control of.

A good Therapist can really help here so if you can get one, get one, but on a practical level, keep a list. Every day, write down one thing that you did by yourself for yourself. List more if you've done them. Keep that list going and watch it grow. It will be your record of all the things the Vampire wanted you to believe you couldn't do. Read it back when you're feeling low. Read it back even if you're not. That list is a permanent record of your success without the Vampire, and I promise you it will contain way more success than anything that occurred when you were with them. They were a millstone around your neck. Now, you are free.

Boundaries and Deal Breakers

There's a reason why this section comes at the end of the Field Manual: It's because it's the most important. Everything has been leading us here, dear Survivor. Heads-up.

During the Big Year, you will have a golden opportunity to figure out the two things that will keep you safe from Vampires as you go forward: Boundaries and Deal Breakers. These two things are absolutely vital in recovery from Narcissistic abuse because they allow you properly take excellent care of the New You that you build during that time. Get this right and you will be such a massively tough target to Vampires that you won't need to avoid them; they will avoid you.

Not only that, but the maxim: "We attract what we are" is so true here. When you have good, solid Boundaries and a list of Deal Breakers; you will attract people who also have solid Boundaries and understand Deal Breakers. Healthy people understand and respect each other's sovereignty; their right to have their own mind, life and decisions. Boundaries and Deal Breakers are a clear demonstration that you have sovereignty over your life and not only will healthy people respect that, they will love it.

Vampires don't have Boundaries or Deal Breakers because they don't have or understand rules at all. What's more, they can't stand people who do have Boundaries and Deal Breakers because they are sovereign; they are in control of their own mind, life and decisions and therefore can't be manipulated or controlled in any way. It's like having a food allergy: they just can't "process" people with Boundaries and

Deal Breakers. Nothing scares a Vampire away quicker than someone who can't be manipulated or controlled.

Think about it. Vampires are always attacking, right? They want to Strike and Retreat and if the work involved is more than the Narcissistic supply gained, they will just move right along to another Target. Having strong Boundaries and clear Deal Breakers sends a hugely clear signal that you are NOT a source of Narcissistic supply. Vampires will take one look at that and get the hell out of Dodge. There is no point attacking someone with strong Boundaries because they can't be manipulated or controlled and won't provide Narcissistic supply. There is no point attacking someone with clear Deal Breakers because they say what they mean and mean what they say; there's nothing to manipulate there.

Earlier in the Field Manual I talked about how I got a security system for my home, not to have a security system, but to make myself a tough target and deterrent to potential burglars. That's what Boundaries and Deal Breakers will do for you; they will make you a walking, talking deterrent to Vampires. Let's have a look at how they work.

Boundaries

Boundaries are essentially the expression of your rights as a person; a Bill of Rights, if you will. They are clear statements of how you expect other people to treat you and what you will and won't accept in other's behaviour towards you. They are usually learned in childhood from our experiences, which is why the children of Vampire parents have a tough time with them. Their parents taught them that having Boundaries was wrong, or unacceptable and violated their Boundaries through their words and actions. That's precisely why recovery from Narcissistic abuse requires the re-learning of Boundaries: we have to teach ourselves not only that we have rights, but we also have the right to assert those rights.

It's all about Self Respect. When we establish Boundaries, we are telling the world that we are to be Respected. When we enforce those Boundaries, we are showing ourselves that we Respect ourselves. Nothing sends a clearer message of Self Respect than the word "No". It doesn't have to be mean, in fact it's the opposite. Using the word "No" when it comes to others crossing our Boundaries is how we tell other people where they stand with us and mature adults actually like that. Healthy people actively want to know who you are and how to treat you best and your Boundaries will tell them. Telling a healthy person "No" when it comes to your Boundaries is simply showing them where the line is and they will not only respect you for that, they will like you for it. We're not being mean when we're asserting a Boundary, we're telling and showing people how to treat us and we all want that kind of consistent stability, right?

When we're recovering from a relationship with a Vampire, our Boundaries will be all over the place. The Vampire will have broken through any that we had using their weapons and tactics in order to exert power and control and drain the Target of Narcissistic supply and resources. In all probability, they will have re-taught the Target that having Boundaries is "mean" or "wrong" because Boundaries get in the way of them exploiting the Target, and they hate that.

During the Big Year, the Boundaries the Vampire trounced can be reinstated and new ones put in place. Once they're there, they have to stay there.

It's so important that happens <u>before</u> looking for another relationship because weak Boundaries is what got the Target involved with a Vampire in the first place. Without strong Boundaries, there is a very high probability they will attract another Vampire, because that's what they're drawn to. If you <u>want</u> healthy, you have to <u>be</u> healthy and setting and maintaining Boundaries is what lies at the heart of that.

I can't overstate the importance of getting a good Therapist to help with this. They will help you to figure out how your Boundaries were crossed in the past, help you rediscover them and learn to assert them. Having Boundaries is the right of every single person on the planet, and no-one has the right to cross anyone else's Boundaries. A good Therapist will help immeasurably in allowing you to get and keep your Boundaries in place.

There are several areas where Boundaries apply:

Material Boundaries

These refer to your belongings, finances and home. You get to decide what to do with those things; who you lend or give to, how much and for how long; who you allow in your home, why and for how long; when and under what conditions you allow others to use your resources. The Big Year will allow you to take stock of your material resources and decide for yourself how you want to handle them and how you expect others to show that they respect them, and therefore you.

Physical Boundaries

These refer to your personal space, privacy and body. You get to decide how close people get to you physically, when, for how long and under what circumstances. This is how you show yourself Respect and tell other how to Respect you and your personal space. If you're not comfortable with hugging; don't hug, for example. You'll need to ask yourself some questions here. For example: What is your definition of privacy? Who gets to touch you, when and under what circumstances? How do they get to touch you, when and under what circumstances? What are you comfortable with about how others want you to be with them? How close do you want to be with others? How do you feel about people's activities near you? Under what circumstances will you leave a situation? Under what circumstances will you ask others to leave you alone? What's your view on locked doors? Or closed doors? There are loads of things to consider, and a good Therapist will be able to help you sort it all out.

Mental Boundaries

These refer to your Values, thoughts and opinions. What are your Values; your principles and standards of behaviour; your judgement of what's important in life? That's pretty big, and it's going to take quite a lot of thinking about. The Big Year gives you that time. How do you manage your thoughts? Are you easily swayed by others? Do you stand by your opinions rigidly, or are you more open-minded? Are you a tad suggestible? Are you comfortable in your own head? Are you OK with being alone with your thoughts? To what extent do you doubt yourself?

Just as with our bodies, our minds are our own sovereign territory. Mental Boundaries allow us to state clearly how others should treat us intellectually and how they should respect our thoughts and opinions. Again, a good Therapist will help you figure all that out and I can't state enough how important that is. Vampires will always try to attack the Targets mind, and if they find Boundaries in there, they will just move along. Once we get a handle on our Mental Boundaries, we can teach others how to Respect us and we can show ourselves Respect by being secure with who we are, what our Values are, what we think and what we believe.

Emotional Boundaries

These refer to our feelings. Having Boundaries around our emotions doesn't mean we can't share with other people, what it means is that we are separate from them and can choose what to share. Emotional Boundaries allow you to take responsibility for your own emotions and stop you taking responsibility for other peoples. They prevent you from blaming others, and accepting blame from others; they protect you from feelings of guilt and particularly Shame; they protect you from other peoples' negative emotions and they draw a force-field around you that allows you to decide which emotions you let out to others, and which emotions you let in from others.

As with all Boundaries, Emotional Boundaries tell the world how to treat your feelings. They let you show other people what you will and won't accept from them on an emotional level, meaning they can show Respect to you, and when you enforce an Emotional Boundary, it means you are Respecting yourself.

Healthy people can manage their emotions (in the main) and can separate their own from those of other people. If someone is trying to dump negative emotions on a healthy person, they just do the Tai-Chi thing and gently sweep it away because they know it doesn't belong to them. Vampires excel at trying to get their Target to accept their negative emotions and own them as if they were their own. Having strong Emotional Boundaries prevents that from happening because those negative emotions just bounce off. It takes time, practice and a good Therapist is a huge help, but it really can be done and the Big Year gives you the time and space to do that.

When it comes to creating a defence against Vampires, Emotional Boundaries are vital. Vampires have no Emotional Boundaries whatsoever and expect their Targets to be the same. Narcissistic supply is simply the meeting of emotional needs, and the Vampire can't do that for themselves; they expect the Target to do it. They expect to be able to gather Narcissistic supply from their Targets at will, meaning they want them to push their emotions through their Emotional Boundaries and into the Vampire whenever the Vampire provokes them to do so. They also have no problem with trying to push their own emotions through the Targets Emotional Boundaries whenever they want. It's how they operate, and the only thing they do. All those tactics and weapons are designed to achieve that one thing.

Having strong Emotional Boundaries stops that from happening. If a Vampire tries to provoke an emotional response in someone with strong Emotional Boundaries; nothing happens. The emotions remain behind the Boundary and the person concerned remains calm; the attack fails. If the Vampire attempts to push their own emotions through a strong Emotional Boundary; again, nothing happens. The emotional outburst dissipates into the air because it's got nowhere to go; it's just an outburst. The person with strong Emotional Boundaries knows that their emotions are their own to do with what they will; that the Vampires emotions are their own and that they have nothing to do with them. The Vampire has nowhere to go with that.

Emotional Boundaries are the fortress that the Vampire cannot invade. This is why it's so important to get a good Therapist to help. If it is at all possible, please do. If not, read and study. Talk with other Survivors. Watch videos, listen to podcasts. Above all, use the Big Year to work hard on those Emotional Boundaries. Get that right and Vampires will just plain leave you alone.

Sexual Boundaries

These refer to your sexuality. As with all other Boundaries, they are there to protect your sovereignty and in this case, that's about your mind, body, beliefs and identity regarding sexual activity. Your sexuality is your own; no-one has a right to dictate it or judge it. It is yours and yours alone.

Sexual Boundaries protect your comfort level with sexual activity, and they will take time to sort out, which is what the Big Year is for. Again, you'll need to ask some questions: What are you comfortable with when it comes to touch? Who do you want to touch you, how, where, when and under want circumstances? What are you not comfortable with? What do you like? What don't you like?

Sexual Boundaries are vital in sexual relationships. As with all other Boundaries, they protect you from sexual contact you don't want and allow you to tell others how to Respect your sexuality. When you enforce them, you are Respecting your sexuality, and therefore yourself.

Sexual Boundaries are the fundamental basis of healthy sexual relationships. It doesn't matter what they are, they are yours, and when we communicate them to healthy partners they are Respected. Intimacy is not about sex; it is about knowing someone deeply and being able to be completely free in that persons presence. Sex and intimacy are often inextricably linked, but Sexual Boundaries tell our partner who we are sexually so that we can know each other better and build intimacy. When we have Sexual Boundaries and they are Respected, we build trust in the other person and we build Respect in ourselves.

One of the features of a relationship with a Vampire is that Sexual Boundaries will have been crossed. The Big Year allows you to reassert those Boundaries, put in some new ones and be able to communicate them clearly to others. Again, I cannot overstate how important a good Therapist is here. Sexual Boundaries are sometimes confusing in today's society and learning yours will be vital in your recovery and moving on to have a healthy relationship.

Spiritual Boundaries

These refer to your beliefs. Spirituality is however you choose to conceive of the world around you. It doesn't matter how you do that, or what your framework is for making sense of the world; just like sexuality, you spirituality is yours and no-one has the right to dictate it or judge it. Spiritual Boundaries protect your sovereign right to your beliefs and your comfort level with how you engage with the world based on them.

Spirituality is an enormous part of what it is to be human, and Spiritual Boundaries exist to protect your right to live your life the way you see fit, to engage in practices that Respect your spirituality, and therefore yourself and to protect your right to believe whatever you want. When you enforce Spiritual Boundaries, you are telling people how to Respect you, and you are Respecting yourself.

As with other Boundaries, it may take time to figure out what your Spiritual Boundaries are and you need to ask some questions: What do I believe about how the world works? Do I believe in a higher power? Are there forms of Spirituality that appeal to me more than others? Am I open-minded about Spirituality? Do I feel secure in my beliefs? This may take you some time, and that's what the Big Year is for. Again, a good Therapist can help you here by encouraging you to explore that part of who you are.

Your Personal Constitution

During the Big Year, you will have a wonderful and unique opportunity to draw up your Personal Bill of Rights and that; dear Survivor is a truly beautiful thing.

But it's more than that. Once you have gained independence from the Vampire, you can draw up not only your Personal Bill of Rights, but your own Constitution; your system of Government; the way you define the Sovereign state that is who You are. It is a set of Principles that tell others how to Respect you, and that you uphold in Respecting yourself. You get to create your own life now, and it is entirely the life of your own choosing.

I like to use the Founding Fathers of the United States as my example here. Having won their independence from British Rule, they had to create something that laid out how the United States would proceed from that point on. You get to do that during the Big Year, and I strongly recommend it. As you go along and decide where your Boundaries are going to be, write them down. There's no set format for this; it's up to you. I will say this, though: They are statements of what you want or don't want, and you don't have to be aggressive about it, so you might like to start them with phrases like "I don't like", or "I won't accept", or "I will allow X but not Y".

Sometimes it's hard to know where to start with all this, so I'll quickly highlight some Rights that other people use to formulate their Boundaries. Maybe it will start you thinking.

The Right to seek professional help
The Right to be listened to respectfully
The Right to make your own decisions, and change your mind
The Right to develop your own talents
The Right to privacy and personal space
The Right not to be responsible for other people's feelings
The Right to your own needs
The Right to your own beliefs
The Right to have your own friendships and relationships
The Right to choose how you live
The Right to walk away from a relationship
The Right to be independent
The Right to choose who to share your body with
The Right to express your feelings and emotions
The Right to say No and live without guilt
The Right to make mistakes

That's just a few, and the Big Year will give you the opportunity to do your own research on your rights and formulate your Boundaries. As always, if you can, get a good Therapist to help you.

Deal Breakers

Deal Breakers are the things that make it clear which actions on the part of other people will lead you to end your relationship with them, or not even start one. That can be a friendship, romantic relationship and even family relationships. Deal Breakers set out what you simply won't accept and being able to tell yourself and others what they are is empowering, shows them how to Respect you and shows yourself Respect. In practice, if someone does something that you consider to be a Deal Breaker, that's it: Relationship over.

It's a feature of healthy relationships that both partners know each other's Deal Breakers because they tell each other early on. Once a Deal Breaker has been stated, everyone works on the understanding that if one happens, the relationship ends. Healthy people will want to know what your Deal Breakers are, and will have their own; their very existence in a relationship is a sign of emotional maturity.

Deal Breakers are personal. During the Big Year, you'll have the opportunity to set yours by reflecting on what you've experienced in the past and never want to experience again, what your preferences are in others and how you want the landscape of your relationships to look. As with Boundaries, Deal Breakers are not negotiable and no-one outside of you has the right to deny them, change them, criticise them or otherwise interfere. They're yours, you mean them and that's that.

Many people have shared Deal Breakers. Cheating and Lying are very common for instance, but just because one of your Deal Breakers might not be commonly held doesn't mean it's not valid. If anyone thinks one of your Deal Breakers is unusual; too bad. It's yours and you have the Right to have it. As with Boundaries, you can use the Big Year to formulate them and a good Therapist can help you sort out what they will be. It's a good idea to write them out, too; it forms part of your Constitution. Here are some of the more common Deal Breakers as a start:

Cheating
Lying
Stealing
Abuse (of any kind)
Differing views on commitment and/or children
Selfishness or Greed
Being unkind
Being a financial liability
Addiction (of any kind)
Being rude
Being critical
Manipulation
Being disrespectful
Being unsupportive

These are just a few and your list can be as long as you like. It doesn't matter how many you've got or whet they are; this is your life now and you get to live it for yourself and by your rules. You've probably noticed that almost that entire simple list is things the Vampire does. Maybe not in the Idealisation Stage, but they can't keep up that façade for long, so pay close attention and if you get any sense that a Deal Breaker is in evidence, walk away.

Which brings me on to my final point:

Trust Your Instincts

How many times do we look back at the relationship we had with the Vampire and think "I knew something was off, I just couldn't put my finger on it"? That was your Instincts screaming at you. During the Big Year, you will have the amazing opportunity to start trusting your Instincts again, because there is something that is true all day every day: "If it feels wrong, it is wrong".

Survivors will have had their ability to trust their Instincts eroded by the Vampire. They hate Instincts, so they use Gaslighting to try to get their Target to second-guess themselves and doubt their Instincts. Right here and now I'm going to say that there isn't a human on the face of the planet that doesn't have good Instincts about other people. It's hard-wired and it's there for our own survival. The only individuals who don't want you to trust your Instincts are Vampires, because they know damn well that humans can tell what they are on an Instinctual level.

Go to a healthy person and tell them that something fells wrong about a situation and they will want to know more. They will respect your Instincts and actively seek to explore what they are telling you, even if it's about them, <u>because they have nothing to hide</u>. The Vampire is a living lie, and if you tell them that something feels wrong, they will minimise and dismiss your Instincts, or try to make you feel wrong for having them <u>because they have everything to hide</u>.

Because of that, the Vampire will have spent the entire time with the Target doing everything in their power to stop them trusting their Instincts so their cover didn't get blown and now's the time to reverse that. The Big Year, and if you can get one, a good Therapist will allow you to learn to "Trust Your Gut" again. There is no greater defence against the Vampire than the early-warning system of good, strong

Instincts that you trust implicitly. Trusting yourself is Respecting yourself; simple.

Initially, you'll probably be on a hair-trigger and your Instincts will look for danger everywhere and actually, that's a far better starting point than where the Vampire left you. It's far better to see Vampires everywhere than to miss the one that gets in. As time goes on, though, please don't stay there. It's really stressful and it's not good for you. Thankfully, using the Big Year to sort out your Boundaries and Deal Breakers will help enormously here. As you develop these, you'll be able to observe people out in the real world and how they behave. If you see someone behaving in ways that would cross your Boundaries, or doing something that would be a Deal Breaker, notice how you feel about that person. That feeling is your Instincts talking.

Wherever you see or hear individuals doing or saying stuff you know you wouldn't tolerate and you become mindful of the way that person makes you feel, you're rebuilding your relationship with your Instincts. It's incredibly valuable, will take time and a good Therapist can really help.

A good start point is to Watch AND Listen. When you observe others, see if their actions match their words. If they say one thing and do another, that will trigger your Instincts. Notice how you feel about that person and remember that sensation: That's your Instincts. People don't tell you who they are; they show you. If there's a mismatch between their words and actions, they're lying; plain and simple. If their words and actions do match, notice how you feel about that person. They won't "feel" the same as the other type. And when you start to notice the way different types of people make you feel, and you have a few examples under your belt, start trusting that.

As a final point, I'm going to say it again. If at all possible, get a good Therapist.

Phew! There we are, Dear Survivor. This is the end of Chapter 12 and effectively, the Field Manual overall. All that's left to do is the last Interlude. Join me?

Interlude 12

"I ain't much for begging." – Dillon, "Alien 3"

Hello again, dear Survivor!

I've always had this weird thing where I have a bank of quotes in my head. You may have noticed that all of the interludes start with quotes from various places. But my all-time favourite comes from the movie Alien 3. The full quote is longer, but here's the version that runs in my mind:

"You're all gonna die. The only question is how you check out. Do you want it on your feet? Or on your fucking knees... begging? I ain't much for begging."

Those words spoke to me the moment I heard them and they have got me on my feet every time I feel like I can't go on because I absolutely refuse to die on my knees. That strength doesn't come from nowhere; it comes from my experiences as the child of a Vampire. Growing up, the unrelenting emotional attacks from the Vampire that is my mother showed me that my responses to her hostility made absolutely no difference. She showed me again and again that she felt entitled to attack me at will and for whatever reason she saw fit and nothing I did made the slightest difference.

Eventually, I realised that all I could control was the way in which I received her attacks. I could kneel in submission, or I could stand in defiance; I learned that since the attack would come anyway, I might as well take it on my feet rather than on my knees. My strength of will was created by my mother's own mindless brutality. I'm actually grateful for that because, like all Vampires, she was in my life to teach me something.

People that attract Vampires are strong. It's what the Vampire sees in us. Somewhere in our history, when the shit hit the fan, we stood where others fell. We stood because others fell. We stood because we didn't believe there was anyone else who would stand for us. At some point, we found ourselves standing alone and yet we still stood, because that's what we do.

And that's precisely why we attract Vampires, because Vampires are weak and will fall when the shit hits the fan. We are strong and we will stand because that's all we know. They are weak but convince themselves and us that they are strong. Their False Self appears strong, but their True Self is weak. Their life is a lie, but we believe the lie because we want to believe it, just as they want us to believe it. We want to believe that the people we love are just like us. That they are strong like us, that they will stand with us, that they will weather the storm with us, that they will have our back as we have theirs. And when they fall, we forgive them because we know that if we fall, we will stand and fight again and we believe that they will do the same.

Vampires won't. They never do.

And that's the hardest lesson of all to learn. That the person we loved was a lie; that we trusted a traitor. That they were weak, and yet needed us to believe that they were strong because that is what they told themselves in their denial of their True Selves. We believed the lie because we wanted to and in my case, as with so many others, because I needed to.

When I was eight years old, my father died. I wouldn't discover it until many years later, but while he lived, he was a barrier between me and my mother. After his death, nothing stood between her and her children and she was free to attack us at will. My sister was eleven years old at the time and from that day forth her childhood and mine came to an end.

My mother was the product of an extremely abusive upbringing. The youngest of eight children, she was starved of attention and became the victim of the paedophile father of one of her school-friends. Her own mother died when she was still in childhood and, unwanted by her father, she was passed to various sisters to be cared for. It was not until she came into early adulthood that she finally met my father, married him and finally found someone that would take care of her. My father carried out that role until the day he died.

Like all Vampires, my mother never developed emotionally beyond the level of a small child. Following the death of my father she became the youngest child in a home that contained two older children. In essence, my sister and I were cast in the role of parents to an individual with little to no capacity to manage her own emotions. We became the unwitting parents to a monstrous child that was full of rage, shame, envy and self-loathing. It was an experience that would set the template for all my adult relationships for many years to come.

As a child, what I learned from growing up with a Vampire was that my value as a person was defined by my ability to make my mother happy. When she was unhappy, my sister and I received none of the attention and nurturance that children deserve and need. When she was happy, we received that which she felt she could spare, and my mother excelled at being unhappy. As a result, my childhood became an endless quest to find ways to make my mother happy so that I could receive that which all children have a right to expect without qualification: unconditional love. In other words, both my sister and I had to work to receive that which should have been given freely.

Ours was the prototypical emotional experience in children of a Vampire parent. Our mother, incapable of showing her children the love and affection that was our birth-right and instead placing her needs before ours, created in us her own emotional experience.

This is what the Vampire does to their children: They behave towards them the way they themselves were treated because they are incapable of anything else. Through their inaction, both involuntarily because of inner lack and voluntarily because of the primacy of their own emotions, they communicate into their children their own inner emotional state. Children that grow up without love feel Unlovable. Children that grow up without a sense of worth feel Unworthy. Children that grow up without a sense of pride feel Shameful. My sister and I were no exception.

And, of course, we grew up in an atmosphere of Fear, Obligation and Guilt. We were both afraid of my mother's childish rage, we both felt obliged to take care of her and we both felt guilty because of our inability to make her happy. In short, my childhood was a toxic mess. Instead of being surrounded by the unconditional love of emotionally developed adult parents, I spent it as an emotional parent to an individual who operated at the level of a spiteful child. The day my mother met the individual who would become my stepfather, it all got much, much worse.

Up to that point, my mother had created a home environment in which my sister and I walked on eggshells and tried to survive in a home dominated by an emotional child. From the time that she introduced her new partner, she began to model adult relationships for us, with predictable results.

My stepfather was introduced to the family when I was 12, and my sister was 15. We had been a single parent family for 4 years, so adapting was not easy. To add to the complication, my stepfather brought his daughter to the mix. She was 5 years old. My stepfather loved her, and my mother hated her intensely.

My stepfather and I had little in common. In all the time we lived together we never formed a bond. Looking back, I know that was because my mother would not allow it. Vampires do that. Instead of promoting unity, they seek to divide and conquer. As soon as it looked like my stepfather and I might be finding common ground, she would find fault with it, or a reason why she should take precedence over it. A drama would ensue, and it was by far easier to walk away from what we were doing than face her wrath for daring to do something that she could not control. We tried sea fishing. It didn't last. We tried computer gaming (this was the eighties). My mother threw the computer in the fire in one of her rages after she had driven my stepfather from the house.

It took my mother less than two years to convince my stepfather to send his daughter away. As part of that machination, she moved the family to a new house in the country outskirts of town, effectively cutting my sister and me off from our friends. In one fell swoop, my mother managed to capture an entire family unit, move them to an environment she could control and then set about the systematic destruction of each and every one of us.

To this day I don't know what became of my stepsister. All I knew then is all I know now: she went to live with her grandparents and we never spoke of her again. My mother had once again achieved primacy of her emotional needs in the house by removing the one person with the greatest needs; my stepsister, and replacing her as the centre of attention. She had also placed herself in the position of control over her domestic domain. It was a state of affairs that would remain in place until the day I finally escaped several years later.

What I've just said might sound preposterous. It might sound like I am claiming that this woman would coldly and calculatedly sacrifice the child of the man she claimed to love in order to establish herself as the one and only centre of attention for the emotional lives of those around her. That is exactly what I am claiming. My mother is a Vampire, and they have absolutely no problem with doing that. My mother, a full grown adult human was so threatened by a child that she forced her partner to exile his own daughter so that she could feel safe. Having done so, she then set about dominating the lives of me and my sister. By now, we were 14 and 17 years of age respectively.

What ensued, now that my sister and I were reaching maturity and therefore presenting a threat to my mother's control was nothing short of an emotional warzone. From my mother's perspective, my sister and I were reaching a point from which we could abandon her in favour of living our own lives. It was at this point that she descended entirely into madness. Her disordered mind, having learned exactly how to control those around her was now fully unleashed because no-one around her was fit to stand in her way.

My sister and I had learned to cope in our own ways. My sister became avoidant and would take every opportunity to be elsewhere. I escaped into fantasy. To this day, I treasure the weird and bizarre because I know full well that the real monsters are all too human. Her now husband had learned to disengage from her insanity by ignoring her wherever possible. In her desperate attempts to exert control over those around her, she incited frequent and violent arguments between her and my stepfather. On more than one occasion, one or both of them sustained physical injuries. On more than one occasion, he would leave the family home. On more than one occasion she was admitted to hospital because of her attempts to commit suicide by drug overdose.

By the time my sister and I had reached the point that we could take control of our own lives, my mother was truly insane. Thanks to her husband's job, she had no need to engage with the real world, and she had no desire to do so. Hers was the only reality that mattered in her life, and she forced that reality on us with impunity. Any and all attempts to question her reality were met with emotional attacks and the threat of abandonment.

Both my sister and I were "cast from the kingdom" when we defied her by giving our love to people other than her. In my sister's case, she married the man my mother ejected her for loving and was only "allowed" back in when she herself became a mother. In my case, I pursued the girl I was ejected for loving and left the country.

Again, it's worth pausing here. It sounds like I'm describing some insane villain: A spiteful, psychotic lunatic that would stop at nothing to render the lives of their own children and that of their partner subservient to their will. That's exactly what I'm describing. My mother is a Vampire and that's what Vampires do. Such individuals are disordered and incredibly dangerous. When allowed, as was the case with my mother, to exert their disordered will on others without fear of retribution, these individuals delight in the systematic destruction of those around them. They seek to destroy them as a means of alleviating their own pain, however temporary, and the relief from that pain is of more importance to them than anything else, including the needs of their own children. Vampires don't raise children, they feed on them. My mother is no exception.

I carried what I had learned from growing up with a Vampire into my adult relationships. My view of what love should be like and what relationships looked like was hopelessly distorted by what my mother and stepfather had shown me. Like so many Survivors, I unconsciously recreated the chaos and abuse of my childhood through a series of toxic relationships, a pattern that would be repeated until I was well into my forties. My boundaries and Self Respect had been all but destroyed by my mother and her disordered behaviour, so when I went out into the world I was the proverbial "lamb to the slaughter".

In adulthood, my relationships fell into two broad patterns; either my partner was emotionally healthy, in which case I ended the relationship, or my partner was a Vampire. Healthy partners capable of giving and receiving unconditional love made no sense to me. I could not understand why there was no drama, no conflict. I could not get my head around how a relationship could exist in which I didn't feel Fear, Obligation and Guilt. These things were familiar, and I believed that they were a necessary part of relationships. Hence, when they were absent in the relationship, I left. So many Survivors report the same thing. Such relationships feel "cold", "uncomfortable", even "boring", and bring a sense of unease rather than peace.

Like so many others, I only felt comfortable when I felt I was earning love, rather than receiving it freely. Vampires are more than happy to make their partners earn what they call "love", so relationships with them become an enmeshment. The Vampire withholds more and more while the Target works harder and harder to earn scraps of affection while all the time the Vampire moves the goalposts, demands more and sets more and more conditions. My mother had prepared me perfectly to be in relationships with women just as disordered as her, and left me completely unequipped to be in relationships with healthy women.

Supporting the skewed reality of the Vampires False Self was second nature to me, as was placing the emotional needs of another before my own. I was conditioned to accept that any problems were my responsibility and I was familiar with withholding, criticism, rage and drama. In short, what my mother and her enabling husband had programmed me to be was the perfect Target. However, I should point out that it was through these relationships that I finally came to see the truth about Vampires and for that I am truly grateful to all of them.

So how then am I here today, writing this? How is it that I became a Survivor, and did not remain a Target? I believe it's because of one simple thing:

Vampires always go too far.

My mother left me no choice other than to receive her abuse on my feet. Her bewildering psychotic episodes and the inevitable attacks that accompanied them would occur regardless of the actions or inactions of those around her; she simply could not contain her disordered rage. If I went to my knees, the attacks didn't end, they intensified. If I stood, they would end when she had burned herself out, because all Vampires don't know when to stop. Their disorder drives them to self-destruction through the destruction of others, and that means they will inevitably hit a point where the Target is left with only one choice: Collapse and submit entirely to the will of the Vampire, or stand and say "No". I believe that all Survivors have that strength in them and, because you're reading this, you clearly have it too.

In my case, and in my relationship with my final Vampire, the turning point came when I started therapy. I had taken responsibility for all the issues she claimed were present in the relationship and I committed myself to resolving whatever was in me that was causing them. By claiming that issues existed that didn't, she drove me to the very thing that would ultimately save me, and it would lead to two things; her undoing and my freedom. I initially presented in therapy for "anger issues". Like many Vampires, mine was prone to creating deliberately frustrating, anger-inducing drama in order to meet her needs for attention. I would be blamed for the entire episode and punished in order to satisfy her need to hurt me and her need to place herself in the dominant position in the relationship.

Through working with my Therapist, I resolved not my "anger issues", because they didn't exist, but my responses to the attacks of my Vampire; I took away her ability to provoke me. Once that particular tactic had failed, she shifted to my sexuality. Suddenly, she wanted a baby and the fact that she was not pregnant was my fault and, if it wasn't sorted out, she would leave. She didn't want a baby, of course, but that wasn't the point. By creating the issue, she could follow the same tactic via a different route; provoke, play the victim, blame, shame, inflict pain and establish dominance. It didn't work.

Once again, therapy saved me. I addressed the issue with my Therapist and returned with calm logic and reason: If it was my fault, why was she not engaging with me? If it was my fault, why was she refusing contact? I did not provide the necessary Narcissistic supply, only calm reason.

Checkmate.

The end result was the Discard. It happened on Sunday 5th November 2017 and lasted 24 hours. My Vampire discarded me in one of the most impressive psychotic episodes I have ever seen, and I've seen a few. Her reasons made no sense, she could not string a coherent argument together and she spent the entire discard in a state of emotional meltdown.

Throughout, I remember thinking "this person is insane". Her mask was fully off and I saw an all-too-familiar face: the Vampire. She had finally gone too far. Throughout the discard, I didn't do what I was supposed to do: I didn't beg. In the 24 hours after her departure, I was devastated. Not because I'd been discarded but because I had allowed another Vampire into my life and I never saw her coming. And then I heard it. I heard that voice:

"You're all gonna die. The only question is how you check out. Do you want it on your feet? Or on your fucking knees... begging? I ain't much for begging"

So I got to my feet, called a friend who agreed to put me up while I sorted my life out and left the building. I returned that weekend to remove my stuff into my storage unit, returned the stuff she had in it, left the keys and closed the door. I took that final act of abuse on my feet, just as my mother had taught me. And then I started on the long, agonising road to recovery. I went No Contact and started my research on Vampires. In the months that followed, I intensified my therapy and I learned. I learned about personality disorders, Narcissistic abuse, everything in this book in fact. I'm still working on me, I'm still researching and I'm still learning.

Dear Survivor, I know where you have been. And if there's one thing I know about you without ever needing to meet you it is this: You have such strength. You are not on your knees. You are on your feet. I know that because you're reading this. If you were on your knees, your reality would still be that of the Vampire and it would never have occurred to you to pick up this book, or any other like it. You have the strength to stand when others fall. I know you will continue to do so.

As I start to wind this up, there's something else I'd like to share with you. See, there is another quote that I live by. I believe it in my heart and in my bones. I believe it so much I had it tattooed on my left forearm so I can see it every day. It's from the great Dr. Seuss and it's this:

"You are You! Now, isn't that pleasant?"

For me, it means that we all, every single one of us, are beautiful, wonderful and unique. We all walk this Earth for a time and we all deserve to enjoy our lives to the fullest. You, dear Survivor, are You! You are a child of the Universe, and it is my sincerest wish that you will know in your heart and your bones that being You is everything that You will ever need.

Thank-you for witnessing my story, maybe one day I'll get to witness yours, and thank-you for reading this book. I say that because we've come to the end. For now, it's time for us to part ways. I sincerely hope that you have found it useful. I set out to help Survivors and if I have helped you, then my mission is accomplished. I also hope that you've had a chuckle at the Interludes. What's the point of life if we can't laugh, eh?

I could do some fancy, extended goings-on in signing off but I think we're past all that, don't you? Instead, I'd just like to take a moment to recognise you and what you've achieved. You have survived, dear Survivor, and in doing so have become a world-class human. I'm proud of you and I hope you're proud of you too.

So here we are. I'm off now and I'll wish you safe travels. I'd wish you good luck but you don't need it. You have all that is required to lead a full and happy Vampire-free life. You have knowledge, strength, courage, and above all, you have You. You'll be just fine.

With love,
Matt

About the author

Matt is a psychologist, writer, coach, teacher and Survivor of Narcissistic abuse. He continues to be alive in Hastings, East Sussex, UK where he enjoys himself far more than is recommended for a man of his years.

The Vampire Hunter's Field Manual is his first book, and if we're not careful he might write another one.

His website: modernvampirehunter.com has all sorts of interesting things on it and is worth a look. If you send him an e.mail there, he'll almost certainly reply. He's good like that.

Printed in Dunstable, United Kingdom